Nationalism in Contemporary
Latin America

STUDIES IN CONTEMPORARY LATIN AMERICA
JOHN J. JOHNSON, STANFORD UNIVERSITY
GENERAL EDITOR

THE ARTS IN LATIN AMERICA
*By Gilbert Chase, Inter-American Institute for Musical
Research, Tulane University*

GOVERNMENT AND POLITICS IN LATIN AMERICA
*By Philip J. Taylor, School of Advanced International
Studies, The Johns Hopkins University*

ORGANIZED LABOR IN LATIN AMERICA
By Robert J. Alexander, Rutgers University

NATIONALISM IN CONTEMPORARY LATIN AMERICA
*By Arthur P. Whitaker, University of Pennsylvania, and
David C. Jordan, University of Virginia*

INTERNATIONAL COMMUNISM IN LATIN AMERICA
By Rollie E. Poppino, University of California, Davis

NATIONALISM IN CONTEMPORARY LATIN AMERICA

Arthur P. Whitaker

and

David C. Jordan

THE FREE PRESS, *New York*
Collier-Macmillan Limited, *London*

Foreword

LATIN AMERICAN NATIONALISM, drawing life from its own historic roots and enrichment from the worldwide nationalist experiences of this century, currently is flourishing as never before. The nationalist ferment in the twenty "Latin" republics of this Hemisphere, as in the developing states of Africa, the Middle East, and Southeast Asia, reflects the determination of millions of people to improve their material well-being, to establish their own identity, and to attain greater status in the community of nations. The multiple requirements that emerging societies impatient to rush into the modern world have placed upon nationalist leaders have caused them at times to focus upon social integration and state building, at other times to direct attacks against foreign interests that threaten or are made to appear to threaten a republic's cultural, economic, and political sovereignty.

From the above abbreviated remarks, one might conclude that Latin American nationalism is by nature monolithic. Such a conclusion would, in fact, have little relationship to reality. The republics are not approaching their "nationalist goals" at the same pace. For prolonged periods of time there often persists wide-scale inter- and intra-group discord over whether nationalist programs are, in fact, promoting the public interest, or are masquerading policy failures and administrative weaknesses.

This perceptive and tightly argued volume reveals that its co-authors Arthur P. Whitaker and David Jordan are abundantly aware of both the complexities of nationalism and the danger of pushing the case for nationalism too far. It seems to me that they have achieved a quite reasonable balance between those who would treat nationalism as an abstraction with little political sex appeal and those who would make it, depending upon the given author's orientation, a political or economic football to be scrambled for and run with by first one group and then another. This

v

volume is notable for its clarity of style. Also, Professors Whitaker and Jordan are to be commended for withstanding the temptation to resort to the use of jargon as a substitute for carefully developed argumentation. The volume adds immeasurably to the breadth of *Studies in Contemporary Latin America*.

John J. Johnson

Department of History
Stanford University,
Stanford, California

Preface

ABOUT 1930 the repercussions in Latin America of the world-wide economic depression combined with other developments there and with contagions from abroad to promote the escalation of Latin America's multiform nationalism. That escalation is still going on today. The thirty-five years since it began is the period with which our book is mainly concerned. But periodization is always artificial, and diversified Latin America is particularly recalcitrant to it, since historical processes move very unevenly in the twenty countries of that area. Accordingly, the following pages frequently examine the period before 1930.

Nationalism appears in many guises and serves widely different purposes. We believe that our book covers all its principal forms in contemporary Latin America. Because of limitations of space and time, only ten countries are discussed individually, but these contain four-fifths of Latin America's population and wealth, and represent its whole range of cultural and economic development and all its principal ethnic groups. Each Latin American country is unique in some respects, and our findings about those we have discussed are not necessarily transferable to the rest. Yet there are situations in which some transfer can be made to good advantage. One is in the Dominican Republic, highlighted by the armed strife of April and May, 1965 which broke out just as the present study was completed. Unless we are mistaken, this situation shows that our conclusions about the

vii

political vulnerability of Cuba, and the reasons therefor, are also useful in analyzing the Dominican case.

Politics is our central theme, for nationalism is an essentially political concept, and in developing the theme we rely mainly on historical analysis of words and deeds. We interpret politics broadly and try to give due weight to the conditioning factors, economic, social, and cultural. Yet, for reasons that we explain, a scientific correlation of nationalism with these other factors is impossible in the present state of knowledge regarding the latter, and we do not pretend to offer one. Similarly, we do not try to settle the vexed question whether there is such a thing as national character; there is an abundant literature on this question for the reader who wishes to explore it. On the other hand, we devote considerable space to the belief in national character, for this is often a chief ingredient of nationalism, especially of what we call nostalgic nationalism.

The book grew out of a group study of nationalism in Latin America, conducted at the University of Pennsylvania from 1959 to 1964, in which we both participated. It is a product of our joint labors throughout, but Whitaker made the primary contribution in Chapters I, IV, V, IX, and X, and Jordan, in Chapters II, III, VI, VII, and VIII. Both the study and our work were made possible by a grant from the Rockefeller Foundation, which was later supplemented by one from the Ford Foundation. We wish to express our gratitude to both foundations and the University, and to the following members of the group in question, by whose labors we profited: Samuel L. Baily, Earl T. Glauert, Marvin Goldwert, Peggy Korn, James Levy, George Strawbridge, and Winthrop R. Wright. We are also grateful to Albert Michaels, a former member of the group, and Frederick B. Pike for most helpful criticism of drafts of Chapters III and VI–VII respectively, and to the following, who served as advisers or consultants on the group study, particularly in its Argentine phase: Robert J. Alexander, Joseph R. Barager, Ricardo Caillet-Bois, Elizabeth Flower, Gino Germani, Otis H. Green, Hans Kohn, Howard Perkins (deceased), and José Luis Romero.

Arthur P. Whitaker
David C. Jordan

Contents

Foreword   v

Preface   vii

I. Nationalism in Latin America: Varieties,
     Sources, Uses   1

II. Modernization and Contemporary Nationalism   19

III. Mexico: Revolutionary Nationalism Contained   32

IV. Argentina: Nostalgic and Dynamic Nationalism   53

V. Brazil: Modernization, Independence, and Great-
     Power Status   76

VI. Colombia and Peru: Defensive Nationalism and
     Practical Reform   94

VII. Chile, Uruguay, and Venezuela: Revolutionary
     Nationalism and Evolutionary Change   113

VIII. Bolivia and Cuba: Revolutionary Nationalism
     and Revolutionary Change   139

IX. Continental Nationalism   161

X. Summary and Prospect   180

Selected Bibliography   205

Index   221

ONE

Nationalism in Latin America: Varieties, Sources, Uses

AT THE CLOSE of World War II, "One World" sentiment and reaction against the fanatical chauvinism best represented by Adolf Hitler led competent authorities to forecast the early extinction of nationalism, not only in Europe, its birthplace, but in the world at large. Instead, since 1945 nationalism has flourished as never before and has become so widespread and all-embracing that one of its foremost historians, Hans Kohn, has recently described the present era as one of global pan-nationalism.[1] Whether in deeds or merely in words, it finds expression in every continent, in countries at every stage of development, and in the Communist world and the free world alike. It has even had a vigorous revival in Europe, where its chief exponent is General Charles de Gaulle, head of one of the oldest and most civilized nations in the world; it has spread like wildfire among the new states of Asia and Africa; and it has become the greatest single force at work in Latin America.

Our concern in this volume is with twentieth-century Latin America, which is a particularly rewarding area for the study of nationalism. It embraces twenty independent and highly diversified countries, with a population which already numbered 210 million in 1964 and whose growth rate, about 2.5 per cent per annum, was more rapid than that of any comparable area in the

1. Hans Kohn, *The Age of Nationalism: The First Era of Global History* (New York, 1962).

world. Latin America also provides the student of nationalism with important points of comparison with the rest of the world. Politically, it is much older than most of the Asian and African states but much younger than Europe, having won its independence in the early nineteenth century.[2] Economically, too, thanks to the stimulus of foreign capital, enterprise, and markets, it occupies a middle ground between the highly developed countries of the North Atlantic area and the underdeveloped Africa-Asian countries, but it is a composite of both types and its people increasingly resent its "economically colonial" dependence on the United States and Europe. It contains some of the largest and most modern cities in the world, such as Mexico City, Buenos Aires, and São Paulo, and also some of the world's most primitive communities, and in the early 1960s, per capita income ranged from about $1,100 in Venezuela to $100 in Haiti. Latin America is also an ethnic composite. Its principal elements are European, Indian, and Negro, but the combinations of these vary from country to country. In several countries, notably Mexico, the preponderant type today is the mestizo, of mixed white and Indian ancestry. Culturally, Latin America is a land of contrasts. It has the oldest universities in the Western Hemisphere but half its people are still illiterate. Its intellectual elite make sophisticated contributions to Western culture and it has produced winners of Nobel Prizes for literature, science, and peace, but millions of its inhabitants still speak only one or another of the many Indian languages that survived the conquest and four centuries of serfdom. Although the great majority of its people are Roman Catholics, idols still linger behind its altars.

These traits help to explain why Latin America at large has never been hospitable to the racist variety of nationalism, although it has developed almost every other known variety. They may also help to explain why no variety of nationalism gained a wide popular following there until, within recent decades, modernization, urbanization, and the growth of mass communications

2. Cuba (1902) is the only exception. Though Panama did not become a separate republic until 1903, it had been a part of independent Colombia for more than eighty years before that.

created something like a national audience, with a new elite to exploit the opportunity. And finally, they help to explain why there has been a shift from nostalgic to dynamic nationalism; that is, away from the retrospective nationalism that glorifies the nation's past and is mainly concerned with preserving and fortifying an established national character, real or fancied, and toward a revolutionary nationalism concerned, almost to the point of obsession, with completing economic development, so as to throw off the yoke of foreign "economic imperialism" and complement political with economic independence.

The following pages will develop more fully these and other aspects of the complex nationalizing process in twentieth-century Latin America. First, however, the reader should be told the sense in which the term nationalism is used in these pages, and should be put on his guard against some common misunderstandings about the term.

DEFINITIONS

The meaning of nationalism is elusive. Boyd Shafer noted in his 1955 roundup of the literature of nationalism that no one had ever produced a universally acceptable definition of the term. The quest has continued but the statement still stands. Hans Kohn, one of the keenest exegetes, has not substantially modified his classic definition of nationalism as "a group consciousness," based on "the individual's identification of himself with the 'we-group' to which he gives supreme loyalty," this "we-group" being, increasingly since the French Revolution, the nation. This formula is one of the best, for it pinpoints the essentially historical and psychological character of nationalism. Yet it fails to satisfy, if only because in most cases it is manifestly impossible to determine whether the nationalists do in fact give supreme loyalty to the nation, or whether, as must often be the case, they are merely using the nationalist idea to promote some other purpose.

Recent efforts to define nationalism have been no more successful. Rupert Emerson, writing in 1960 with special reference to Asia and Africa, fell into the common error of identifying nationalism exclusively with anti-foreignism or xenophobia when he wrote: "Reduced to its bare bones, nationalism is no more than the assertion that this particular community is arrayed against the rest of mankind." This formula excludes the whole large body of liberal nationalism, which is directed primarily towards the internal consolidation and strengthening of the nation and is not only not "arrayed" against foreign nations but may even be positively benevolent towards them. In 1963, K. H. Silvert, a Latin American expert, made nationalism too absolute and totalitarian when he defined it as "the acceptance of the state as the impersonal and ultimate arbiter of human affairs." If this means, as it must, *all* human affairs, it is open to the same objection as the test of "supreme loyalty"; it fits some nationalists but not others, and often we cannot be sure which.

Least satisfactory are the definitions, or appraisals implying definitions, that comprehend only one of nationalism's many facets—usually its militancy. In 1916 J. Holland Rose called nationalism "an intolerant and aggressive instinct."[3] Four decades later the Swiss historian Herbert Lüthy described it as a "terrorist theory which imposes conformity in ideas and conduct." Other definitions, though broader, are still not broad enough. A century ago Lord Acton saw the "new conception of nationality" as marking "the end of the revolutionary doctrine and its exhaustion." "In proclaiming the supremacy of the rights of nationality," he continued, "the system of democratic equality . . . falls into contradiction with itself. . . . The theory of nationality is more absurd and more criminal than the theory of socialism. . . ." In 1946, Don Luigi Sturzo hurled an anathema that was almost equally sweeping. While admitting that "there are strictly political and sentimental nationalisms which are benign in nature," he maintains, in a passage echoed by Louis Snyder (see note 3) that the concept of nation has been deformed

3. This and some of the other quotations given below are conveniently brought together in *The Dynamics of Nationalism,* ed. with introduction by Louis J. Snyder (Princeton, N.J., 1964).

by making it an "ism," for this has turned it into a political, sociological, and ethical *primum,* so that "nationalism is interpreted as being the principal efficient and final cause of the community." Who puts this interpretation on it? I daresay most nationalists have never bothered their heads with philosophical speculations of this kind, just as many nationalists have never joined Lord Acton in equating nationalism with "the system of democratic equality."

The truth is that broad though they are, Lord Acton's and Don Luigi's definitions do less than justice to the protean varieties of nationalism. The term means so many different things that it might well have been included in Theodore Roosevelt's list of weasel words. As Kohn writes, "nationalities . . . defy exact definition . . . Nationality is therefore nothing absolute." He adds that some have raised it to an absolute by the two fictitious concepts of race or blood and *Volksgeist,* but, as noted above, few have done so in racially mixed Latin America.

Obviously, profitable discussion of any subject is impossible without agreement as to its meaning. In the case of nationalism, however, we should be content with broad and general definitions, such as those given in a dictionary: "National spirit or aspirations; devotion to the interests of one's nation; desire for national advancement or independence." Beyond this, the meaning of any particular nationalism can be determined only by discovering what its advocates said about it and what they did about it. The overarching question in any study of nationalism should be: "What function does it perform?". For nationalism is a tool, and the things we need to know about it are, who uses it, and why, how, and with what results. And since it is a tool, we should approach the problem without ready-made judgments as to whether nationalism is inherently and necessarily good or bad, terroristic or benign. As Ernest Barker said in this connection years ago, "We can only judge tools by the efficiency with which they fulfill the purposes for which they are used; and if we pass any moral judgment, it can only be passed on purposes."[4]

4. *National Character* (rev. ed., London, 1948), 228.

VARIETIES

For the present study, one special merit of this approach is that it accounts for a phenomenon common to most Latin American countries, namely, the existence of several different and competing varieties of nationalism in the same country at the same time. Argentina provides the most striking example. As a later chapter on that country will show, most Argentines are nationalists of one kind or another, but the kinds range over the whole spectrum of nationalism, from right to left, from traditional to revolutionary, from benign to terroristic.

As this fact suggests, we should be on our guard against the common error that nationalism does not exist, or, at any rate, that it is not worth studying, unless it rests on a consensus or perhaps even a majority vote. All of us, of course, are interested in the effectiveness of nationalism, but there are many situations in which more than one variety of it can be effective without a consensus or even a 51 per cent majority. The world is still largely ruled by elites, and even in the most democratic societies choices are generally determined by the interaction among power groups directed by their own elites. Hence, in studying nationalism, close attention should be paid to the varieties of nationalism in each country.

In any such study the question of the uses of nationalism is basic. These can be classified in various ways. Classified according to their orientation, they fall into two main categories: domestic and foreign. The domestic variety is primarily concerned with a country's internal arrangements, with building a nation through overcoming particularism and other factors, and is often relatively pacific and benign. Foreign-oriented nationalism, on the other hand, aims at strengthening the country's international position and is often marked by xenophobia and aggressiveness. The importance of the domestic variety should be stressed here in order to redress the balance of much recent discussion of nationalism which, through an obsession with the horror of Hitlerism, has greatly overemphasized the aggressive variety. This overemphasis is unfortunately reflected on the jacket of Snyder's otherwise excellent book (see note 3), which shows only a row of bayoneted rifles against a blood-red sky.

The fact is that the domestic and pacific type has bulked large in the history of nationalism ever since the eighteenth century. At times it has been preponderant, as in Europe and the United States through the early nineteenth century and in most of Latin America until about 1930. Even Theodore Roosevelt stressed this domestic type in his book, *The New Nationalism,* published in 1910, for he described "the New Nationalism" as putting "the national need above sectional or personal advantage" and as aimed at making the nation "efficient . . . for that which concerns all [its] people. . . ." The same kind of orientation is important in the nationalisms of Latin America and of many emerging states of Asia and Africa today. If these are in part xenophobe and militant, they are also in part designed for the domestic market as a cement for fragile and uncertain unions.

Distinguishing foreign and domestic nationalisms from each other should not be understood as segregating them in watertight compartments, for the two are often closely interrelated. The point is admirably illustrated by Latin America, where anti-imperialism, which is foreign-oriented, is closely linked with attacks on the domestic oligarchy—all in the name of nationalism. Moreover, contrary to the common misconception that nationalism is necessarily irreconcilable with internationalism, it could be said of other countries, as Ernest Barker said of England, that they have produced the kind of nationalism that runs easily into internationalism.

The relation between nationalism and internationalism is illustrated by the history of Catholicism and communism. Both are theoretically antagonistic to nationalism, yet both have coexisted rather peacefully with it. Catholicism has done so in France from the time of the Liberties of the Gallican Church to that of Charles de Gaulle; it has done so in Spain, at least from the time of Menéndez Pelayo (if not of Ferdinand and Isabella) to that of Generalissimo Franco; and it has done so in Argentina, where one of the most articulate nationalist groups since 1930 has been the Catholic. In all these cases there was an approximation to the Anglican position described by Ernest Barker when he said, "Queen Elizabeth held that citizenship involved churchmanship, and that men could not be full members of the nation unless they also belonged to the national church."

As for communism, its leaders have made a wide departure from the line laid down in 1913 by Lenin that "Marxism is irreconcilable with nationalism, even the 'justest,' 'purest,' most refined and civilized." The change appears to have been begun by Trotsky, who, from about 1930, in exile, gave strong encouragement to Communist collaboration with nationalist revolutionary movements, both bourgeois and popular, as a transitional device. This, together with the fact that much of Trotsky's preaching of the new gospel was done from Mexico City, explains the otherwise puzzling fact that *Trotskismo* (Trotskyism) has been an influential factor in Latin America's left-wing nationalist movements ever since the 1930s. As we all know, this particular "heresy" of Trotsky's was ultimately taken over by the Kremlin—witness its support of the Cuban nationalist Castro, among others.

CHANGES

The Latin American states won their independence just after modern nationalism took shape in Europe, and Europe has always been a major source of their ideas. Since then they have responded in some degree to the various changes that the nationalist idea has undergone among the great powers. In the twentieth century, however, and mainly after the catastrophic depression beginning in 1929, nationalism was greatly intensified in Latin America and ultimately assumed a form that assimilated that area to underdeveloped Africa and Asia rather than to Europe. The main reasons for these changes can be grouped under three headings: socioeconomic, technical, and political, as follows:

Socioeconomic

The economic and social stimulus to nationalism in the underdeveloped or "peripheral" world has received increasing attention since Karl Deutsch highlighted it in a penetrating study published in 1953. He wrote:

> Since the Industrial Revolution, nationalism has drawn much of its strength from the successively lower levels of material civilization. . . . Everywhere on this ladder of economic inequality, nationalists found richer neighbors to resent and envy; poorer neighbors to despise and fear; but few, if any, equals to respect. . . . *Not before the vast poverty of Asia and Africa will have been reduced substantially by industrialization, and by gains in living standards and in education . . . will the age of nationalism and national diversity see the beginning of its end.*[5]

This forceful statement of the correlation between underdevelopment and nationalism is true in the main. Nevertheless, two of its implications are questionable: first, that the intensity of nationalism increases in direct proportion to poverty; and second, that gains in industrialization, living standards, and education will progressively diminish the intensity of nationalism. In at least some countries, notably Uruguay, Argentina, and Brazil, the early stages of economic development have had the opposite effect of intensifying nationalism. The correlation is stated more accurately in a recent Brazilian book whose very title, *Nacionalismo e desenvolvimento*, links the two.[6] Its author, Cándido Mendes, argues that Brazil's political independence and policy of economic liberalism opened it to an economic penetration that has reduced it to more truly colonial status than ever before, and that, while the country has developed rapidly in recent years, the only instrument by which it can free itself from its age-old domination by foreigners is accelerated economic development under the aegis of nationalism.

The equation "political independence plus economic liberal-

---

5. Karl W. Deutsch, *Nationalism and Social Communication* (New York, 1953), 165; italics in original.
6. For further discussion of this book, see Chapter Five.

ism equals economic colonialism" is by no means new in Latin America; it was explicit in the Mexican and Uruguayan revolutions after 1910 and in Juan Perón's formal declaration of Argentina's economic independence in 1947. But today it has become an article of faith in most of Latin America. Moreover, this variety of economic nationalism has been closely identified with the demand for structural economic and social changes, mainly for the benefit of the exploited masses and at the expense of the *vendepatria,* or sepoy or Quisling oligarchy, bound by a corrupt alliance to the foreign exploiters. Left-wing nationalism is one of the main expressions of rising aspirations in Latin America.

Technological

Technological change in Latin America began in the nineteenth century with steamboat, railroad, cable, and telegraph, but since 1900 it has been intensified by automobile, radio, air transport, and television. In many ways it has directly promoted nationalism. The ramifications of this subject are so numerous that only three examples can be given here. First, it led to a great expansion of the means of communication and transportation, which in turn stimulated a sense of nationality. Second, it promoted the extraordinarily rapid growth of urban centers and their agglomerations of uprooted masses of immigrants and internal migrants who, with their other ties and loyalties broken, were highly susceptible to the nationalist appeal.

Third, and perhaps most important of all for our theme, it gave most Latin Americans keener awareness than ever before of what was going on in other parts of the world, which seemed to be advancing while they stood still. The effect on them was perhaps deplorable, but certainly not surprising. They gained a clearer vision of the United States' presence, which they deplored; of its wealth, which they envied; and of its power, which they resented and feared. Fresh impetus was thus given to anti-Americanism, which had long been one of the chief ingredients of nationalism in Latin America. In somewhat the same way a growing sense of difference and inferiority has alienated many

Latin Americans even from Western Europe. Conversely, they have developed a fellow feeling for the underdeveloped nations in Asia and Africa and have made some essays in collaboration with them; but there is clearly no sound basis for a close and enduring connection between Latin America and Africa-Asia. As will be shown in Chapter Nine, the final result has been to turn each Latin American nation in upon itself; that is, to stimulate nationalism.

The only important exception to this rule is the Central American Customs Union; and that represents a revival rather than an innovation, for Central America was united for the first fifteen years after it began its independent career in the 1820s. To be sure, there is also the Latin American Free Trade Association, or LAFTA, created in 1960 and consisting in 1965 of eight South American countries and Mexico. But this is only a loose and, so far, rather ineffectual association for promoting the minimal trade (less than 10 per cent of their total foreign trade) among member countries, whose economies are oriented towards the United States and Europe, and however little they may like it, must long remain so.

Political

In explaining the political aspect of the postwar stimulus to nationalism in Latin America, we revert again for convenience to the categories of domestic and foreign. On the domestic side, the principal countries of the area have already moved so far along the path of modernization that most of their major problems, such as the promotion of manufactures, agriculture, power production, education, social legislation, and reforms in the land and tax systems, are of such magnitude that only die-hard traditionalists would deny the primacy of the national government in dealing with them. In addition, these countries have built up national bureaucracies, including the armed forces; and these, like bureaucracies elsewhere, are not only self-perpetuating but self-multiplying.

Among the larger countries, only Brazil, which is half a con-

tinent, comes close to being an exception, for regionalism and
the individual states still count for something there. No such
situation exists in the other two largest countries, Mexico and
Argentina. Both, like Brazil, are federal in name, but neither is
federal in fact, for Mexico is run by its president, and Argentina
has long been a unitary state. Chile and Peru have never been
anything but unitary since the 1830s; Colombia, once a confederation of city-states, is approaching the same status; Venezuela
has recently achieved it; and everyone knows who runs Cuba.
These countries contain more than four-fifths of the Latin American people.

In some important respects, the foreign or external stimuli
to nationalism since 1945 have been much the same in Latin
America as in the underdeveloped countries of Asia and Africa.
In both areas a strong stimulus has come from the nature of
international organizations, as indicated by their very names:
United *Nations,* Organization of American *States.* For most purposes it is only through national governments that people can
participate in world affairs and that underdeveloped countries
can obtain aid for development. Once this national pattern is
established, it tends to harden and sharpen through competition
for funds, prestige, or other advantage. In the case of Latin
America, two special stimuli need to be mentioned, both added
in the past generation. One is the absolute Inter-American rule
of nonintervention. First adopted in 1936 by the Buenos Aires
Conference and reinforced by the OAS Charter in 1948, this rule
is the quintessence of political nationalism in its affirmation of
untouchable national sovereignty. The other stimulus is the
pressure exerted by the Alliance for Progress in favor of national
planning.

The only other stimuli to Latin American nationalism that
space permits us to note can be grouped under the label, contagion. The group includes communism, which did not by any
means create nationalism in Latin America but which has es-
calated its intensity and demands. There has also been contagion
from noncommunist sources abroad, including, in the 1930s,
Nazi fascism and Spanish Falangism and, since World War II,

other underdeveloped countries, especially Nasser's Egypt. Today we must add the influence of General de Gaulle, who is hailed by many Latin Americans as a champion of the increasingly popular policy of nonalignment, which is also known as the Third Position or neutralism, and which, whatever the label, is an expression of nationalism.

What is distinctive about Latin American nationalism? Nationalisms in all countries have much in common, but also differ according to the circumstances of each, such as history, culture, social and economic development, and power position. History and culture link Latin America with the West—in the first century after independence Latin America's rather elementary nationalism was little more than a replica of the European liberal, politically focused variety. After about 1910, however, it became much stronger, more diversified, and more distinctive. It became less nostalgic and benign and more dynamic, with a strong tinge of xenophobia. Its focus shifted from political consolidation to economic and social development and to economic independence. It gained a wider appeal than the old nationalism through political slogans and was "institutionalized in the state."[7] It has shown a tendency to bifurcate into left and right wings and to take on an integral, authoritarian character. Finally, since 1945 it has shown some resemblance to the nationalism of the new and underdeveloped countries of Asia and Africa.

The latter resemblance, however, is rather superficial. The Latin American countries in which nationalism has had its most substantial growth and which contain the great bulk of population are the ones that have either already risen to the intermediate stage of development (Argentina, Chile, Uruguay, Venezuela), or are approaching it (Brazil, Mexico, Panama). Even the latter are much more highly developed than the Afro-Asian nations in standard of living, literacy, and technical proficiency. All these countries have therefore produced a different kind of nationalism from that of the Afro-Asian group. It is more firmly based, more likely to retain some degree of affinity for democracy

7. John J. Johnson, "The New Latin American Nationalism," *Yale Review*, Winter 1965, 192.

and the West. It is more concerned, in external relations, with economics than with politics and, in domestic affairs, with social and economic problems than with political unification.

CLASSIFICATION

There is much truth in Silvert's observation that the prevalence of "traditionalism and an over-simplified universalism" in Latin America hampers the acceptance of the nation-state as a "social device or artifact."[8] Although this situation is not peculiar to Latin America, and is changing there, it helps to explain the fragmentation that characterizes the nationalist movements in most of that area. Both as between countries and within each country, the varieties of nationalism are so numerous that we can do little more than list them here. Most of them could be fitted into the classification drawn up by Carlton Hayes for Europe, which distinguishes five types of nationalism: Humanitarian, Jacobin, Traditional, Liberal, and Integral; but for Latin America the following categories are more appropriate.

Traditional-rural. This was one of the first types to appear and has been one of the commonest. Its apogee in late nineteenth-century Brazil, for example, was characterized by a kind of nostalgic nativism in the form of *sertanismo* or glorification of the *sertão* (the Brazilian backlands) in a campaign to shake off the cultural yoke of Europe.

Old bourgeois. This was an even earlier type, supported mainly by the commercial-professional middle class. It was also the mildest and the most concerned with national unification. It was marked not only by political liberalism, but also by an economic liberalism and cultural cosmopolitanism which are now generally reprobated as *vendepatria*, but which held that the best way to strengthen the nation was to draw as fully as possible on foreign investments, foreign enterprise, and foreign culture.

New bourgeois. This is associated with the *burguesía nacional*

8. K. H. Silvert, "Nationalism in Latin America," quoted in Snyder, *The Dynamics of Nationalism*, 294, 295.

or national bourgeoisie—a new upper middle class, primarily industrial-entrepreneurial, whose interests are rooted in the country, in contrast to the foreign-oriented, old middle class. Today, Mexico, Brazil, and Argentina provide outstanding examples of this type. It stands for economic nationalism and for a modified statism that still allows a wide role for private capital and private enterprise.

Populistic. This corresponds roughly to Hayes's Jacobin type, but the use of the term Jacobin in the Latin American context would require too many qualifications. Populistic nationalism first emerged in the Mexican Revolution of 1910, and later appeared in the 1940s in Perón's Argentina, in the 1950s in Víctor Paz Estenssoro's and Juan Lechín's Bolivia, and after 1959 in Castro's Cuba. João Goulart, President of Brazil from 1961 to 1964, was suspected of setting the stage for it in Brazil when he was ousted. It represents the most complete form of the fusion of nationalism with social revolution. Communists (first Trotskyites, then the orthodox) support it, but they are far from monopolizing or controlling it.

Nasserist. This is a kind of military-socialist nationalism. It resembles the populistic type in most respects except that Nasserism assigns the dominant role to the armed forces, in alliance with as much support as they can get from the masses. It has something of a precedent in the Perón regime, which Gamal Abdal Nasser is said to have imitated. Rupert Emerson does not mention this possibility in his study of the rise to self-assertion of African and Asian peoples, but his account of Egyptian nationalism reminds one of Argentina.

KEY GROUPS

Some references have already been made to the roles of key groups in Latin American society in relation to nationalism. More will be said on this important subject in discussions of individual countries and in the final chapter, where the obstacles to a scientific investigation of it will be noted. But the following general observations, though necessarily impressionistic, are valid enough to orient the reader.

In most of Latin America, four groups or sectors play a major role in the development of nationalism. These are the armed forces, the middle class, the intellectuals, and organized labor. In a few Latin American countries the bureaucracy, the Church, and the political parties should be added as separate entities, but in most cases they operate through one or another of the four major groups. Among the latter, the armed forces and middle class are probably the most important. The only person who has studied both of them closely in several countries is John Johnson. He first gave the middle sectors the palm for nationalist leadership, but several years later, after a study of the armed forces, he transferred it to them. The shift seems to have been justified, for in the interval the role of the armed forces had become if not more important, at least more visible. In any event, both are key groups. Unhappily for the student, however, neither group even remotely approaches unity on most of the issues of nationalism. The division of the middle class into old and new has already been noted, and it is divided in other ways as well. Likewise, the armed forces (meaning its officer corps) not only reflect the fragmentation of the middle class, from which most of the officers come, but are also divided by interservice and personal rivalries. Yet there are extremes that no substantial part of either of these two groups is likely to tolerate. The populist type is almost certainly such an extreme, especially if it has a Castro-Communist flavor.

The intellectuals, including the university students, present a picture of utter confusion. Most of them are nationalists but their types of nationalism vary with their political affiliations, and these are widely assorted. According to a recent study, they provide "a significant percentage of the new members drawn into the Communist party" and provide most of its top leadership.[9] Many more of them are anti-Communist Marxists or left-wing democrats, and a respectable number are middle-of-the-road lib-

9. Rollie Poppino, *International Communism in Latin America* (London, 1964), 44.

erals or out-and-out conservatives. Socially, too, they are heterogeneous. Although most of them are tagged as middle class, that
class itself is heterogeneous, and some of the most talented of
them are associated with either the upper or the lower class. A
new type of intellectual leader, the economist-in-politics, is ap-
pearing as modernization progresses. Víctor Alba, in his recent
history of social ideas in Mexico, complains that this new type
forms a kind of technocracy which has committed Mexico to what
we would call a nationalism of the new or industrial-entrepreneurial middle class.

Our last major group, organized labor, dates only from the
1930s in most of Latin America (Argentina, Chile, and Mexico
are the chief exceptions), but is already becoming a major force.
If its strongest and politically most active representative, Argentina's C. G. T. (General Confederation of Labor), is any guide,
Latin American labor is most likely to support populistic nationalism. But the C.G.T. is probably not a reliable indicator.
For one thing, labor's political power, though rising in Latin
America, is still curbed in one way or another by strong forces
hostile to that kind of nationalism. Moreover, the labor leaders
themselves are restrained by the risk that populistic nationalism
may end in Castro-type regimes. They are well aware that Castro
destroyed not only the existing armed forces of Cuba but also
the existing labor organization and the freedom of labor.

These facts are highly relevant to our theme, for, as Silvert
observes, "nationalism as a social value is necessary to modernism," and modernism is a major force in contemporary Latin
America. But as he further notes, nationalism is also a formal
juridical concept, a symbolic concept, and an ideology, and
"maladjustments among value systems, ideologies, and social institutions must always exist, especially in developing societies, for
underdevelopment is also uneven development."[10] In addition,
strong forces in Latin America, as in other underdeveloped areas,
are urging the quick completion there of a process that stretched
over a century in Europe: the conversion of the nineteenth-

10. K. H. Silvert, ed., *Expectant Peoples: Nationalism and Development*
(New York, 1963), 18, 31.

century type of middle-class nationalism into popular, integral nationalism.

As E. H. Carr pointed out two decades ago with special reference to Europe, this "socialization of the nation" had its "natural corollary in the nationalization of socialism."[11] Contemporary Latin America has followed much the same pattern, except that its old elites have put up a stouter resistance to change, so that nostalgic, retrospective, traditionalist nationalism still survives along with the dynamic, forward-looking, revolutionary variety. A half-century ago the old elites might have taken refuge in the anti-nationalism with which they were charged, as *vendepatria* allies of foreign imperialists. But it is a sign of the present "massified" times that, on the contrary, they have generally sought to outbid their rivals for popular support in a kind of nationalist auction. Almost all sectors of society in all the principal countries of Latin America, and some of the smaller ones, have been caught up in this process, the complexities of which will be explored in the following pages.

11. E. H. Carr, *Nationalism and After* (London, 1945), 19.

TWO

Modernization and Contemporary Nationalism

FOR MOST LATIN AMERICAN NATIONS, contemporary nationalism has provided the ethical as well as the emotional concept for legitimizing the state's entry into the modernization process. Even to the most casual observer it is apparent that change is occurring at an ever accelerating pace in Latin America and that this change is closely linked to modernization. Although some Latin American countries by no means may be classified as primitive or underdeveloped in the economic sense, all, to some degree, are underdeveloped vis-à-vis the most advanced Western nations and have, as a consequence, responded in varying degrees to the need for greater modernization.

There are several indications that modernization is taking place mainly in urban centers. The most obvious are the creation of large and rapidly growing populations in these centers and increased requirements for specialization for employment. Indeed, in general terms modernization represents the transition from the small, preindustrial, and traditional status society to the big, industrialized, and occupational status society.

Of course, this modernization process is uneven, not only as between states but also, and equally important, as between the segments of society within states. It should be clear that the development process, whether it is political, social, or economic, may attain different stages in an uneven manner within individual countries. Consequently, nationalism, conceived of as a group

19

viewpoint, or "we" concept providing the value structure for legitimizing the state, may reflect the different "we" values of the unevenly developing socioeconomic groups within a state as well as differences in specific content as between states.

This variation in nationalism is approached by observing the close link between the modernization process and the types of nationalism. The labels "process of change" and "level of change" provide a convenient method for linking modernization to various nationalisms.

The process of change involves understanding the social system undergoing change and the means by which this change is implemented. The vital fact about the old semifeudal *latifundio* system is its increasing vulnerability to rapid change. The most likely method of rapid change is the popular and revolutionary nationalist movement. This type of movement may develop within the electoral system (i.e., Peronism) or outside it (i.e., the initial stages of the Mexican revolution).

Ascertaining the level of change involves understanding to what extent the old system has been destroyed or substantially modified by contemporary nationalist movements. The level of change also describes to what extent new values and social norms have been implanted in the society.

THE PROCESS OF CHANGE

The traditional social and economic system is under attack in Latin America. The landed oligarchies have found the whole concept of their rule undermined in both the economic and political spheres. The commercialization of society has produced new sources of wealth and has undercut the hacienda as a self-contained economic unit. Many of the landed oligarchs have turned to the commercialization of their lands and thereby released large numbers of peasants as they were either displaced by machines or were attracted by higher wages elsewhere.

A substantial part of Latin America has come into contact with industrial societies and is, in fact, industrializing not over a relatively long period of time as occurred in Western Europe and the United States but in a compressed and agonized period that represents hardly more than a man's lifetime. Thus we have the peculiar popular nationalist movements of Latin America which so clearly represent the method many of these nations have chosen to effect rapid change.

Gino Germani, a distinguished Argentine sociologist, has postulated six stages in the process of political development in Latin America, as follows: (1) revolutions and wars for national independence; (2) anarchy, *caudillismo,* and civil war; (3) unifying dictatorships; (4) representative democracies with limited participation; (5) representative democracies with enlarged participation; and (6) representative democracies with total participation, or, as a possible alternative to these traditional democratic forms, "total" participation through "national popular revolutions."[1]

All the Latin American countries treated in this study either have had or seem near to having national and popular revolutions that are closely tied to the modernization process. All have unique features and all have certain similarities. Some seem to be more or less adapted to a constitutional and democratic structure; others, to dictatorships. One purpose of this analysis is to indicate some of the elements that favor or hinder an emerging democratic and constitutional pattern. This requires an understanding of the means by which social change is being brought about in Latin America.

Since the "we" concept behind nationalism tends to stress differences rather than similarities between peoples, it should be evident that when, as in contemporary Latin America, popular and revolutionary nationalist movements are linked with the modernization process, conceptualization that covers several countries is difficult. Such movements vary considerably from one country to another, in the nature and composition of both their mass base and their elites, in the content of their nationalist ideologies, and in the organizational agent chosen for achieving their goals.

1. *Política y sociedad en una época de transición* (Buenos Aires, 1962), 147.

THE MASS BASE OF POPULAR AND
REVOLUTIONARY NATIONALIST MOVEMENTS

Since the publication of Ortega y Gasset's famous book, "the revolt of the masses" has faded almost to a cliché, but the rising aspirations of the masses are very real. The fact itself needs little if any documentation, but the meaning and form of this popular upheaval require close examination. It would be a grave error to assume that the "masses" are an undifferentiated group. Indeed, for Latin America, and perhaps for other areas as well, such a view might well distort the implications of the various nationalist movements and our interpretation of them.

For example, if the popular support of a nationalist movement is chiefly drawn from an urban rather than a rural mass, then there are significant implications for the goals and appeals of that movement, in terms of the needs of that mass. Of course, there may be overlapping appeals, but the main popular pillar can still be identified.

Whether the principal mass base of a nationalist movement is urban or rural, certain conditions are necessary before the populace will support the leaders and their ideologies. William Kornhouser, in his study *The Politics of Mass Society* (New York, 1959), has suggested a fundamental point. Although he makes the well-worn observation that the lower groups of society are more receptive to mass appeals than the higher strata, he also points out that within all social groups those with the fewest social ties are the most responsive to mass appeals. This implies that a populist movement may be latent whenever social ties are weak, and that an explosive situation may exist in urban as well as rural societies.

There are various ways of mobilizing the rural masses. The classic example in the United States is the populist revolt which reached its apogee in the 1890s. The Latin American variety, although likewise based on real grievances, has often been exploited by a far more utopian propaganda than its prototype in the United States. Some of this propaganda seems to be aimed more at discontented urban intellectuals than at the real needs of the rural masses. The latter have apparently been most stirred when the issue was redistribution of land. As these masses have received tangible benefits from revolutionary movements (or in some cases merely the promise of such benefits) they have provided them with considerable popular support. In several countries, even when these rural-based movements have not dominated the governments, they have influenced them significantly.

Urban discontent, on the other hand, requires a peculiar set of circumstances in order to be mobilized in support of popular and revolutionary nationalist movements. One prerequisite seems to be that a large proportion of the working class not be organized or disciplined by a strong labor union bureaucracy. Another is the existence of a fairly well-developed national electoral system through which frustrated special interests can find expression.

The requirement of a weak labor organization and bureaucracy is fundamental. With a strong union the urban masses have not only an organization to express their interests but also a bureaucracy to interpose between them and the government. Without this intermediary association urban workers are, of course, greatly dependent on the government to protect their interests.

In Latin America two chief factors have contributed to the organizational weakness of the working-class movement. First, most of the working-class bonds were voluntary because the labor movement developed chiefly among immigrants whose ties were ethnic and whose philosophies were often strongly anarchist and international, if not openly antinational. Second, under the impact of a heavy internal migration from the countryside to the cities, the labor ties that did exist were often broken and overwhelmed by rural masses conditioned to the *patrón* system of the hacienda.

It is not mere coincidence that this urban mass was mobilized into a nationalist force when the electoral process had been well established. A representative democracy in some form appears to be a necessary prerequisite to the mobilization of the urban masses. Because a strong and independent interest organization is not available to these masses for articulating their demands, whereas the electoral process does provide them with such a means, it has been possible to create popular, even revolutionary, movements directed by national leadership. Furthermore, like the rural masses, the urban populace, lacking organized interest representation, may be exploited and manipulated by the aspiring elites.

The mass base of these nationalist movements, whether it is urban or rural, is often manipulated by the elites through the mass media. This manipulation may be the first indication of the authoritarian cast or character that the movement may take. Nevertheless, some of these movements have been contained within relatively stable and progressive constitutional systems of government. One intriguing problem is to determine how and why constitutionalism has been achieved. Another is to identify the barriers to achieving constitutionalism for nationalist movements. Such an assessment requires an understanding of the leadership of these movements.

THE ELITES OF NATIONALIST MOVEMENTS

C. Wright Mills has defined a power elite as those who can gain their goals even if others resist. On the basis of this definition, the most significant elite in Latin America for revolutionary purposes is the military. In the venerable Latin American tradition, the military elites, to paraphrase Harold Lasswell, have taken the most of what there was to get. Nevertheless, in the last thirty to forty years these elites have not always sought power purely on the basis of personal enrichment. Indeed, some have apparently made the modernization of society their first goal.

They have a strategic interest in an urban and industrial society which they were able to further because of their control of organized force. For example, Colonel Juan Perón demonstrated the interest of the Argentine military in an industrialized society by his important speech as Minister of War on June 10, 1944, when he called for a heavy industry owned and operated in Argentina. Gustavo Rojas Pinilla in Colombia, Carlos Ibáñez del

Campo in Chile, Manuel Odría in Peru and other military leaders were sympathetic to similar goals for their countries. Control of the military aided them considerably in their aspirations. Furthermore, some of these military leaders represented the hopes of the rising industrial middle classes. If the armed forces were the chief source of such social mobility as existed, their sensitivity to the prevailing social immobility was heightened by being linked to the status quo—the lack of rapid industrial progress and so to the lack of a representative community leadership. Thus Perón, Ibáñez, and Rojas Pinilla, though they differed in other respects, were alike in their unwillingness to maintain the status quo.

Military elites have not provided the only leadership for popular nationalist movements. Some of the most important leaders in twentieth-century Latin America can be best classified as members of the civilian intelligentsia. Some of them are: José Batlle y Ordóñez (Uruguay), Rómulo Betancourt (Venezuela), Víctor Raúl Haya de la Torre (Peru), Hipólito Irigoyen (Argentina), and Jorge Eliécer Gaitán (Colombia).

The nationalist commitments of these men generally involved them in modernizing their societies and in running their governments efficiently and justly. They were deeply concerned with political doctrine and often made important contributions to the political philosophy of their countries. Their contact with more advanced economies, foreign ideologies, and higher education provided an important stimulus to their thought. The usual result was their united hostility to the status quo. Undoubtedly, the civilian intelligentsia provided (and still provides) a crucial element in the mobilization of the masses into a nationalistic movement. When conditions allowed this intelligentsia to ally itself with revolutionary military elites, the rate of change was greatly accelerated. The MNR-led revolution of 1952 in Bolivia is a classic example. It should be borne in mind, however, that revolutionary military and intellectual elites may oppose each other, as, for example, in Bolivia, where they clashed soon after their joint victory in 1952, and in Peru, where the *Apristas* (American Popular Revolutionary Alliance) and the military have generally been on opposite sides since 1930. Indeed, military leaders often have joined with conservative intellectuals in right-wing or reactionary nationalist movements; Argentina since 1930 provides some of the best illustrations.

One other fact about revolutionary elites should be noted. Their commitment to certain defined ideologies and organized procedures of government must be understood. When the personality of a leader takes precedence over definable goals the movements thereby created may be captured by a more coherent ideology and organization and the original goals changed. The ideology of these nationalist movements is fundamentally important because it reveals the responsibility of the elites and the aims that they consider most important.

IDEOLOGY AND NATIONALIST MOVEMENTS

In any study of nationalist movements the most complex feature for analysis is the ideology used to mobilize the masses. Here, to know that something is useful does not explain how it developed or why its content is what it is, though it may provide valuable clues to the explanation. Ideology has a functionalist purpose in a mass nationalist movement, but it can probably be best understood as a mobilizing instrument in historical rather than teleological terms. In other words, though the ideology may serve a specific mobilizing function, its significance for the purpose is best discovered by a historical approach. A nation's historical animosities, conflicts, aspirations, and many other factors must be understood for the nuances of meaning and implications of a nationalist ideology to become clear.

The traditional terms of left and right are so much a part of the current political vocabulary that despite their ambiguities they must be used in discussing ideology. But it should be made clear at the start how such terms are employed. Seymour Martin Lipset presents a convenient scheme. He maintains not only that "extremist ideologies and groups can be classified and analyzed in the same terms as democratic groups, i.e., right, left, and center," but also that the "three positions resemble their democratic parallels in both the compositions of their social bases and the contents of their appeals."[2]

Although there are situations where left-center-right categories are inappropriate, here they are useful for both the democratic and nondemocratic ideologies. But the situation is even more complicated than this six-fold division. For example, despite the difference in ideologies between the right which is democratic (constitutionalist and republican) and the right which is not democratic, both groups view man as essentially bad, support hierarchical rule based on class distinctions, and share a fundamental anti-intellectualist irrationalism. The same sort of comparability exists between the democratic and the nondemocratic left. To both lefts, man is by nature good and this assumption is the source of the anarchistic tendencies and utopianism that they often exhibit.

What is striking about this situation is the fact that within democratic ideologies there is a tendency to borrow viewpoints from both the left and the right extremes in a pragmatic manner, as may be witnessed in many Western democracies. This is also observable in nondemocratic ideologies; Peronism, for example, developed as an *ad hoc* blend of elements drawn from antidemocratic extremism of both the right and the left. Furthermore, democratic and neodemocratic ideologies may have left and right-wing tendencies which vary according to which social groups are most important to the power base of the manipulating elites.

The ideology of the nationalist movement remains perhaps the best means for interpreting the ills, problems, frustrations, and goals of the society. By examining and understanding the ideology one may well be on the way to interpreting the nationalist movement. Because the idea of nation is an intellectual construct, the content that is given to the idea must be understood and its implications assessed.

2. Seymour Martin Lipset, *Political Man: The Social Bases of Politics* (New York, 1960), 128.

THE ORGANIZING AGENT

An idea will not triumph of itself; there must be an organization to carry it out. Thus, the study of nationalism involves an inquiry into the organizations that impose an identity upon a nation. Foremost among these in twentieth-century Latin America are governments, trade unions, the military, and political parties.

It may be further postulated that when these organizations attempt to define the national identity they are acting as binding agents, in the sense that they are carriers of specific ideas of the common interest.

This can present problems. Since there may be different nationalist ideas within a state, different binding agents may be at work. The result, in some cases, is chronic instability, as in Brazil since 1951 and in Argentina most of the time since 1930. To the extent that a developing nationalist consensus becomes based on substantive rather than procedural norms, rigidities are inevitable, and these, in a rapidly changing society, cause fundamental conflict. When the consensus is maintained on what the government must do rather than on how it is constituted, any resulting conflicts may strain the society's ability to adjust to new realities. Mexico may be an exception to this rule, as will be explained in a later chapter.

THE LEVEL OF CHANGE

The transition from the hacienda system to the industrial and commercial system seems inevitable in Latin America, even though the kinds of emerging society may vary a great deal in concepts of social justice and types of economic management. But the old hacienda system is doomed because it simply is not economically efficient. Will contemporary nationalist movements be able to replace the old regime with a viable social order? The answer is not at all self-evident. There are many indications that the old ruling class is neither prepared nor willing to rule under the new conditions and that in the agonizing gap between its rule and that of the new leaders many countries will suffer needless strife.

The modern society, which is the major justification for contemporary nationalist movements, requires definition. First, the modern society involves a change in attitude toward knowledge. Traditional knowledge is idealistic: subjective, religious, and dogmatic, while modern knowledge is empirical: objective, materialistic, and inductive. For the new leaders, bringing about a change in knowledge, particularly if they are dealing with a large Indian population, is a major undertaking.

Second, in a modern society the role of government is greatly enhanced. The government tends to pick up functions that often had been left in the hands of the private sector in the traditional society. Education, social security, and even economic decision-making become increasingly centralized governmental functions. Such change probably requires the new leaders to increase government monopoly of public force to maintain order in society, until the private sectors voluntarily support the government's expanded activities.

Third, in the economic area modern society is characterized by increased specialization, rapid industrialization, mass markets, mass transportation, and mass communications. The economic aspect of the modern society is one of its most dramatic features. For the new leaders, the management of such a society requires highly specialized skills which cannot be created by demagoguery or indoctrination.

Finally, the social characteristics of modernization are no less demanding than the economic ones. Social mobility, partially the result of great internal migrations from the countryside to the urban areas, is a most significant characteristic. New status values based on universal principles are features of modern society and indicate the degree to which modernization is at the same time both creative and destructive in the developing area. For the new leaders status changes are essential but obviously dangerous.

In running a modern society efficiently, the nationalist values used to destroy the traditional system often must be adjusted or even abandoned. When this adjustment cannot be made because they have too much political support among key groups, although they are unrealistic for maintaining a modern society, the country stagnates. This may very well describe the present dilemma in both Argentina and Chile.

Latin American countries have reacted in a variety of ways to the problem of modernization and nationalism. Some, so far, have had only a fairly mild modernization process cloaked in the trappings of a reformist nationalism. This modernization, with its accompanying nationalism, is mainly defensive. Its leadership is drawn largely from the traditional ruling groups and is designed to thwart the political challenge of rising social groups. If the defensive nationalist and modernizing leaders are successful, they will be able to preserve traditional institutions by adapting them to the times. Peru and Colombia currently have defensive nationalist leaders although these countries are still threatened by revolutionary nationalist movements.

Some Latin American countries have actually passed from traditional to revolutionary and modernizing leadership. The leadership is drawn from new social groups and often has developed new institutions and processes—sometimes borrowed from more advanced societies—to modernize the society.

These modernizing leaders have been faced with serious problems. The seizure of power was comparatively easy compared with the complicated and specialized problems of the economic and social transformation of their societies. All have had difficulty at this stage. Within this modernizing and ruling leadership, there are two main approaches toward transformation: evolution and revolution.

When in power the evolutionary leaders tend to experiment with a variety of methods to attain a modern society and to be responsive both to some traditional values and to a fairly gradual reorientation. The revolutionary leaders tend to have a fixed program and to be inflexible in their image of the modern society. Venezuela, Chile, Uruguay, and Mexico have leaders who represent the former approach while the leaders of Bolivia and Cuba represent the latter. The case of Brazil is mixed.

For the new elites, providing effective leadership is an unenviable task. They must somehow gain the support of the people while creating and sustaining a modern economy. They must create a government which is considered legitimate by the necessary number of supporters and, at the same time, they must demonstrate the government's modernizing abilities.

The difficulty of this task is manifest when it is noted that many of the slogans and ideas used to destroy the old system conflict with the most efficient and rapid methods for modernizing society. This may be the most embarrassing dilemma facing contemporary Latin American nationalism after an old system has been overturned. More simply, the three main questions facing these nationalist movements in power are: First, can they reconcile the popular demand for a quick rise in the standard of living with the requirements of long-range development? Politically, this is their most pressing problem. If they fail, they will either lose popular support or else fail in their economic objectives. Second, can the new national identity, based so extensively on political, economic, and cultural independence, be modified to meet the demands for rapid economic growth without falling prey to some form of tyranny? Finally, can the new nationalism be restrained from developing into xenophobia and self-defeating isolationism? This last question always arises in the nationalist process, but it is particularly important to developing countries in Latin America, for they must have foreign aid if they are to achieve their goal of rapid growth.

THREE

Mexico: Revolutionary Nationalism Contained

BETWEEN 1910 AND 1940 the Mexican Revolution destroyed the sources of power of the traditional Porfirian society and created the bases of a new social order, but in 1940 the Revolution reached its Thermidor. Since then, Mexico's rulers have worked to perfect their technique of satisfying at the same time mass aspirations and economic growth. The goal of reconciling the demands of social justice with economic expansion are thrashed out in a well-organized political party which has a discreet leftist philosophy toward social justice and encourages private enterprise draped in economic nationalism. So far this amalgamation has been Mexico's dominant type of nationalist expression since 1940.

There is not, however, a complete consensus on nationalism in Mexico today. Even within the revolutionary family hierarchy there are competing groups. The most important split concerns the problem of economic growth and social justice mentioned above. One view, stemming from Plutarco Elías Calles stresses economic growth whereas the other, represented by Lázaro Cárdenas, puts the equitable distribution of wealth ahead of growth. So far, both views have been contained within the pragmatic consensus that the revolution's leaders have sustained. For the most part, since 1940 the dominant nationalism in Mexico has been introverted, progressive, and restrained. As the following analysis indicates, this is a remarkable achievement.

Mexico's history as an independent country began in 1810 when a *criollo*[1] priest led his ragged followers against the *gachupines*.[2] Shortly thereafter, a constitution was adopted, but the subsequent years have seen a struggle to determine just what that nation is and to whom it belongs.

For many, the nation was what the *criollos* said it was. They were the great property owners and they felt the government should represent their interests. In the colonial period, political power had been in the hands of the *gachupines,* but the 1810 revolution initially turned this power over to the *criollos*. While political power shifted, the economic system remained unchanged. An economic system that had been imposed by the Spaniards became "native" to Mexico, the hacienda and the *latifundio* became the economic pillars of the new nation. Nevertheless, this state of affairs did not go uncontested.

On the contrary, political strife was rampant, with two major political groups developing: the Conservatives, who advocated monarchism, centralism, and a state church, and the Liberals, who desired republicanism, federalism, and separation of church and state. Their political conflicts agitated the Mexican scene and were only interrupted by abrasive clashes with foreign powers.

Two of these clashes gave particular impetus to the ever-growing self-identity of Mexico. One, the Mexican-American War, practically dismembered the country, while the other, the short-lived domination of the country by the French puppet Maximilian, turned the federalist leader who successfully spearheaded the Mexican resistance into a national symbol.

This leader, Benito Juárez, became the symbol not only of resistance to foreign domination but of economic and social reform, as well. In this fortunate juxtaposition, Frank Tannenbaum gives Juárez "the credit of having created a common people out of the many diverse groups on Mexican soil."[3] This perceptive statement is important in the study of contemporary Mexican nationalism

1. A *criollo* is a native born Mexican of Spanish parents.
2. A *gachupín* is a native born Spaniard residing in Mexico.
3. *Mexico: The Struggle for Peace and Bread* (New York, 1962), 15.

because many of the values that Juárez supported were, for the most part, betrayed under the subsequent dictatorship of Porfirio Díaz.

For twenty-odd years Benito Juárez led a federalist movement of protest. In Mexican history, this period (1855–1876) has come to be known as *La Reforma*. As Howard Cline has noted "the avowed objectives of the Reform group . . . were to make Mexico a modern, middle-class state, based on a federal republican constitution, the supreme law."[4] Anticlerical legislation was passed, and a liberal constitution (1857) was enacted. Even more important, the first basic attack on the economic system that sustained the power of the conservative *criollo* elite was initiated. A major purpose of the attack was to put an end to the abuses of the hacienda system.

THE PROCESS OF CHANGE

The Reform came to an abrupt close during the ruling era of Porfirio Díaz. In his rise to the presidency in 1876, Díaz raised the Federalist cry of "No Re-election and Effective Suffrage." (The Federalists opposed the common practice of the President's serving consecutive terms.) Initially, it appeared as though he might retain the goals of The Reform during his rule, but this hope soon proved illusory.

From 1880 to 1884 when Díaz' puppet ruler Manuel González formally held the presidency, all pretense of following The Reform was dropped. In this period, the policy of distributing the communal lands of the Indians to individuals and privately owned (including foreign) companies was increased.[5] By 1910 the Díaz policy of surveying and selling Indian communal lands—

4. *The United States and Mexico* (Cambridge, 1961), 45.
5. The first attempts at breaking up the communal lands of the Indians began under Juárez. The Liberals wanted to encourage industrialization and to develop a rural middle class, and they felt that the Indian communities hindered these goals.

some 135 million acres or 27 per cent of the national territory—resulted in 85 per cent of the land being owned by one per cent of the families. The property was sold to favored landowners for an average of nine cents an acre.

From his "re-election" in 1884 until the 1910 revolution, Díaz ruled without the pretense of presidential puppets or the mask of The Reform. He erected his regime on the basic forces that The Reform had opposed. He gained the support of the clergy by not enforcing The Reform's anticlerical laws, he obtained the loyalty of the old *criollo* elite by not touching their haciendas, and he earned the gratitude of the "new *criollos*"—new industrial and commercial rich of European origin—by granting them valuable business advantages. Thus Díaz's administrative slogan, *Pan y Palo* (Bread and the Stick), came to mean only benefits and concessions to his supporters, and repression and exploitation to his adversaries.

Besides the support of the privileged and wealthy, the Díaz regime had its own ideological justification. A group of new *criollos*, the *científicos,* provided the intellectual justification for the Díaz policies.

The *científicos* proposed the application of scientific principles to the problems of public administration. They were convinced that Mexican society was so backward that it must be directed by the superior classes. Mestizos and Indians were considered inferior while foreigners—particularly North Americans and Europeans—were admired. The *científicos'* views were officially propagated in their political party, the *Unión Liberal.*

Understandably, these attitudes led the *científico* advisors of Díaz to urge him to deliver much of Mexico's natural wealth to foreigners. His compliance was exemplary. During his rule, over half of Mexico's oil and nearly three-quarters of her mineral wealth fell into American hands alone. In 1910, as estimated by the *Nacional Financiera,* Americans controlled nearly half of the entire net worth of the Mexican economy. Although there were ominous rumbles of discontent and even a few revolts, these policies were considered sound and were furthered under José

Ives Limantour—Díaz's most trusted *científico* advisor in his last years in power.[6]

Whether or not Díaz appreciated it, his policies were changing the make-up of Mexican society. Those that stimulated economic growth were affecting the lives of the urban and rural workers. His check, indeed reversal, of agrarian reform produced discontented rural groups, but he made no effort to gain the support of the growing number of industrial workers. Díaz and his advisors never understood the importance of incorporating the working classes into the society they were developing. By 1910, the would-be leaders of both the urban and the rural workers were well aware of their position outside the governmental structure.

Another significant change had occurred which the Díaz regime did not meet. By 1910 the mestizo proportion of Mexico's population was at least half the total. To consider the predominant ethnic group inferior, as the *científicos* did, was untenable. Obviously there were many reasons for deserting this system of rule.

For well over a decade before the 1910 revolution, many Mexican intellectuals began to do so. The unifying concept of their desertion from the Díaz regime was the desire to encounter, or forge, or return to the essence of the Mexican nation. (As Crane Brinton has so aptly noted, one deserts to something.)

Heriberto Frías wrote the novel *Tomochic* (1892) to express his belief that the Indian ought to be considered the ethnic base of the Mexican nation. Alberto Santa Fe wrote in his *Revolución Social* that the proper governing principles for Mexico could be found in the radical ideas of nineteenth-century Europe. Wistano Luis Orozco demanded that the government rectify public want by distributing public lands to the people. Harsher and more specific attacks followed these early signs of intellectual desertion from the Díaz regime.

6. There is some revisionist writing which suggests that Díaz's role as a *vendepatria* is exaggerated. The fact that Mexico needed capital and could only obtain it from abroad is considered a partial justification of Díaz's policies.

One group of intellectuals attacked the "scientific" viewpoints of the *científico* advisors to the *Díaz* regime. Most representative of this approach were Antonio Caso and his disciples, who argued that positivism as employed by Díaz and his *científico* advisors did not aid the masses and was, therefore, neither scientific nor idealistic. This criticism eroded much of the authority of the ideology that sustained the regime.

Another group assailed the economic and social values of the Díaz government even more directly. Ricardo Flores Magón, a well-known anarchist, was easily one of the most important figures in this group. Along with his brother Enrique, he organized a political party that had as one of its objectives "to foster love of the fatherland." He published and edited a newspaper, *La Regeneración* which not only attacked Díaz but also propagandized Ricardo's syndicalist ideas. Through *La Regeneración*, Ricardo demanded better pay for industrial workers, better working conditions, the eight-hour day, the right to strike, and other improvements. Also included among his demands were the traditional liberal objectives of The Reform: freedom of speech and press, lay education, land reform, and the like.

Another intellectual in this category was Andrés Molina Enríquez. He based his evaluation of Mexican society on an analysis of its ethnic composition and of its socioeconomic structure. Estimating that of Mexico's total population 50 per cent was mestizo, 35 per cent Indian, and only 15 per cent *criollo* and foreign, he argued that in terms of this ethnic composition the basic nationality for a Mexican nation had to be mestizo. Furthermore, he felt that all the evidence indicated that the *criollos* were antinational because of their foreign orientation. The Indians, he concluded, were anational because their vision of society did not extend beyond the plot of land on which they lived. It followed that Mexico's future lay with the mestizo not only by a process of elimination but also by an objective understanding of the essential national needs, which ranged from a common language and religion to common aspirations and frustrations—requirements which only the mestizos shared.

In addition, Molina Enríquez felt that the socioeconomic

structure of Mexican society made the mestizos the crucial population group for creating a truly independent and genuine Mexican nation. In his opinion, Mexican society was badly deformed, with the privileged classes, which included *criollos* and foreigners, owning the country while the mestizos were excluded from positions of influence. Molina Enríquez took particular delight in assailing foreign interests both for deforming the nation's economic structure and for blocking the growth of a broadly based national identity.

In addition to the intellectuals who deserted the Díaz regime for philosophic, socioeconomic, and ethnic reasons, there were others who did so because of their political beliefs. In his work *Explotadores Políticos de México,* Juan Pedro Didapp is probably best representative of the political criticism of the Díaz government. Didapp held the standards of the 1857 Constitution up to the government's performance and found little correspondence. Moreover, he reasoned that political reforms were necessary prerequisites for social and economic change. If the government could be compelled to return to proper political practices, then other problems could be handled, as well. This line of thought seems to have been the one most influential on and similar to Francisco Madero's thinking and suggests why the revolution started off in 1910 as mainly political and moderate in its aims.

In reviewing the genesis of the Mexican revolution, the mildness of its beginning seems startling when contrasted with the major upheavals it subsequently engendered. Several interlocking factors could have given this revolution, at least in the beginning, a high potential for bringing about change in an evolutionary rather than a revolutionary manner.

Internally, the regime began to show severe strains despite the considerable economic growth before 1910. The hacienda system, which had benefited so much by Díaz's give-away program of the Indian lands, was hurt by the government's industrial policies. The relatively immobile labor force that supported the hacienda system was undermined by urban competitors, and the commercialization of some haciendas upset the prevailing wage scale. Some of his most important landowning supporters lost confidence in Díaz. Also, under the urging of Limantour, Díaz took control of major segments of the Mexican railroad system, which made some of his foreign supporters uneasy. Internally, the regime had seriously weakened the confidence of landowners and foreigners. Externally, it was already faced with the widespread opposition of the urban and rural masses and the growing mestizo middle class.

At the same time that the regime was weakening internally, a scion of a wealthy landowning family was quietly organizing and popularizing a broadly based national movement. Both the background and ideas of Francisco Madero seemed to make him unlikely to launch one of the greatest revolutions of the twentieth century. He was independently wealthy and belonged most closely to the Juan Pedro Didapp group of democratic intellectuals.[7] Nevertheless, his political instincts were appropriate for the times.

Francisco Madero's opposition to Díaz began slowly and on the local level. He attempted to win elections in his home of San Pedro de Las Colonias, and, as early as 1904, he formed a political club. He also attempted to diffuse his moderate political ideas through two newspapers. Quickly he learned that Díaz could mobilize too much force against him, so he decided that the best way to overcome this opposition was to organize his protest movement throughout the country.

On the principal ideological basis of free suffrage and no re-election, he formed political clubs throughout the country. Travel was the only way to do this, in the days before radio and television. Beginning in June 1909, Madero took his cause around the country, and everywhere he went he left political clubs in his wake. Apparently, his successes in such places as Querétaro, Jalisco, Colima, Sinaloa, Sonora, and Chihuahua led him to believe he could rely on support in much of the country. In the course of all his trips, Madero visited a total of seventeen

7. According to Moisés González Navarro, neither Madero nor the other democratic revolutionaries had read Andrés Molina Enríquez's famous book, *Los Grandes Problemas Nacionales*. Moisés González Navarro, "La Ideología de la Revolucion Mexicana," *Historia Mexicana*, X, 4 (April-June, 1961).

states and twenty-six cities, and he had reached the point where he could now create a truly national party. He believed in the need for a national party because it seemed obvious that Díaz might never be disposed to permit a genuine opposition to develop.

A convention was called in April of 1910, at which the clubs were welded into the *Partido Nacionalista Antireelectionista* (Nationalist Antireelectionist Party), with Madero as its presidential candidate. The platform maintained the traditional rule against re-election and also suggested the need for improving the social and economic conditions of the masses. It was apparently during this national convention that Madero became convinced that Díaz would not voluntarily give up power. Nevertheless, he did not begin his revolt until after Díaz declared himself "re-elected."

The pattern that developed was complicated but in retrospect logical and understandable. An educated elite had been excluded from power in blatant disregard of the principles the government itself had professed. The excluded leaders had a widespread popular base to exploit. Madero's movement was primarily based on the widely held liberal principles of correct political behavior, the traditional anticlerical bias of reformers, and the support of the commercial middle-class mestizos who resented the foreign economic domination of Mexico. In the belief that it would be enough if Díaz were ousted and Madero made president, the movement neither tapped the potential revolutionary resources nor destroyed the traditional system with its still viable sources of influence.

In 1911 the aging Díaz was ousted and Madero became president. What chances he might have had to mount reform were cut short by his murder in February, 1913. In one of the sorriest chapters in American diplomatic history, much of the blame for Madero's murder can be laid on the head of Henry Lane Wilson, the United States Ambassador to Mexico, who was responsive to the views and interests of the old Díaz backers.

But the revolution continued. Under Madero, it had created its own military arm. The new military elite and the intellectuals had a common interest in furthering the revolution. The military needed the intellectuals to help recruit troops to destroy the professional army that backed Díaz. With the help of the appeals developed by the intellectuals, the revolutionary military leaders turned to gain the support of the masses, both rural and urban. The rural workers were promised land reform and the mestizo mine and factory laborers were promised social and economic legislation. With this sudden broadening of its goals, the revolution became an almost irresistible force. Such intellectuals as Luis Cabrera, who was influenced by Molina Enríquez, linked up with Venustiano Carranza. Under their influence and the pressure of his rivalry with the famous peasant leader Zapata, Carranza espoused agrarian reform and workers' rights. He also joined forces with Alvaro Obregón and the two rallied around them great popular support with their drive for internal reform and their efforts to undercut foreign monopolies in Mexico. Peasants and workers formed fighting battalions in support of Carranza and Obregón.

The benchmark of this renovating nationalist drive was the Constitution of 1917, which soon demonstrated just how national the revolution was. The Constitution was a substantive document of Mexico's nationalist ideology—an ideology that was not internally or rationally consistent but was a monument to that nation's history. Because this nationalism grew historically, it was complicated and full of conflicting and interlocking customs, attitudes, and beliefs. It was the work of countless lives and many minds.

Almost two-thirds of the provisions were similar to those of the 1857 Constitution, but it also expressed the social and economic ideas of the intellectual precursors of the revolution. Article 27 put the ownership of the land and the subsoil resources in the hands of the nation. The article maintained that property rights had a "social function" and stressed the need for both small private holdings and collectivized communal systems. Article 123 called on the government to aid the Mexican labor movement while giving the State power to regulate unions. The underlying feeling in all these measures is expressed in Article

32: "Mexicans will be preferred to foreigners, other circumstances being equal, with regard to all government concessions and all government jobs, posts, or commissions where the citizens' qualifications are not an indispensable requirement."

This document required an organization or force or both to impose it, no matter how ably it incorporated the nation's experience and goals. The groups that benefited most happened also to be the ones that had demonstrated the greatest potential force: the military, the peasants, and the urban workers. Nevertheless, it was to be more than a decade before power would be institutionalized to begin the imposition of the new consensus.

If the policy of relying on the support of urban and rural masses began under Carranza's rule (1915–1920), it was an even more conscious feature during that of Alvaro Obregón (1920–1924). His policies clearly foreshadowed the alliance of peasants, workers, and the military that Calles institutionalized in 1929.

Obregón wooed the peasants by distributing uncultivated lands to them under the Constitution of 1917, but he relied even more on labor and furthered its interests far more than those of the peasants. Article 123 in the Constitution of 1917 encouraged the growth of the emergent labor movement. Shortly after 1917, the idea of forming a national labor organization became widely accepted. In May of 1918, such an organization was drawn up and named the Regional Confederation of Mexican Labor (CROM). Under Obregón, CROM became an organ of the government. Its membership grew from a mere seven thousand in 1918 to well over one million before Obregón left office in 1924. Obviously the nationalist ideology as expressed in the constitution drew popular support. It is instructive to note too that most of the anarcho-syndicalism that had infused the labor movement before 1917 withered away under the impact of the practical advantages gained by labor's cooperation with the government. This change signified the growth of nationalism among the workers, since anarcho-syndicalism was anti-national. Also, more specifically, it signified the increasing growth of populistic nationalism.

There was, however, considerable hostility between several of the key labor and peasant leaders. Toward the end of Obregón's term, Luis Morones, the head of CROM, openly broke with Obregón's agrarian supporters, Soto y Gama and Aurelio Manrique. It remained for the next military President, Plutarco Elías Calles, to keep the broadly based nationalist movement going.

As Frank Tannenbaum has correctly noted, "Calles crystallized the ideas of Mexican nationalism and saved the Mexican social revolution from internal disintegration and external pressures."[8] Under Calles, labor gained an even stronger influence than it had held under Obregón. Luis Morones was placed in the cabinet as head of the Ministry of Industry and Labor. Calles liked to call his regime a "labor government."[9]

Calles needed his strong labor support because his anticlerical views stirred up a serious revolt by Catholics, who opposed Articles 3 and 130 of the 1917 Constitution. Article 3 secularized education and prohibited the Church from operating primary schools; Article 130 prohibited the Church from engaging in politics or criticizing the laws and government of Mexico. Catholic protest turned into an open revolt which became known as the Cristero Rebellion. The struggle that followed was bitter, but in the end the rebels, including their Church leaders, capitulated.

Calles' government was threatened by the military, as well. To prevent the rise of local chieftains he attempted to shape the local armies into a national institution by rotating the assignments of the generals. This maneuver was successful in limiting their influence.

During the Calles era, the struggling revolution faced possible intervention from the United States over the issue of the expropriation of American-owned property. With both sides making concessions, the situation was eased after Dwight Morrow became the United States ambassador to Mexico.

As Calles' term came to a close, Obregón prepared to return to the presidency, but he was assassinated in the interval between his election and his inauguration. Again Calles rose to the challenge and maintained that the time was at hand when Mexico

8. *Op. cit.*, 65.
9. It may be doubted that Calles' government was in reality pro-labor. Labor's rights seemed secondary to economic stability and anticlericalism.

should no longer depend on heroic leaders and should turn instead to institutional regularity. A civilian president, Emilio Portes Gil, was chosen to serve. Following this innovation, Calles turned more directly to the organization of institutional stability.

At Querétaro, in March, 1929, the National Revolutionary Party was created. Mexico's new revolutionary ruling class took its first step toward establishing internal stability and regularity by conciliating the social forces that had shown the greatest capability for organized violence.[10] These groups had been the military, labor, and peasants. The interests they represented were given group or "sector" representation in the new national party; Mexico had started the formal organization of its popular and renovating nationalist movement. But besides this attempted institutionalization of the developing national consensus, the new party was based on political realities, and it integrated the three principal power groups into one organization where they acted as mutual checks. It was now possible for Mexico to begin to seek a new level of development within a relatively stable institutional framework.

Immediately following the formation of the National Revolutionary Party, there was no marked trend toward moving the revolution forward. In the period between 1928 and 1934, when Calles controlled the movement from behind the scenes, Mexico had three short-term presidents; Emilo Portes Gil, Pascual Ortiz Rubio, and Abelardo L. Rodríguez. This period was characterized by Calles' motto, "Consolidate gains already made before attempting new advances."

When Lázaro Cárdenas was elected President the government again became exceedingly active in reform. Cárdenas, the son of a Zapotec Indian, had absorbed completely the nationalist spirit of the revolution. His nationalist program was, as he said, "not to Indianize Mexico, but to Mexicanize the Indian." In no small way, he accomplished this Mexicanization by distributing land.

During his presidency, Cárdenas distributed over seventeen

10. See the interesting comments on this development by Martin C. Needler, "The Political Development of Mexico," *The American Political Science Review*, LV. 2 (June, 1961), 308–12.

million hectares to 771,640 peasants. This was almost twice the amount of all the land given to the peasants prior to his administration.[11] The distribution under Cárdenas, coupled with that under the earlier leaders, meant the end of the hacienda system as the dominant economic and political institution of the country. His rule marked the high point of the agrarian emphasis of the Mexican revolution and the final destruction of the semi-feudal and semi-slave economic system of the hacienda. In a sense, Cárdenas terminated the preparatory stage for industrial growth by liquidating the old social patterns in rural areas. Despite the fact that later Presidents continued agrarian reform, the basic change had been accomplished by the end of the Cárdenas period.

But Cárdenas did more than appeal to the rural masses by his land reform programs and thereby end the possibility of the resurgence of the old hacienda system. He organized these peasant workers into the structure of his party and government. Portes Gil and the PNR staff had the principal responsibility for initiating this incorporation. In July of 1935, Cárdenas issued a decree which organized the members of the *ejidos* (Mexico's communal farms) into a national union. This organization (League of Agrarian Communities and Peasant Unions) was incorporated into the PNR under the name of the National Peasant Confederation (CNC) as the peasant sector. It was kept separate from the labor sector and represented only the rural base of the nationalist party and movement.

The urban masses were also reorganized and re-incorporated into the party and movement under Cárdenas. Since 1928, when CROM opposed Calles' decision to return Obregón to the presidency, the labor support of the revolution had fragmented. While factionalism struck CROM, its rival, the more recently organized CGT (General Confederation of Workers), grew rapidly. In 1930, there were some ninety-six unions with 80,000 members in the CGT. But this organization with its anarcho-syndicalist orientation was not in step with the organizational movement of the

11. 10.08 million hectares of land were distributed by the revolutionary leaders up to 1934.

revolution. In early 1936, Cárdenas bluntly told labor that he wanted it united.

A congress was held and a new labor confederation (Confederation of Mexico Workers, CTM) was formed. Under the leadership of Vincente Lombardo Toledano, the CTM had a Marxist orientation, but nevertheless represented urban workers in the nationalist revolution. The CTM was government-controlled and, along with the CNC, represented the organized base of the revolution's popular urban support. It grew from a mere 200,000 members when it was founded to an estimated one million at the end of Cárdenas' term of office in 1940. Thus the CTM became one of the main components of Cárdenas' political power structure and of the PRM, in which it was known as the "labor sector."

Cárdenas also attempted to incorporate Mexico's businessmen into the revolutionary party. Two organizations were designed to represent commerce and industry. Cárdenas created the National Federation of Chambers of Commerce (CONCANACO) to bring the members of Mexico's chambers of commerce under state control. Included in the same organization under Cárdenas, but separate since then, was the Confederation of Industrial Chambers of Mexico (CONCAMIN) which represented Mexico's developing industrialists. Both organizations could voice business attitudes to the government, while the government could accommodate them or control them as it deemed necessary.

Impressive as this organization of the nationalist revolution was, during the Cárdenas era significant opposition to it arose among nationalists of other types. As Víctor Alba has suggested, some of their attacks reflected middle-class hostility to the economic direction of the revolution. Theorists like Díaz Defoo, for example, attacked the Cárdenas government on the grounds of its anticapitalist tendencies and its excessive economic isolation. The thrust of his argument was that without economic development the revolution would ultimately fail. Gómez Morín held somewhat similar ideas, but represented Catholic nationalism. In 1939 he organized the National Action Party (PAN) which favored private enterprise and the Church.

The most violent nationalist attack, however, came from an extreme right-wing group organized in 1937, the *sinarquistas*. Their name signified the opposite of anarchism but, specifically, they represented fascist nationalism. Associated in the public mind with European fascism, they rose during the latter's ascendancy and declined rapidly after its defeat in World War II.

Most of these attacks on Cárdenas and the revolution had two chief features: defense of the Church and defense of private property. The seriousness of the attack was lessened, however, because the expropriation of the foreign oil companies identified Cárdenas with the kind of economic nationalism that had the widest appeal in Mexico,[12] and because his successor in the presidency, Manuel Avila Camacho, was a protector of private property and openly professed himself a believer in Roman Catholicism.

By the end of the Cárdenas administration, the dominance of the large landowner in national politics had been ended. Agricultural workers were no longer politically or economically helpless; on the contrary they were organized into one of the chief "sectors" of the ruling political party. To be sure, the government still had to appeal to agricultural interests, but that appeal was to the peasants and not to the *hacendados*.

By 1940, Mexico's complex nationalist movement had as its mass base two nationally organized groups of workers, one rural, the other urban. Both groups were officially incorporated into the movement, and each acted as a check on the excessive ambitions of the other. It may be significant that this unity within the movement of the two separate "sectors" acted as a restraint on the movement's potential authoritarianism. A similar restraint resulted from the junction of two other groups, the intellectual elites who had deserted the old regime and the new military leaders who arose early in the revolution mobilized by these intellectuals. Under their joint propulsion, the movement gained even more momentum, but at the same time they became de-

12. The international hazards of the expropriation were reduced by the absolute nonintervention protocol of 1936 (Buenos Aires) and Franklin D. Roosevelt's support of the Good Neighbor Policy.

pendent upon each other both for their new-found power and for their new social and economic system.

The ideology that sustained the movement during these years was completely nationalistic. It preached an independent nation based on a constructed image of Mexican society which, while it drew on the past, demanded a new internal identity based on popular sovereignty, social equality, and economic justice. Despite the fact that this ideology served to destroy an old economic system, it drew on creative impulses deep in Mexico's past and had as its principal feature a constructive goal for the country.

From the beginning of the revolution under Madero, reform was based on the political party as the fundamental binding agent. Even though this type of organizing agent disappeared during the more chaotic years of the revolution, it was recovered when the movement sought to stabilize itself, in the latter years of the Calles era. As in its mass base, in the composition of its new ruling elites, and in its ideology, so also in its structure, the party incorporated the complex and diverse components of the movement. This incorporation of diversity seems to be a source of the restraint developed by Mexico's nationalist revolution even at its apogee in the administration of Cárdenas.

THE LEVEL OF CHANGE

Manuel Avila Camacho, who succeeded Cárdenas in 1940, became, as John J. Johnson has pointed out, "the spokesman of a generation that was prepared to come to terms with the sons of the opponents of reform."[13] Such an accommodation, however, was possible only because Mexico had been irreversibly changed by its revolution. With the break-up of large landholdings and the distribution, between 1915 and 1960, of over 100 million acres of land to the peasants, the semi-feudal agrarian economy was permanently altered. Foreign control over the economy was reduced and organized labor was supported by the government. The economic wealth of the upper class no longer could be based

13. *Political Change in Latin America* (Stanford, 1958), 142.

mainly on landholding, but it could be built in finance, industry, and commerce.

Although for many observers Camacho's presidency marked the end of the revolution, it seems more enlightening to regard 1940 as the benchmark year for the revolution's efforts to unify the Mexican people within the revolution's nationalistic goals. After all, if modernization was implied in the basic aims of the revolution, then the newly created industrial classes of the nation would have to be incorporated into the governmental structure.

During Camacho's presidency, the military sector of the revolutionary party was dissolved. The military leaders were allowed to associate themselves individually with other sectors of the ruling party, and many chose to join the "popular" sector. Made up mostly of white-collar workers, this sector represented Mexico's growing middle class. The military leaders' decision to join this sector on an individual basis was a significant indication of the increased social mobility and growth of Mexican society. Had the situation been different, politically astute military leaders would probably have joined either the labor or the agrarian sector, thereby producing the narrower alliances characteristic of societies where the rulers have less support among the various industrial classes.

Besides this important popular support, which included a growing middle class, the fear of foreign economic domination had been significantly lessened after Cárdenas' successful nationalization of the oil industry. Writing in 1961, Howard Cline noted that "better than 90 per cent of financing underlying the current Mexican boom is local, with outside funds, direct and indirect, still welcome to flow into critical areas under carefully imposed conditions."[14] To the extent that this was true, it was so just because the people felt that their domestic economy was predominantly controlled by them.

Despite the indications that Mexican leaders were now conciliating traditional opponents, they still had to have the support

14. "Mexico: A Matured Latin-American Revolution, 1910–1960," *The Annals,* Vol. 334 (March, 1961), 87.

of most of the forces that had brought them to power. The new rulers were faced with the problem of adapting their nationalist movement from its initial focus on destroying an outmoded political, social, and economic system to its implied purpose of modernizing the society. The legitimacy of the revolutionary government rested on nationalistic norms which did not always jibe with the values needed to develop their economy rapidly. The question inevitably arose as to the capacity of Mexico's new leaders to modernize their country rapidly without modifying in some degree the nationalist consensus.

Some seem to think that the answer to this question is in doubt. Raymond Vernon, for example, maintains that the economic implications of the revolution conflict with reality.[15] He feels that the new leaders of Mexico, in attempting to conciliate their traditional supporters and newer adherents, have only succeeded in avoiding hard and sound economic choices. As a consequence, he argues, economic growth may fail and thereby bring the political system to grief.

There is considerable merit in this contention. Obviously, the government may fall if the country's resources are wasted by inefficiency. Economic reforms, however, are far more accessible to technical expertise than are efforts to restore the loss of faith in the government. In modern political systems as produced by contemporary nationalist movements, the most characteristic feature is that legitimacy comes from "below" rather than from "above." A sound rationale for the elasticity of the nationalist consensus lies in this fact. More than one observer has noted how the Mexican consensus has supported many positions with revolutionary justifications. Nevertheless, hard choices have been made in Mexico at the expense of the "below" legitimacy of the government, and it may well be that the threat to the system from this source is more critical than that from economic inefficiency.

For example, the nagging question of how wealth should be distributed was aggravated by the decision to industrialize rapidly. Many Mexican economists noted that the cost of this industrialization has been borne by the workers. Statistics taken

15. *The Dilemma of Mexico's Development* (Cambridge, Mass., 1963).

from United States, Mexican, and United Nations reports substantiate the charge that the real income of the poor has risen very little, if at all, since 1940, whereas that of the well-to-do has risen substantially.[16] Some observers believe these figures should be partially discounted because a large proportion of the population is rural and in the countryside welfare is not truly reflected by wages.

Since 1940 Mexico's leaders have accepted evolutionary means for modernizing their society. They share the nationalist values that are the pride of the revolution. They are not, however, possessed of a blueprint for a modern society beyond such pragmatic goals as a higher standard of living, social justice, industrialization, and the like. Nevertheless, the traditional system was destroyed by revolution and there remains a strong revolutionary heritage that would describe the ideal modern Mexican society in an inflexible manner.

It is not surprising, therefore, that a variety of nationalist groups have appeared drawing their support from those least benefited by current policies. The Cuban revolution has aggravated this question of the ideal modern society and this fact suggests why outgoing President López Mateos characterized his government as one of the "extreme left within the law."

MEXICO'S NATIONALISM

For the most part, the dominant nationalism in Mexico is restrained and progressive. The nationalist consensus is varied, even elastic. There seems little probability that Mexico's ruling system will degenerate into tyranny. Because the people seem generally to believe in what their government is trying to do, they will probably support its painful adjustment to modernization. In 1934, Samuel Ramos complained that "perhaps the most lamentable truth of our history is to be found in our ancestors' feeling that they had not been themselves with all their vices

16. Oscar Lewis, "Mexico Since Cárdenas" in *Social Change in Latin America Today* (New York, 1960), 285–345.

and virtues but instead had concealed reality behind a rhetorical façade from abroad."[17] The nationalist revolution has, for most purposes, allowed the Mexicans to dare to be themselves. This new-found strength has permitted them gradually to open their international relationships without xenophobic fear of losing their identity. It is true that some resentment against the United States remains. Nevertheless, Mexico as a nation has become a bulwark against adversity and an instrument for improvement for most of the people, most of the time.

17. *Profile of Man and Culture in Mexico* (Austin, 1962), 25.

Argentina: Nostalgic and Dynamic Nationalism

ARGENTINA HAS LED all Latin America in the development of nationalism. She has been first in point of time, first, probably, also in intensity, and first, certainly, since 1910, in the variety of nationalisms strongly supported by rival groups. More particularly, in Juan Perón's administration from 1946 to 1955, she produced for the first time in Latin America a full and explicit combination of nationalism with populism and a foreign policy of nonalignment or, as Perón called it, the Third Position.

Since the first generation of independence in the early nineteenth century, Argentine nationalism has been characterized by two conflicting currents observable in nationalism everywhere: one, nostalgic and traditionalist; the other, dynamic and forward-looking.[1] These currents have manifested themselves both when nationalism was focused on the domestic structure and when its main concern was with foreign relations. Increasingly in the twentieth century the domestic and foreign aspects have tended to converge, as left-wing nationalists, with some aid from other sectors, have popularized the image of a potentially rich country exploited and stunted in its growth by a corrupt alliance between its own oligarchy and foreign imperialists. At all stages the nationalist movement has been related to social change, but

1. For the period before 1916, see the more detailed account in Arthur P. Whitaker, *Nationalism in Latin America, Past and Present* (Gainesville, 1962), Chap. II.

in the space at our disposal the connection can only be briefly indicated from time to time.

RISE AND FALL OF CANONICAL NATIONALISM

The existence of Argentine nationalism in the early decades of independence has been questioned on the ground that Argentina was disunited, that is, not a nation. This is true but irrelevant, for as already noted, nationalism often expresses not a fact but an aspiration, not the existence of a nation but the will to create one. Argentina illustrates this point vividly. National unity was not consolidated until 1880, but from the beginning of independence in 1810 Argentine nationalism found expression in poems, speeches, and other forms, and the present national anthem dates from 1813. The very name "Argentine nation" (*la Nación Argentina*) was adopted by constitutional amendment in 1860, and about the same time myth-makers gained public acceptance of a national hero, the Liberator, General José de San Martín.

There was wide disagreement, however, as to what kind of nation Argentina was to be. In the very first generation of independence a conflict developed between the dynamic, modernizing nationalism of Bernardino Rivadavia in the 1820s and the nostalgic, xenophobe nationalism of the tyrant Juan Manuel de Rosas in the 1830s and 1840s.[2] After Rosas' overthrow in 1852 the dynamic type prevailed again under such leaders as Bartolomé Mitre and Domingo F. Sarmiento, but they were less doctrinaire than Rivadavia, and instead of rejecting Argentina's past, they tried to build on it. Theirs was a liberal nationalism. In domestic affairs, it envisaged an open society, political democracy administered by a natural ruling class, an economy based on free enterprise, and education and equal opportunity for all. In international relations it was pacific, good neighborly, and designed to draw on foreign nations for capital, immigrants, technology

2. Eduardo B. Astesano, *Rosas, bases del nacionalismo popular* (Buenos Aires, 1960), gives a left-wing account of the subject.

and culture, with a view to making Argentina a stronger and more self-reliant nation.

Mitre's generation and the next succeeded beyond all expectations in promoting the country's material development, and by 1914 one would have been justified in calling it the Argentine miracle. Yet in important ways success was self-defeating. Prosperity brought with it the emergence of a corrupt, selfish, and greatly enriched oligarchy, which critics of the new Establishment charged with riveting on Argentina a colonial economy dominated by Great Britain. The very same flood of European immigrants that "washed Argentina white" (a new source of national pride to some Argentines) also eroded the national consensus that had been building up since mid-century. In addition, the immigrant flood stimulated the growth of both a nativist reaction against the foreigners and a new, impatient middle class. By the first centenary of Argentine independence in 1910, there was widespread dissatisfaction with what was to become known in Ezequiel Martínez Estrada's phrase as the canonical or patristic nationalism of the nineteenth century.

One result was a wave of nostalgic nationalism best represented by the new vogue of the gaucho poem *Martín Fierro,* first published in two parts in the 1870s. To many twentieth-century Argentines, the poem has been merely a charming evocation of open spaces and rugged individualism long lost in a country already on the way to urbanization and modernization. Among many others, however, Martín and the gaucho cult built up around him are roughly the equivalent of *sertanismo* in Brazil or Indianism in Mexico; they represent a reaching back into the nation's remote past for the construction of an autochthonous nationalism. More important than this, the myth identifies Martín Fierro with resistance to the liberal, modernizing nationalism of Mitre and Sarmiento, and thereby suggests the rehabilitation of the tyrant Rosas, which was in fact widely attempted in the 1920s and 1930s, and of which more will be said below.

Discontent with canonical nationalism found its best expression in Ricardo Rojas' *La restauración nacionalista* (The Nationalist Restoration, 1909) and later works.[3] Whether or not he was original, Rojas helped to reshape Argentine nationalism in two ways. First, he stimulated its reorientation by arguing that Argentina's major national problem was not (as Sarmiento had maintained in his classic *Facundo*) the domestic conflict between the "civilization" of its cities and the "barbarism" of its countryside, but rather was the defense of its national independence and integrity—cultural, economic, and political—against foreign penetration. Secondly, although Rojas was generally a liberal in politics, he sanctioned the employment of authoritarian means to nationalist ends by urging that the public schools be used by the government to impose one single version of nationalism on all the youth of the nation.

In the political realm, the new nationalism first shaped public policy in the period of Radical domination from 1916 to 1930, but its influence was more clear in foreign than in domestic policy. Most characteristic of the former was President Irigoyen's effort to form a league of neutrals after the United States entered World War I; the effort failed but prefigured Perón's Third Position, or nonalignment policy, of three decades later. A domestic measure of prime significance for foreign policy was the establishment in 1922 of the state oil monopoly, YPF (*Yacimientos Petrolíferos Fiscales*), designed ultimately to make Argentina independent of foreigners for its oil supply. In general, anti-imperialism was one of Irigoyen's most frequent themes, and in developing it he made much of the by now familiar companion theme of the "corrupt alliance" between Argentina's *vendepatria* (country-selling) oligarchy and the foreign imperialists. Yet he did surprisingly little to disturb either of them, and his Radical successor Alvear did even less.

Among the explanations of the Radicals' failure to give full effect to their great leader's economic nationalism, the one most pertinent here is that most Argentine Radicals at that time belonged to the middle class, which was made up mainly of professional men, businessmen, and white-collar employees, all of

3. Earl T. Glauert, "Ricardo Rojas and Cultural Nationalism," Ph.D. dissertation, 1962, University of Pennsylvania Library.

whom were dependent on the country's export economy. The members of this class might and did complain about the corrupt alliance that dominated the existing system, but translating words into action was another matter, for they would be among the first to suffer from any change. Argentina's middle class at that time did not include a sizable "national bourgeoisie" or domestically oriented upper middle class with interests firmly rooted in the country. Such a group did not emerge until the 1930s and 1940s under the impact first of the great depression and then of World War II.

Yet the effect of Irigoyen's preachments against imperialism was great and, indeed, he probably did more than anyone else before Perón to popularize, in Argentina, the theme of economic nationalism. By tireless reiteration he identified himself with that theme, and, although the ouster of the old man's do-nothing government by the revolution of September, 1930, met with general acclaim, his death three years later was followed by a rehabilitation so quick and complete that by the 1940s all politicians except the conservative minority were scrambling for possession of his mantle.

The rehabilitation of Irigoyen was speeded by the character of the two regimes that succeeded his in the next thirteen years. First, for a year and a half, came a military dictatorship which sought to implant an elitist, right-wing nationalism that contained elements borrowed from the France of Charles Maurras, the Italy of Mussolini, and Primo de Rivera's dictatorship in Spain.[4] This was followed by eleven years of oligarchical rule, during which the government promoted nationalism on the home front but sacrificed it in foreign relations. Examples of the domestic nationalism are the central government's increased control over the press, prices, banking operations, and (at the expense of the provinces) domestic commerce. In foreign relations, the oligarchy distinguished itself by its concessions to Great Britain, which tightened that country's already firm hold on the Argentine economy and provoked redoubled cries of "colonialism" and

4. Manuel Río, "Las actuales tendencias social-políticas en la República Argentina" (MS., 1956), Chap. III, "El 'nacionalismo.' "

"imperialism" from a host of Argentine critics. That the limited counter-concessions from Great Britain benefited mainly the hard core of the oligarchy, Argentina's beef barons (*estancieros*), was taken as confirmation of the thesis, popularized by Irigoyen, that the Argentine people were being systematically plundered by a corrupt alliance between foreign imperialists and the *vendepatria* oligarchy.

POLYCENTRIC NATIONALISM

Driven home during the decade before 1943, this belief did much to shape the development of nationalism under Perón after that date. Other factors, however, also went into its making, and these should be examined before we take up the climax of Argentina's whole nationalist process in the Perón period.

The generation of 1910, borrowing elements from the two main nationalist currents of the nineteenth century, produced a new nationalism, best represented by Ricardo Rojas, which was more comprehensive and more fully formulated than its predecessors. It resembled the Rosas-Martín Fierro type only in its nativism, and differed from the patristic type mainly in making the nationalist canon more cultural and economic and somewhat less liberal. More concerned with ends than means, it suffered from lack of appeal to any particular power group in a society that increasingly divided as it multiplied.

An early offshoot of this new nationalism did make such an appeal to the emergent national bourgeoisie. Its first prominent spokesman in Argentina was Alejandro Bunge, an economist well connected in business and financial circles in Buenos Aires. In various writings, principally in a comprehensive analysis of the Argentine economy published in 1928,[5] he warned that dark days lay ahead unless radical measures were taken to strengthen and diversify it. It had not only ceased to grow, he complained, but was also one-sided, vulnerable, and dominated by foreigners. The

5. *La economía argentina* (Buenos Aires, 1928, 4 vols.), especially Vol. I, *La conciencia nacional y el problema económico*.

remedy he proposed was government intervention to build up a strong industrial sector under Argentine control. So strongly did he believe in this solution that he even accepted the military dictatorship of 1930–1931 as the best means of achieving it.

Bunge's hope was disappointed by the early fall of the dictatorship and by the agrarian bias of the conservative regime that grew out of it. Moreover, Bunge did not fully work out a theory of the relationship of nationalism to modernization and the role of the national bourgeoisie in that process, as some post-World War II writers were to do. Nevertheless he clearly indicated both lines of thought and thereby raised a standard to which the national bourgeoisie could repair as it gained strength with the rapid industrial expansion of the 1930s and 1940s. It did not so repair, however, except fitfully, and this type of nationalism has never flourished in Argentina as it did in Brazil after 1950. The explanation is no doubt multiple, but probably a major factor has been the strength of competing types developed since about 1930.

Among these other varieties of Argentine nationalism, two stand out: the Catholic and the populistic (of which there are two main branches, Peronist and Communist).[6] Since in most countries the armed forces are prime agents of nationalism, the reader may wonder why our list does not include military nationalism. The reason is that in Argentina it simply does not exist as a separate category. Argentina's armed forces are at least as nationalistic as those of any other country, but they are deeply divided on the question of nationalism, as on most questions, and each fragment adheres to one or another of the varieties of nationalism already listed. Efforts to establish a specifically military nationalism in Argentina have occasionally been made, notably in 1943, as we shall see, but they have come to nothing.

In the sense that Catholic leaders were avowed nationalists, Catholic nationalism was firmly rooted in Argentina by the 1870s,

6. The best published account of both varieties is contained in *La formación de la conciencia nacional (1930–1960)* (Buenos Aires, 1960), by Juan José Hernández Arregui, whose sympathies are with the left wing but who tries with much success to write impartially about both sides.

as John J. Kennedy has shown.[7] In the next generation, however, anticlericalism combined with other new factors to weaken the solidarity between church and state, and as the twentieth century progressed, new attitudes towards public affairs developed among Catholic leaders, both lay and clerical. The attitudes were based on the common premise that the old order in Argentina would be changed and that the Church should play a positive role in shaping the new order. Beyond this they diverged along two lines that can be described in political terms as left and right. The former, stressing the need for social reform, found significant expression first in the long apostolate among the workers of Monsignor Miguel de Andrea, titular Bishop of Temnos, notably from the 1920s to the early 1940s, and later in the Christian Democratic movement, first openly organized in 1955. But the Catholic labor movement was overwhelmed by Peronism, and Argentina's Christian Democrats, divided among themselves, have never amounted to more than a splinter group even in the aggregate.

Right-wing Catholicism has been far more influential in Argentine public affairs. It is also pertinent to our theme, for it has had a definitely nationalist orientation ever since it first emerged as a significant force in the 1920s. By the early 1940s it had become associated in the public mind with Nazi-fascism, or at least with authoritarianism and military intervention, and its highly articulate exponents had established a virtual monopoly of the nationalist label in Argentina. Once established, this stereotype proved highly durable. An interested foreign observer, visiting Argentina in 1962 and again in 1964, found that when he mentioned nationalism, the great majority of his respondents assumed that he was of course referring to the Right-Wing-Catholic-authoritarian-military variety. This is rather remarkable when one considers that this variety has had a rather small following as compared with others, particularly Perón's populistic nationalism.

A combination of domestic and foreign developments helps to explain the emergence of right-wing Catholic nationalism in the

7. *Catholicism, Nationalism, and Democracy in Argentina* (Notre Dame, Indiana, 1958).

1920s. (It should be recalled that by this time the Catholic Church in Argentina had become identified with the conservative upper class.) On the home front a conservative reaction was provoked by the violent labor disputes culminating in the near-anarchy of the *Semana Trágica* (Tragic Week) of 1919 in Buenos Aires; by the establishment of a Communist party in Argentina in 1920; and by the increasingly secular trend in Argentine society at large. Moreover, this was the period of Radical domination, and while the aging Irigoyen was not anticlerical, many of his fellow Radicals were. A channel for the conservative reaction was indicated by events abroad, such as the rise of fascism in Italy, the Vatican's accommodation with it in the Lateran Treaty of 1929, and the precepts and examples set by Charles Maurras and *Action Française* in France.

Charles Maurras gave a strong impulse to Catholic nationalism in Argentina. Based on an interpretation of history that led him to assign the Catholic Church a key role in the reordering of society, his nostalgic nationalism appealed strongly to many Argentine upper-class Catholics, particularly in Buenos Aires and Córdoba, who regarded themselves as a natural elite wrongfully deprived of power. Since the established version of Argentine history did not suit them, they rewrote it; an extreme example is their rehabilitation of the tyrant Rosas.

This revisionist movement produced some works of sound historical scholarship. One of its chief exponents, Carlos Ibarguren, played a prominent part in politics, notably as a supporter of the dictatorships set up in 1930 and 1943. The movement also produced extremists such as Leopoldo Lugones and Father Julio Meinvielle. Lugones, one of Argentina's leading men of letters in this century, was an anarchist until 1918. After that he became an authoritarian and a champion of the union of the cross and the sword, with the emphasis on the latter. His favorite haunt became the Military Club and his favorite themes, "Democracy is done for" and "The hour of the sword has struck."

Meinvielle was a secular priest who achieved considerable prominence through his writings but otherwise operated largely behind the scenes. His first important book, *Concepción católica de la política* (*A Catholic Conception of Politics*), appeared in 1932. A third of a century later he was still as productive as ever, hammering away consistently at the same themes, with changes of emphasis to suit the changing times. On his highly developed negative side, he attacked with impartial zeal Communists, Jews, liberalism, democracy, toleration, and Yankee imperialism. His positive thought can be summed up as yet another nostalgic appeal for a revival of the "cross and sword" crusading spirit of times past, in support of Catholic nationalism.

The main stream of Catholic political thought in the 1920s and 1930s was more moderate, but the difference was of degree rather than kind. Moderates as well as extremists now asserted a specifically Catholic role in Argentine politics and identified it with right-wing nationalism. The first step was taken in 1922, when the Auxiliary Bishop of Buenos Aires established a kind of seminar, called *Cursos de Cultura Católica* (Courses on Catholic Culture), in which most of Argentina's right-wing Catholic nationalists of the next generation received instruction. Next, right-wingers founded a newspaper, *La Nueva República,* which provided them with a forum. Then, in 1928, an organization of Catholic laymen, formed nine years earlier to promote the Church's social action, was merged with the world-wide Catholic Action movement launched by Pope Pius IX in 1848. Called Argentine Catholic Action, the new organization consisted mainly of laymen, under clerical guidance.

As defined by the Argentine episcopate, Argentine Catholic Action's mission was at first exclusively spiritual; not until 1943 was social action added, and the group was never authorized to engage in political activities. It was difficult if not impossible, however, to segregate any kind of public activity in separate spiritual, social, and political compartments. This was apparent from the start. In 1928 Argentine Catholic Action established a journal, *Criterio,* which, after a brief fling in extremism, was edited by the relatively moderate Monsignor Gustavo Franceschi until his death some thirty years later. Franceschi did not concern himself with the minutiae of Argentina's domestic policies. He dealt extensively with major issues, both domestic and foreign, and pulled no punches in denouncing communism and lauding the European dictators in Italy, Spain, and Portugal who defended Christianity. At the same time he demonstrated his Catholicism by attacking Adolf Hitler and his nationalism by maintaining that no foreign system could meet the needs of Argentina. His stress on the need for social reform in the interest of the workers differentiated him from the extreme right-wing nationalists who would have whipped the masses with scorpions.

Left-wing nationalism had been given expression since the turn of the century by Socialists such as Alfredo Palacios and Radicals such as Hipólito Irigoyen.[8] But in its most significant contemporary variety, the populistic, it began to take shape with the organization in 1935 of a dissident Radical group called FORJA. This name was formed by the initials of its full name, *Fuerza de Orientación Radical de la Joven Argentina* (Radical Orientation Force of Young Argentina), but *forja* is also a common noun which the late Hipólito Irigoyen was generally, though erroneously, believed to have used in a well-remembered revolutionary phrase: "Todo taller de forja parece un mundo que se derrumbe."[9] FORJA represented a rebellion by intransigent members of the Radical party against its leaders, especially Alvear, whom they accused of betraying Irigoyen and of making the party an accomplice of the restored oligarchy by abandoning "abstention and revolution" in favor of normal, legal political action in 1935. These "Young Turks," as some contemporaries inevitably described them, now undertook to clarify, systematize,

8. Divergent accounts of left-wing nationalism are conveniently assembled in Alberto Methol Ferré, *La izquierda nacional en la Argentina* (Buenos Aires, n.d.).

9. Literally, "Every forge seems a world crashing down," implying that din and seeming destruction are essential preliminaries to any constructive change in society. The author of the phrase was not Irigoyen but a Brazilian writer, Paulo Ossório, who used it in a published commentary (April 13, 1921) on a telegram from Irigoyen to Argentine Minister Alvear in Paris. But the phrase summed up Irigoyen's thought so successfully that it was soon attributed to him. He accepted the attribution, and it became a permanent fixture in the Irigoyen myth despite documentary evidence of its inaccuracy. See Ricardo Mosquera, *Yrigoyen y el mundo nuevo* (Buenos Aires, 1951), pp. 93–102. I am indebted to Dr. Roberto Etchepareborda for this citation.

and extend the rather murkily revolutionary and nationalistic pronouncements of Irigoyen on the character and destiny of the Argentine people.

Both of FORJA's original leaders, Luis Dellepiane and Arturo Jauretche, were university students and both sought at first to reform the Radical party rather than to split it, but before long their paths diverged widely. Dellepiane, essentially an organization man, became reconciled with the majority group in 1940, and by the end of that decade he held a prominent place in the party's dominant wing. Jauretche, on the other hand, was a born fighter, with the stubbornness of his Spanish Basque ancestors, who had settled in Argentina in 1854, and he ultimately broke with the party. He was also a gifted propagandist, and is credited with having coined terms that have since become clichés among left-wing nationalists, such as *vendepatria,* with which the reader is already familiar, and the cognate *cipayo,* meaning sepoy or person in the service of foreigners. He likewise helped establish two left-wing stereotypes: first, that the revolution of 1930 was the work of imperialists and *vendepatrias* alarmed by Irigoyen's increasingly clear left-wing nationalism, and second, that since 1930 foreign domination of Argentina had accelerated so rapidly that now the only genuine Argentines left in it were "the humble people," whose poverty proved that their *patria* was in reality only a colony. Yet Jauretche as well as Dellepiane stopped short of advocating class conflict; both men professed to champion the interests of the Argentine people at large, not merely those of its "humble" classes. Accordingly, FORJA's first Declaration of Principles, adopted on June 29, 1935, summed them up in the slogan, "Through Radicalism to popular sovereignty; through popular sovereignty to national sovereignty; through national sovereignty to the emancipation of the Argentine people."

As summarized by a sympathetic Argentine commentator, Juan José Hernández Arregui,[10] FORJA's distinctive features were as follows: (1) A return to the nationalism of Irigoyen and its antecedents in the period before 1852 (which included the Rosas regime). (2) A revival of the original "ideological postu-

10. Cited above, note 6.

lates" of Argentina's celebrated University Reform of 1918 (which were in large part nationalistic). (3) Argentinism combined with Hispanic (Latin) Americanism. (4) Support of the thesis of a coming revolution of the masses in Hispanic America in general, and Argentina in particular. (5) Identification of FORJA initially with the lower middle-class university students in Buenos Aires, though it later had ramifications in the interior of the country. (6) Anti-imperialism aimed against Great Britain and the United States.

FORJA remained in existence for ten years, until 1945. It never won a large following, apparently because its appeal was confined mainly to the middle class, most of whose members remained loyal to the Radical Party, with which FORJA had broken completely by 1940. The break was due in large measure to the latter's nationalistic refusal to take sides in the conflict between Nazi-fascism and democracy, as a result of which it was charged with pro-Nazism—quite unjustly, we are told. As for the masses, FORJA made no direct appeal to them in terms of class conflict; it never sent missionaries into the working class quarters, and its publications seldom if ever used such terms as working class and proletariat. FORJA continued to address itself to "the Argentine people" at large, and that audience it never reached, for the principal newspapers and all the radio stations remained closed to it.

Yet at the end FORJA's leaders felt, with some reason, that somehow—through reaching key persons, through word-of-mouth publicity, with the aid of events at home and abroad—they had succeeded in their missionary enterprise and that the public, so indifferent if not hostile to them in 1935, was now permeated with their nationalist ideas. These ideas had as their core an economic nationalism whose main target was the corrupt alliance between the *vendepatria* oligarchy and foreign imperialists. In addition, they had championed two other ideas that were to be taken over by the Perón regime: the armed forces' collaboration in structuring a new nationalism should be sought, and Argentina's foreign policy should be one of noncommitment in conflicts between the great powers. When Juan Perón scored his crucial triumph on October 17, 1945, FORJA's leaders were satisfied that their mission had been accomplished and accordingly disbanded their organization.

Several of FORJA's nationalist ideas were shared by many Argentines who disagreed with it profoundly on other grounds. The best example is *Acción Argentina,* an organization of 1940–1943, formed by Radicals and Socialists to combat the Axis and defend democracy. Its program called not only for economic independence but also for an intermediate economic policy between free enterprise and state control, as represented respectively by the United States and the totalitarian states.

A third noteworthy variety of Argentine nationalism since 1930 is the one to which Latin Americans have given the apparently contradictory label "continental nationalism." Reference should be made to it here because it was one of the ideas championed by FORJA and later taken up by Perón, but it will be reserved for discussion in a later chapter in the broad Latin American context to which it belongs.

FROM POLYCENTRIC TO PERONIST NATIONALISM

A striking illustration of the strength and diversity of nationalism in Argentina at this time is provided by the three years that began with the military coup of June 4, 1943, and ended on June 4, 1946, with the inauguration of Juan Domingo Perón as constitutional president of Argentina. During these three years, as many different types of nationalism prevailed in rapid succession.[11] First, the Group of United Officers (known as the G.O.U.), who executed the coup, produced one of the few Argentine examples of a distinctively military nationalism. Theirs was not only military but militant. Contained in a secret manifesto circulated among army officers just before their seizure of power, this assigned to the military the role of savior of the Argentine people from their own vices and follies, and to Argentina a

11. These are described in detail in Arthur P. Whitaker, *Argentina* (Englewood Cliffs, N.J., 1964).

hegemonic role in South America. To these ends the military would impose order, discipline, and unity on the nation by every means from physical force to thought control, and would build up Argentina's military might, especially against the "threat" from Brazil.

Almost at once, however, a second type of nationalism came to the fore. Argentina's new military masters found that they must have civilian help in running the government, and since most of them belonged to the top brass, which had conservative leanings, their choice naturally fell on right-wing Catholic nationalists. Chief among these were Carlos Ibarguren, whom we have already encountered; the novelist and anti-Semite Gustavo Martínez Zuviría (pen name Hugo Wast); and Marcelo Sánchez Sorondo, talented exponent of the rather unusual combination of upper-class anti-imperialism and Hispanism. For a brief time men of this kind gave the regime an elitist, traditionalist, Catholic orientation.

But Colonel Perón, a junior member of the G.O.U. and a participant in the revolution of 1930, was convinced by the sequel to that revolution—the failure of dictator Uriburu's effort to establish a similarly oriented system—that the new regime had no future unless it attracted wide popular support. The result was the development of still a third type of nationalism, which we have called populistic. How Perón accomplished his purpose, mainly by organizing the *descamisado* (shirtless) masses in a regimented and greatly expanded General Confederation of Labor (C.G.T.), has already been related in detail elsewhere.[12] Here we need only note that, after a long and bitter struggle, he finally won out on October 17, 1945, which has ever since been a red-letter day in the Peronist calendar.

Perón's position was never again seriously threatened until 1955, and in the not inconsiderable interval he worked out and applied his system of populistic nationalism. Two qualifications of this statement are in order. First, Perón's system was not oriented wholly towards the populace even in theory, much less in practice. On the contrary, the armed forces shared the lime-

12. *Ibid.*, and Germani, *Política y sociedad* (Buenos Aires, 1962).

light in both respects, for the internecine conflict just referred to ended not in a victory of labor over the military, but in a kind of compromise under which these two groups became the main pillars of the regime—with Perón on top of both. Moreover, as things worked out, another major beneficiary of the regime was the national bourgeoisie, mainly industrialists, though that was not part of the theory.

The second qualification is that Perón's system was never fixed and unchanging. Despite his philosophical pretensions and mental agility, he was not a systematic thinker, much less a deep one, and he was an incorrigible opportunist who frequently changed course. To give only one example, in the 1940s he discoursed as eloquently as any Catholic nationalist about the union of cross and sword as the salvation of Argentina, but his last year in power was marked by a sharp conflict with the Catholic Church. As a result, before we describe his system, we must know what period we are talking about.

Yet there is one theme that does run through the whole Perón period, namely its identification of nationalism with social justice and the betterment of the lot of Argentina's plain people, the *gente humilde*. In this respect Perón outdid FORJA in continuing and extending the left-wing nationalism rather vaguely adumbrated by Hipólito Irigoyen. By according the *descamisado* sector preferential consideration, Perón gave nationalism in general a new orientation. As for economic nationalism in particular, his doctrine completely revolutionized its social implications by identifying it with a transformation of society in the interest of the masses. Before this, in Argentina as in most countries, nationalism had been identified with the middle class. He thereby made more plausible his role as integrator of a divided nation, for the *descamisados*—especially their hard core, the new horde of migrants from the underdeveloped interior to Buenos Aires—had been the forgotten men of Argentina.

That Perón stopped short of carrying out his promised social revolution is another matter. As we have already said, one must always distinguish between his theory and his practice, and he continued to preach social revolution almost to the very end, abandoning it only briefly on the eve of his overthrow, in a vain effort to placate his middle- and upper-class enemies. Moreover, his continued preachment of the theory of populistic nationalism was itself a kind of practice, and a very effective one. By dinning it into the Argentine masses for ten years, he gave the doctrine a hold over them that was still strong ten years after he was driven into exile, never to return once in all that time.

In view of the shifting character of the Peronist regime and the opportunism of its leader, anyone seeking documents to define the nationalism of the Perón period must look for them in many places. To begin with official pronouncements, leading examples are the formal Declaration of Economic Independence (1947), which proclaimed the nation's emancipation from the foreign capitalist powers and their Argentine accomplices who had formerly controlled the country; the "Twenty Truths of Peronist Justicialism" (1950), which stressed the third member of the regime's motto (Sovereignty, Independence, Social Justice) for the benefit of the masses; and the amended constitution (1949), which devoted a whole section to "The Rights of the Worker," and included among these not only the rights to work, to a just wage, and to social security, but also to "wellbeing" (*bienestar*) and "economic improvement" (*mejoramiento económico*).

But one must also search widely through other documents such as the speeches of Perón, his wife Eva, and their lieutenants. On May Day, 1952, shortly before her death from cancer, Eva told the *descamisados* massed in the Plaza de Mayo, "Stand by Perón, who stands by you, and we can never be defeated, for we are the real Argentina." Later that same day, in his annual message to Congress on the state of the union, Perón declared that "the capitalist economy has nothing to do in our country," that its "remaining redoubts will be the objects of our implacable destruction," and that "by a natural evolution of our political system, the workers will progressively acquire direct ownership of the capital goods of production, commerce, and industry." A fair sample of the pronouncements of Perón's lieutenants comes from a speech delivered in December 1953 by one of his top cabinet officers, Angel Borlenghi, who described the regime as "the government of the working class" and the late Eva Perón as its guiding spirit. He concluded: "We shall continue to fight against the oligarchy, against oppression, against class privilege. We shall continue to champion the cultural, social, and economic betterment of the workers. We shall continue to carry forward our social program, which is the heart of Peronism."[13]

There was enough truth in Borlenghi's final phrase to distinguish Peronism from Hitler's nazism and Mussolini's fascism, with which careless commentators have often bracketed it: his nationalism was populistic, theirs was not. But his also contained a strong military component; indeed, its main strength lay in the joint support of it by the military and the regimented masses. This gave it a family resemblance to the system built up in Egypt in the 1950s by Gamal Abdel Nasser, and the latter has now found would-be imitators in Latin America, including Argentina, under the label of Nasserism. This is ironical, since Nasser is said by some to have borrowed from Perón. One could find still other analogies between Perón's and certain foreign varieties of nationalism, notably the decisive importance of the charismatic leader. Also, despite its generally revolutionary, dynamic character, Peronism contained a strong strain of the traditionalism and nostalgia so frequently found in other varieties of nationalism, including some in his own country.

But when all is said and done, the most striking thing about Perón's populistic nationalism was its predominantly Argentine character. When he borrowed or imitated or reproduced foreign models, he Argentinized the product, and he gave the abstractions of the student of nationalism a local habitation and a name, which in turn gave them vitality. For instance, he often made the appeal to tradition by invoking the names of the Liberator San Martín and the mythical Martín Fierro, both of whom were generally admired by most Argentines. At the same time, he avoided the name of Juan Manuel de Rosas, for though many of his followers admired the tyrant, the weight of tradition was against Rosas. Perón also asserted his fidelity to most of the

13. Quoted in Arthur P. Whitaker, *The United States and Argentina* (Cambridge, Mass., 1954), 172.

country's democratic traditions and institutions (this is another thing that differentiated his nationalism from the Nazi-fascist type), and when his henchmen in the constitutionally elected convention of 1949 reformed the Constitution of 1853 for him, they reproduced the original framework of government in almost every detail. Finally, when he set about institutionalizing his regime, he gave one of the key institutions, the General Confederation of Labor, the same name that its smaller counterpart had borne under his predecessors.

In short, Perón's was one of the most traditional revolutions the world has ever seen. Yet his populistic nationalism was planted in it like a time bomb, which, as he predicted in his May Day address to Congress in 1952, would some day eliminate the last vestiges of control by foreign imperialists and their Argentine allies and give the workers "direct ownership of the capital goods of production, commerce, and industry."

The thoroughly Argentine character of Perón's type of populistic nationalism helps to explain why the rival type launched by Communists has not flourished in Argentina.[14] The latter has been the work mainly of Trotskyites, for Trotsky, by encouraging nationalism in under-developed countries at a time when it was still under the Stalinist ban, won over many of the rather few Argentine Communists (estimated at 30,000 in 1947, 90,000 in 1957, and 50,000 in 1963). Trying sometimes to rival the Peronists and sometimes to merge with them, these Trotskyites have made a great show of Argentinism, as is illustrated by the queer labels they attach to their nationalist concoction: "creole Marxism," "Trotskyite Peronism," and, queerest of all, "gaucho socialism."[15] They do not mind taking leaves out of other people's books. The most prominent of them, Jorge Abelardo Ramos, calls for a "re-

14. Although Perón never hesitated to use tractable Communists, he denounced communism, along with socialism, from 1944 on, describing them as "foreign ideologies" which constituted the "worst malady of the working classes" and which "the politicians" had always employed to divide and exploit the workers. See for example Juan Perón, *El trabajo al través del pensamiento de Perón* (Buenos Aires, 1955), pp. 19, 21. I am indebted to Samuel L. Baily for this citation.

15. Examples occurring in Methol Ferré, cited, n. 8, are "marxismo criollo," "socialismo gauchesco," and "trosko-peronismo."

union" of the military with the masses in terms redolent of both Peronism and Nasserism, and since 1949 Ramos has been honing Argentine nationalism on the razor-strop of Pan Latin Americanism, as did FORJA in the decade after 1935.[16]

THE LATEST PHASE

Since Perón's overthrow in 1955 no important new variety of nationalism has appeared in Argentina, but there was already an embarrassment of riches, and the competing nationalisms, reflecting the fragmentation of Argentine society, have kept the country in an uproar the whole time. The first provisional military government, under General Eduardo Lonardi, was ousted after less than two months by another, under General Pedro Aramburu, which, surviving a rebellion, lasted until constitutional government was restored with the inauguration of President Arturo Frondizi on May 1, 1958. In the next three and one-half years Frondizi weathered nearly three dozen attempted coups, but was at last forced out early in 1962 by the military, who squabbled among themselves most of the year. The winning faction restored constitutional government again, and the new president, Arturo Illia, inaugurated on October 12, 1963, was still in office though sorely beset, in mid-1965.

Throughout these ten troubled years nationalism in its various guises has been in the thick of the trouble. Catholic nationalism, for instance, dominated Lonardi's administration and provoked a reaction that helped to cut it short. Military nationalism played a brief return engagement during the armed forces' internecine contest in 1962, but the faction that espoused it lost out. Populistic nationalism, on the other hand, was a constant. Preached by Peronist leaders, who controlled most of the C.G.T. unions and garnered from one-fourth to one-third of all the votes cast in successive elections, populistic nationalism seemed about

16. Jorge Abelardo Ramos, *Historia política del ejército argentino* (Buenos Aires, 1959), 74–77; and *América Latina: un país* (Buenos Aires, 1949). Also, in 1953 Ramos led in the "rediscovery" of the Pan Latin-Americanist Manuel Ugarte (see below, Chap. Nine, "Continental Nationalism").

to triumph again when Frondizi was inaugurated. He himself had professed it even when leading the opposition to Perón before 1955, and in 1958 he owed his election to Peronist votes.

Once elected, however, Frondizi did an about-face. Sobered, as they say, by the responsibility of power and convinced that Argentina could not solve its problems without foreign aid, especially from the United States, he soon adopted a plan for stabilization and development that gave his economic policy a misleading resemblance to the liberal nationalism of times past. Actually, he appears to have been trying to fuse populistic nationalism with a bourgeois nationalism reminiscent of Alejandro Bunge.

The latter strain was best represented by Frondizi's close adviser, Rogelio Frigerio, a self-made millionaire who was now dedicated to politics. Frigerio accepted nationalism as a datum, calling it "the distinctive feature of this second half of the twentieth century." But he distinguished his own variety of it sharply from the Marxist nationalism of the left wing and the "aristocratic, reactionary" nationalism of the right. His reasoning was quite simple. Our once rapidly developing economy, he said, has bogged down and disaster threatens. If this is to be averted, quick structural changes and diversification will be necessary, but these require capital, which can be obtained in only one of two ways: either through forced savings that lower the standard of living, which would be unacceptable, or through foreign investments, to which the only objections are doctrinaire and "ideological." "For the Argentines [he declared] there is nothing above the nation itself, and history teaches us that whenever we confuse national interests with vague ideological interests such as 'liberty,' 'democracy,' 'anticommunism,' the tangible results are prejudicial to those [national] interests." . . .[17]

Accordingly, Frondizi welcomed foreign investments and even permitted foreign companies to lay their profane hands on that sacred symbol of Argentine nationalism, the country's petroleum resources. He also made concessions to the Roman Catholic

17. *Unidad nacional o lucha de facciones* (Buenos Aires, 1961), 127, 129, 153–54.

Church, particularly in the field of education, that won him, for a time, the support of moderate Catholic nationalists. Yet, in the fields of politics and organized labor he also made concessions to the Peronists, and these were the immediate cause of his downfall in 1962.

Finally, under the Illia administration after October 1963, public affairs were dominated by two competing nationalisms. One was President Illia's own neo-liberal nationalism, which was firm in some respects and moderate in all. His prompt cancellation of Frondizi's foreign petroleum contracts was balanced by encouragement of foreign investments and business enterprise on terms compatible with Argentina's national interests and dignity and by a reasonably prompt fulfillment of its international commitments. These were interpreted in favor of the West, and in July, 1964, Argentina joined with the majority of members of the Organization of American States in imposing sanctions on Cuba. In its domestic aspect Illia's nationalism was of the older, benign, comprehensive type based on the concept of a plural society combining diversity with unity. Applying this specifically to the country's foremost domestic problem, he sought to end the almost unbroken proscription of the big Peronist minority since 1955 by reintegrating it with the rest of the nation.

Whether the Peronists would ever accept this olive branch was an open question. At any rate, though they were divided among themselves, the dominant faction rejected it now, opposing Illia's neo-liberal nationalism with an uncompromising reassertion of populistic nationalism. This found its clearest expression in the C.G.T.'s "battle plan." In the familiar way, this combined anti-imperialism and the Third Position with implications, if not open threats, of social revolution. Among other things, it aimed at the immediate realization of Perón's prophecy in his address on May Day, 1952, that "the workers will progressively acquire direct ownership of the capital goods of production." Perón had forecast that this could come about through the "natural evolution of our economic action," but the battle planners now resorted to direct though nonviolent action and the turmoil mounted. To speed the process they demanded that the exiled Perón be permitted to return to Argentina. Early in October, 1964, they reinforced the demand by noisy demonstrations on the occasion of the visit of French President Charles de Gaulle to Buenos Aires and Córdoba, bracketing him with Perón as a Third Position nationalist. The demonstrations were repeated on the Peronist red-letter day, October 17, but with no decisive results. In early December Perón did return as far as Brazil, but its government stopped him there and sent him back to Spain, and at the end of the year the issue still remained in doubt.

In any case, it seems likely that Argentina will remain for an indefinite period a battleground of competing nationalisms, for these reflect the nation's deep divisions, which appeared during the period of rapid growth before 1950 and have been deepened by the frustration of arrested development since that time.

FIVE

Brazil: Modernization, Independence, and Great-Power Status

B RAZIL'S NATIONALIST MOVEMENT is marked by several features which are unique in their combination, though not individually. (1) It flowered late, mainly after 1930, for reasons suggested below. (2) Since 1930 it has become exceptionally explicit, elaborate, and broadly based, with special attention to other countries of the developing or, as Brazilian nationalists prefer to call it, the "peripheral" world, particularly those of Africa. (3) Its exponents show a high degree of consensus on aims—modernization, independence, and great-power status. (4) They have shown increasing agreement on the thesis that modernization (meaning development in the broadest sense) is the key to the achievement of their aims. (5) They disagree most widely with reference to the domestically revolutionary implications of this thesis. (6) Agreement is most frequent on foreign relations. Indeed, in this last area nationalism has won apparently overwhelming public support in Brazil in the last few years, though even here there are differences between moderates and extremists. Yet the foreign and domestic aspects of nationalism often overlap, and when they do, consensus easily breaks down, as it did in the coup of April 1, 1964, that ousted the left-wing, nonaligned government of President João Goulart.

LATE BEGINNINGS

It may seem surprising that the development of nationalism in Brazil was comparatively slow—much slower than in neighboring Uruguay and Argentina—for there are reasons why it should have grown at least as rapidly. For one thing, Brazil is the only non-Spanish American country in South America. From the beginning of the national period it has had common boundaries, and hence boundary disputes, with several of its neighbors, as well as a power rivalry with Argentina, which, though it produced only one formal war (1825–1828), has been incessant. Moreover, Brazil's ties with Europe, the original source of all Latin American nationalisms, have been exceptionally strong.

Why Brazilian nationalism grew so slowly despite these favoring factors is a question that requires further study, but the following reasons may be tentatively suggested. Brazil was always much the largest South American state, in population as well as area, and militarily the strongest until the rapid rise of Argentina after 1880. Until its imperial government was overthrown in 1889, the monarch served as the symbol of national unity. The Brazilian upper classes, on the other hand, were either particularistic or oriented abroad, towards Great Britain economically and France culturally, and, it has been argued by some, were stopped by slavery from favoring nationalism. Finally, there was no middle class capable of fomenting the usual nineteenth-century type of nationalism, and no organized working class to foment the modern populist type. Even after the advent of the railroad and the telegraph, the country was so poor in means of transportation and communication that it long remained, in effect, an archipelago, a cluster of loosely connected islands of settlement. In short, until the last decade of the nineteenth century Brazil had neither the need for a nationalist movement, nor the raw materials for it.

Beginning with the 1890s the environment became more favorable to the growth of nationalism. Brazil was now a republic, the nation replaced the monarchy as the chief symbol of the country's unity, and slavery had been abolished (1888). The reaction which had already set in against the cosmopolitanism of the imperial period was intensified. Booming Argentina, always a rival, now emerged as a much more formidable one than ever before.

Some of the forces making for nationalism were economic. Stanley J. Stein has noted those arising from the wide fluctuations of Brazil's basic coffee economy, which "stimulated Brazilians to criticize economic dependence upon one staple subject to the vicissitudes of a world market controlled [by foreigners]. . . ." "In large measure," he writes, "here are the roots of Brazilian nationalism of the 1890s and the early decades of the twentieth century."[1] On the other hand, Nicia Vilela Luz stresses the impulse given to nationalism by the early struggle for industrialization.[2] In the 1890s, for example, came the first demand for the "nationalization" of industry; the demand was far more modest than the term suggests today, for then it meant only that manufacturers in Brazil should be required to use Brazilian rather than imported raw materials, but at any rate the seed of the nationalist idea was planted in this fertile field. Shortly thereafter, in 1903, began the long series of attacks on foreign capital investments in Brazil. The economic impulse was reinforced by Brazilian nativism, which emerged in the 1890s in the guise of a *sertanismo* that glorified the *sertão,* or backlands, in a campaign to shake off the "cultural yoke of Europe." (Simultaneously, Frederick Jackson Turner was glorifying the American frontier in somewhat the same spirit, and before long Argentina produced the cult of its own backlands hero, the romanticized gaucho.) Another manifestation of nationalism about the turn of the century was Brazil's territorial expansion at the expense of her neighbors, particularly Bolivia.

World War I and the establishment of the League of Nations gave a stimulus to nationalism in Brazil, as in certain other Latin American countries. Finally, after 1920, one barrier to nationalism was gradually lowered by new studies of race which exploded

1. *Vassouras, A Brazilian Coffee Country, 1850–1900* (Cambridge, Mass., 1957), viii.
2. *A luta pela industrialização do Brasil (1808 a 1930)* (São Paulo, 1961), Chap. III, "Aspectos do Pensamento Nacionalista Brasileiro," 61–95.

the myth, once generally accepted in Brazil, that nonwhite races, and especially the mixed races, which predominate in Brazil, are irretrievably condemned to inferiority.

Among all these developments, a leading Brazilian authority, João Cruz Costa, holds that the most important for the growth of nationalist thought was *sertanismo* as represented by Euclides da Cunha's now classic book of 1902, *Os Sertões* (published in English as *Rebellion in the Backlands*). To Cruz Costa, Euclides da Cunha is "the forefather of contemporary Brazilian thought," for he announced and combined two of the dominant themes of early twentieth-century nationalism in Brazil: nativism and social justice for the masses.[3]

EFFLORESCENCE AFTER 1930

Unquestionably, however, Brazilian nationalism developed much more rapidly from 1930 to 1945 under Getúlio Vargas, and its character changed. The former year, marked by the "depression revolution" that brought Vargas to power, is described by Cruz Costa as a "turning point for the Brazilian mind." Since then, he holds, an "evolution of conscience" has taken place under the impulse of multiplying socioeconomic changes, and he quotes with approval his fellow-Brazilian Nelson Werneck Sodré's statement that: "A new criticism, history, and fiction became manifest from the 1930s on, when the power of the landed gentry was challenged by a politically very active middle class, and by the appearance on the political scene of the working class."[4] Also, another authority tells us, new elites now emerged which were "national in character, rather than traditionalist or regionalist in loyalties" and which supported "dynamic national development."[5]

3. "Nationalism and the Evolution of Brazilian Thought in the Twentieth Century" (Mexico City, 1962, mimeographed), 5, 6. The same author discusses *sertanismo* in *Contribuição à história das idéias no Brasil* (Rio de Janeiro, 1956), 420–25.

4. João Cruz Costa, *op. cit.*, p. 9.

5. Irving Louis Horowitz, *Revolution in Brazil. Politics and Society in a Developing Nation* (New York, 1964), 302.

To the question "Why nationalism?" Werneck Sodré answers that "nationalism . . . combats the economic, colonial, imperialistic forces and their internal allies and leads to liberation." The validity of economic nationalism, he notes, has been denied by some, but "various aspects of economic pressure speak for themselves." As for political nationalism, this "can be equated with the democratic ideal supported by the aspiring classes, whose need for liberty is similar to that of the human body for oxygen."[6]

This "new nationalism" in Brazil has recently been described by an American writer, Frank Bonilla, as having been "weighed more with an eye to its usefulness than for its mere capacity to charm" and as a "credo for men of power with a job to do rather than for zealots out to refashion the world."[7] On the other hand, its emotional voltage has been given a much higher rating almost as recently by two leading Brazilian authorities, Werneck Sodré and Cruz Costa, who hold that the new nationalism's "liberating feature makes it so passionate that its opponents characterize it as passion rather than politics."[8]

In Brazil as in other Latin American countries, the "liberating feature" of nationalism has had implications for both domestic affairs and foreign relations. The connection is indicated by the passage quoted above which links foreign "imperialistic forces" with their "internal [i.e., Brazilian] allies"; in other words, with those foreign-oriented domestic elements identified by their critics in Spanish America as the *vendepatria* oligarchy and its henchmen. Thus the new nationalism in Brazil contained the usual double dose of potentials: on the one hand, xenophobia and anti-imperialism; on the other, a drive for sweeping social, economic, and political reform, with revolution as the alternative to reform. The former potential was the more deeply rooted of the two. Xenophobia was already finding vigorous expression in the later years of Brazil's Empire, whereas serious social unrest did not

6. *Raízes históricas do nacionalismo brasileiro* (Rio de Janeiro, 1959), 34–35.
7. "A Nationalist Ideology for Development: Brazil," in K. H. Silvert, ed., *Expectant Peoples: Nationalism and Development* (New York, 1963), 260–61.
8. Cruz Costa, article cited in n. 4, in which he cites Werneck Sodré.

become endemic until a generation later, when a numerous proletariat began to pile up in the rapidly growing cities. Both phe-
nomena are familiar enough in the records of other Latin American countries, but, as will be shown below, both have so far been
developed in Brazil with a moderation peculiar to that country.

Important steps towards putting nationalist ideas into practice
were taken in both administrations of Getúlio Vargas. In the
first (1930–1945), immigration was severely restricted and limitations were imposed on the employment of foreigners in business
and in the liberal professions. Brazilians who were not native born
were excluded from public office. Foreign railroads were nationalized by purchase, federal aviation was promoted, the armed
forces were built up, and an iron and steel plant ("the finest symbol of Brazilian economic nationalism" under Vargas, says John
J. Johnson) was started at Volta Redonda.[9] But economic nationalism made perhaps its greatest stride forward in the provision in
the Constitution of 1934, which required the progressive nationalization of key sectors of the economy, including minerals, water
power, and petroleum. Although Vargas scrapped this constitution three years later when he became a dictator, he adhered to
its nationalist policy until the armed forces ousted him in 1945,
ostensibly for flirting with Brazil's rapidly growing Communist
Party.

For the next six years, and under a new constitution (1946),
the nationalist pace abated as the control of public policy passed
into more conservative hands, favorable to the foreign-oriented
economy and free enterprise. In fact, the new constitution stipulated that Brazil's economic structure is based on free enterprise
(livre iniciativa), subject only to limitations imposed by the common welfare.

In 1951, however, Vargas was again elected to the presidency,
this time for the new five-year term prescribed by the Constitution of 1946, although his term was cut short by his suicide three
years later. Nationalism flourished again, as evidenced by three
noteworthy features of his administration. First, an act of Con-

9. *Political Change in Latin America. The Emergence of the Middle
Sectors* (Stanford, 1958), 167.

gress of October 3, 1953, established Petrobrás, a government petroleum agency similar to the older Y.P.F. in Argentina and Pemex in Mexico. It was vested with a monopoly of the search for and exploitation of petroleum deposits in Brazil and the refining and maritime transportation of Brazilian petroleum and its derivatives. Petrobrás was not, however, empowered to engage in the marketing of petroleum products, such as gasoline and fuel oil; this function remained in the hands of private companies, which were overwhelmingly foreign, as were the products they distributed. Second, a stimulus, which long outlived this administration, was given to congressional investigations of such subjects as the administration of the state petroleum monopoly, the activities of foreign oil companies, the production of atomic energy, and the export of Brazilian minerals useful for such production. A collection of reports of such investigations was published in 1959 under the significant title "The Reasons for Nationalism."[10]

Finally, toward the close of Vargas' administration steps were taken which resulted, in 1955, in the establishment of a social science institute, the Instituto Superior de Estudos Brasileiros (ISEB), "with a view to the elaboration of theoretical instruments that will permit the stimulation and promotion of national development." ISEB never developed a single "party line," but in the opinion of a close student, Frank Bonilla, it "unquestionably shaped the thinking of a substantial number of importantly placed Brazilians through its extensive publications, courses, and public lectures." And, he adds, by bringing "the knowledge of social science systematically to bear on the analysis of Brazil's present situation and prospects for growth," ISEB innovated "in an area where more advanced countries continue to lag."[11] ISEB's achievements are all the more notable because it received less government support than had been promised under Vargas and because its assorted nationalist doctrines were strongly combated in influential quarters whenever they threatened the domestic *status quo.*

10. Dagoberto Salles, *As razões do nacionalismo* (São Paulo, 1959).
11. K. H. Silvert, *op. cit.*, 235–39.

The latter point should be stressed, for it indicates the nature and strength of nationalist sentiment in contemporary Brazil. As already suggested, most Brazilians respond to the nationalist appeal against foreign control, but dissidence becomes formidable when nationalist measures impinge on the interests of domestic sectors. In addition, there are grey areas, involving both foreign and domestic interests, where the nationalists themselves disagree. The most obvious example is foreign private investments: some nationalists argue that these will accelerate the winning of economic independence, others, that they will retard it. Almost equally obvious are the hotly debated questions involving the leadership in national development: whether this should be entrusted to the national bourgeoisie or some other group, and the rate at which national development should be pressed with reference to considerations of social and political justice.

REPRESENTATIVE WORKS

How the problems of nationalism in Brazil are presented can be seen best by examining representative works of two leading Brazilian nationalists. One of these is Hélio Jaguaribe's little book "Bourgeoisie and Proletariat in Brazilian Nationalism," the other, a stout volume, "Nationalism and Development," by Cándido Mendes. Although they differ widely, both identify Brazilian nationalism with the urge for national development.

Jaguaribe was a pioneer member of the ISEB group and the author of its first major publication, *The Brazilian Crisis* (1953). On the Brazilian scale he is classified as a right-wing nationalist, but his is a dynamic, forward-looking nationalism. Moreover, the left-wing Argentine publisher of a Spanish translation of his *Bourgeoisie and Proletariat* lauded it for its realistic use of "the dialectical method of Marxism," and, while disagreeing with some of the author's propositions, held it up as a shining example of the superiority of the enlightened bourgeois nationalism of Brazil to the blind, reactionary nationalism of Argentina's bourgeoisie and oligarchy, "which, on every decisive occasion," he moaned, "is wrecked by a pact with the enemies of their country."[12]

Basic to Jaguaribe's book is his concept of nationalism as an "historical-social phenomenon," as a transient but essential function of the development of a given community, and as expressing, not "national characteristics" acquired in the past, but a goal to be achieved in the future. Indeed, Jaguaribe has no sympathy with *sertanismo* and handles all nostalgic nationalism roughly, asserting that "nationalism is anti-nativist and anti-folklorist." For Brazil, he holds, the goal of nationalism is economic development on terms that will assure modernization as well as national independence, social justice, and domestic harmony. As he sees it, the chief problem facing Brazilian nationalists is not class conflict, as in eighteenth- and nineteenth-century Europe, but is the division between the "dynamic" and "static" elements, which cuts across all classes of Brazilian society. His examples of the static element include not only most of the old cosmopolitan oligarchy, which does not wish to risk its present privileges under the existing semicolonial economy, but also large parts of the middle class and the proletariat, such as middle-class bureaucrats who are, in effect, pensioned supporters of the *status quo,* and laborers who, deceived by "charismatic demagogues," turn their backs on long-range economic development requiring hard work and austerity, in order to gain the immediate comforts of shorter hours, higher wages, and job security.

On the other hand, Jaguaribe found strong "dynamic" groups in all Brazilian classes, and among these he regarded the national bourgeoisie, or big business-entrepreneurial group, as best qualified for national leadership. He defended this choice on practical, not theoretical, grounds (he is nothing if not antidoctrinaire). The national bourgeoisie were by definition rooted in the nation, they had a special aptitude for the central task, economic development, they already had the support of many of the intelligentsia, and they could hope to win support of the middle class and labor by proper enlightenment. Just how their leadership was to be

12. Hélio Jaguaribe, *Burguesía y proletariado en el nacionalismo brasileño* (Buenos Aires, 1961), 8, publisher's preface.

established he did not make clear, further than to say that it must be "assumed"; but he insisted that this must be done, and done within one generation. Then development might be achieved "through the maximum efficiency of the entrepreneurial function under a policy that will bring about the closest possible cohesion between Brazilian capitalism and the exigencies of social and mass democracy, particularly with a view to reducing class privileges and equalizing opportunities." The alternative, he warned, would be radical and revolutionary socialism.

Jaguaribe's vote for the bourgeoisie as leader in Brazil's nationalist movement was only one of several features of his book that precipitated attacks on it from the left or the right or both together. The doctrinaires on both sides were offended by his refusal to commit himself wholly to either capitalism or socialism and by his flat assertion that each of these systems has been so modified by the other that, even as represented by the opposite poles, the United States and the Soviet Union, the two are now tending to converge. Most challenging of all, perhaps, was the forthright way in which Jaguaribe applied his antidoctrinaire thesis to the explosive issue of foreign investments and enterprise, even to the extent of laying his profane hands on that new symbol of nationalism, Petrobrás. The important thing, he maintained, is the end, not the means:

> What makes the present petroleum policy nationalist is not the fact that Petrobrás is an enterprise of the Brazilian state, directed by native-born Brazilians, etc. In a general way, the nationalist petroleum policy could as well be realized through the Standard [Oil Company] or any other firm, provided only that, in the actual situation of the country, this proved the most efficient way of exploiting Brazil's petroleum and providing the national economy with the full use and control of that raw material. . . . Nationalism . . . is effective only when it keeps its eye on its goal, which is development. . . .

This was nationalist heresy to Cándido Mendes de Almeida, who set forth his view of orthodoxy in the much longer, left-wing, and otherwise quite different book, *Nationalism and Development*.[13] Though comparatively young (born in 1928, in Rio de

13. *Nacionalismo e desenvolvimento* (Rio de Janeiro, 1963).

Janeiro), Mendes had already written books on "political sociology," the current Latin American scene, and the problems of the Catholic left, to which he belongs. After taking his doctor's degree in the National Faculty of Law in 1950, he taught in various institutions, including the Getúlio Vargas Foundation and the Pontifical Catholic University. In 1961, during the brief administration of Jânio Quadros, who injected a strong note of nationalism into Brazil's foreign policy, Mendes held an important government post in the economic planning section and in August of that year he was a member of the Brazilian delegation to the Inter-American economic conference at Punta del Este, Uruguay.

Nationalism and Development was published by the Instituto Brasileiro de Estudos Afro-Asiaticos, whose foundation in 1961 illustrated additional dimensions of Brazilian nationalism. One of these was the ambition to play a leading part in world affairs, especially among the underdeveloped countries; another, a tendency to identify Brazil with the latter group, of which it is one of the more advanced members, and at the same time to show its independence of the Western powers, in comparison with which it is decidedly underdeveloped. Both the ambition and the tendency had basis in precedent as well as fact. In the 1920s, Brazil had sought to gain a permanent seat in the League of Nations Council, alongside the recognized great powers. In the 1940s, it tried to be the spokesman for Latin American at the close of World War II, during which it had been the only Latin American country to send an expeditionary force to fight in Europe. Both bids for leadership failed, but now Brazil's exploding population made it one of the largest countries in the world in population as well as area, and a large part of it, led by São Paulo in the south center, had made rapid progress in industrialization and modernization since 1945. Moreover, Brazil had long-standing ethnic ties with Africa through the large Negro element in its population, and commercial and cultural ties with Asia dating from the time when it was a part of Portugal's globe-girdling empire.

These wide ties and high aims are reflected in the design of Mendes' 398-page book. Although it deals mainly with Latin

America, as does Jaguaribe's, it treats the theme of nationalism globally, and, unlike Jaguaribe's, it devotes much space to Africa and Asia. From references in the text and footnotes (there is no bibliography), it would seem that the author made extensive use of works by European and North American writers such as Arnold Toynbee, Max Weber, Karl Mannheim, Max Millikan, and W. W. Rostow, and leaned heavily on a Spanish translation of Alfred Weber's *Sociology of History and Culture,* part of which first appeared in German in 1921. Mendes mentions few Latin American works except those of his fellow Brazilians, among them Hélio Jaguaribe's study of Brazilian nationalism published in 1958, *O nacionalismo en la atualidade brasileira.*

As the title suggests, Mendes assigns development, meaning primarily economic development, the key role in his nationalist planning. Like Jaguaribe and many other Latin Americans, he bases his position on the thesis that the advanced nations (mainly Western Europe and the United States) have imposed a kind of colonial economic servitude on the rest of the world, which Mendes and others call the "peripheral" countries and the "historical proletariat." Mendes agrees that Latin America forms a part of this peripheral proletariat and that the Latin Americans, like the other subject peoples, can emancipate themselves only through economic development. On the question of how this is to be accomplished, however, his nationalism is exceptionally hard-bitten and, it would seem, rather doctrinaire. In contrast to Jaguaribe, he turns thumbs down not only on foreign investments but also on aid from such agencies as the International Monetary Fund, on the ground that these institutions are controlled by the very nations from which the "peripheral" world must emancipate itself, and so tend to perpetuate the old regime, including the corrupt alliance between the foreign exploiters and the underdeveloped countries' own oligarchies.

Mendes' views on this question are made clear by his discussion of *Fidelismo* in Cuba and *Frondizismo* in Argentina. Castro, he says, was doing a fine job of producing in Cuba an authentic economic and social revolution of the type all underdeveloped countries require—uncompromisingly nationalist, and geared to his country's needs—until the hostility of the United States forced him to denature it in order to win Soviet protection. Frondizi, on the other hand, says Mendes, provided an "anthological" example of the application of "classical remedies" for inflation (he refers to Frondizi's commitment to the stabilization plan of December, 1958, drawn up by the International Monetary Fund), and maintained the traditional economic structure in alliance with only one of the classes interested in development. In so doing, Mendes asserts, Frondizi chose a path that could only lead to a neocapitalist system of production, through an austerity regime imposed on the masses, thereby closing the door to the structural changes essential to economic development and national emancipation. As for Brazil, Mendes charges that its rulers since 1955 have deliberately used a systematic policy of inflation to create a "climate of ambiguity," that is, to cloud and evade the issues involved in national development. Since such ambiguity postpones decisions and makes them more difficult, he does not like it; apparently, he prefers Castro's more forthright, early approach.

Nothing if not thorough, Mendes rounds out the picture by counseling for the underdeveloped countries a foreign policy of "positive neutralism," which bears a family likeness to Juan Perón's Third Position. But Mendes is franker than Perón, for he openly justifies this policy as a means of increasing the bargaining power of the underdeveloped countries vis-à-vis the great powers by playing them off against one another. This is certainly not a novel tactic in the history of the world, but circumstances— particularly the protracted cold war, in which many Latin Americans feel involved against their will and interests—have recently given the tactic a special attraction for them. This has been even further enhanced by the success with which Egypt's Nasser has exploited it.

FROM FOREIGN TO DOMESTIC FOCUS?

Whether for its tactical value, or as an emotional release for xenophobia, or for some other reason, this Third Position type of foreign policy had won widespread support in Brazil by the 1960s

—wider than any other variety of nationalist policy or position. Although it had been foreshadowed to some extent in the 1950s and briefly asserted by Quadros, the policy was first put into sustained practice by President João Goulart, who had been a protégé of Getúlio Vargas and, reputedly, an exponent of a Brazilian variety of Peronism in the closing years of the Perón regime. As Goulart summed it up early in his administration, Brazil still regarded itself as culturally a part of the West but was no longer committed to any alliance; instead, it would henceforth follow an independent foreign policy aimed only at promoting its own national interests, and to this end would seek friends and trading partners in all parts of the world, whether Communist, anti-Communist, or uncommitted. Stated in these broad terms, the nationalist policy of positive neutralism is reported by two foreign observers, Lloyd Free and Frank Bonilla, to have won strong support in all sectors of Brazilian society.[14]

It has been quite otherwise with the domestic phase of Brazil's new nationalism, for the obvious reason that although the nationalists' ultimate aim is to unite the nation, many of them begin by dividing it into mutually antagonistic sectors and plumping for the victory of one over the other. On the domestic scene, they equate nationalism with sweeping social reform or revolution, depending on their position in the political spectrum. Those on the left are more extreme in foreign as well as domestic policy and seem to be gaining control of the movement with the aid of such groups as the Brazilian Labor Party (P.T.B.) and the National Student Union (U.N.E.). A French observer noted in 1963 that Brazil illustrates the truth of a *Pravda* editorial to the effect that "the malady of leftism is a product of nationalism and in turn nourishes nationalism." Left-wing identification of Brazil with the recently emancipated colonies was being carried so far, he said, that even Augusto Frederico Schmidt, well-known Brazilian statesman and writer, complained that Brazil was being transformed into an "imaginary colony."[15] Others protested still

14. Bonilla, *op. cit.*, 250–51, and Lloyd A. Free, *Some Implications of the Political Psychology of Brazilians* (Princeton, N.J., 1961), cited by Bonilla, 251, n. 1.

15. Jean Jacques Faust, "Brésil 1963: La 'bossa nova' ou la mort," *Preuves* (Paris), No. 148, 32.

more vigorously. One of them, in 1964, accused the "so-called leftists" of espousing an "antinational" nationalism based on a denial or distortion of Brazil's history, and quoted with approval the noted Brazilian writer Alceu Amoroso Lima's statement that "What Brazil needs is a policy that is national but not nationalist."[16] In a similar vein traditional nationalism was defended against so-called nationalists of the left wing who rejected "national values modeled by time in a long process of sedimentation," thereby situating themselves at "the antipodes of nationalism."[17]

As already suggested, there is no sharp dichotomy between the domestic and foreign aspects of Brazil's new nationalism, for the two frequently overlap. This, for example, is one reason why the Alliance for Progress has not prospered in Brazil, at least until the ouster of Goulart's nationalist government in April, 1964. Brazil's static sector disliked the Alliance for its dedication to revolutionary reform, but the dynamic sector, the new nationalists, though liking it for the same reason, looked askance on the Alliance as an engine of Yankee imperialism; they distrusted Achaeans bringing gifts. Hence, although Goulart himself was pragmatic, opportunistic, and no doctrinaire, and tried to work both sides of the street, during his administration Brazil remained the leading example of the failure of the Alliance for Progress to progress.

Another illustration, related to Goulart's fall, was his maintenance of friendly relations with the Castro regime in Cuba. He persisted even in the face of circumstantial charges, upheld in February, 1964, by an investigating committee of the OAS, that Castro was promoting guerrilla warfare and subversion in Venezuela. Goulart may have regarded his Cuban policy as simply an exercise in positive neutralism, but increasing numbers of Brazilians, placing it alongside his tolerance of agents of Communist China and the Soviet Union in Brazil and his pro-

16. João Camillo de Oliveira Torres, *Razão e destino da revolução* (Petropolis, 1964), 114.
17. Fred P. Ellison, "The Writer," in John J. Johnson, ed., *Continuity and Change in Latin America* (Stanford, 1964), 98.

jected agrarian and other reforms, concluded that it had a sinister domestic significance as well. When this view gained acceptance among the bulk of Brazil's armed forces, they overthrew Goulart's regime in a bloodless coup, to widespread, though by no means unanimous, civilian applause.

What this overturn may mean for the long-range development of nationalism in Brazil remains to be seen. Its first effect was dampening but not catastrophic. The new provisional regime, headed by the former Army Chief of Staff, Marshall Humberto de Alencar Castelo Branco, promptly severed relations with Cuba, on the ground that Castro was trying to sow subversion in Brazil. However, it reserved its position on the question of joining with other OAS members in imposing multilateral sanctions on Cuba. Though it finally went along with the majority favoring sanctions,[18] there is no reason to believe that it thereby abandoned the whole popular policy of nonalignment. In domestic affairs, it clearly favored extensive though pacific reform as against revolution. The fact that the new regime was in effect a military dictatorship provided no firm basis for forecasting the further development of Brazilian nationalism. For one thing, the Brazilian military are internally divided by "severe conflicts,"[19] and like the civilians, although most of them are nationalists, they are nationalists of widely different kinds. For another, their provisional regime was expected to lead to a restoration of civilian rule by 1967.

What the nature of the latter will be is the important question. One is tempted to think in terms of Argentina's experience after a similar coup in 1930, which was likewise carried out by the military to loud civilian applause: first there was a military dictatorship for eighteen months, then a restored oligarchy for a decade, and after that another military coup and, for another decade, the Perón regime, which, based on an uneasy alliance

18. Arthur P. Whitaker, "Cuba's Intervention in Venezuela: A Test of the OAS," *Orbis*, VIII: 3 (Fall, 1964), 523, 525.

19. Edwin Lieuwen, *Arms and Politics in Latin America* (New York, 1961, rev. ed.), 167. A paper by Hélio Jaguaribe illustrating this "military factionalism" as it operated in 1961 is included in Horowitz, *Revolution in Brazil*, 138–64.

between the military and regimented labor, produced a kind of populistic nationalism. But the temptation should be resisted. Brazil is not Argentina and the 1960s are not the 1930s.

In comparison with the Argentina of that time, contemporary Brazil has a much stronger national bourgeoisie, a much larger group of "nationalist-minded technicians and planners" (Bonilla's phrase), and a body of nationalist doctrine which, though full of contradictions, is in the main far more forward-looking and better adapted to the specific situation of a developing country than was its counterpart in pre-Perón Argentina. Other differences are that Brazil's armed forces and Catholic Church are more sympathetic than Argentina's had been to modernization, which all the jarring sects of Brazilian nationalists are now demanding, and that the country's great landlords, though still a potent force, are less strong.

Finally, while the political party system in Brazil seems to be as weak as that in the earlier Argentina, the resulting vacuum of political power is not likely to be filled by a nationalist military-labor alliance of the Perón type, for the Brazilian labor movement, while much larger than Argentina's a generation ago, lacks independence and leadership. It might have found a charismatic leader in Luiz Carlos Prestes, the former army officer, who headed Brazil's burgeoning Communist Party in the 1940s, but communism in Brazil has proved a dead end,[20] to which Prestes has remained steadfastly devoted.

Perhaps the solution will be an alliance between the military and the national bourgeoisie and its intellectual cohorts. That might be the way in which the national bourgeoisie would "assume" the leadership in Brazil, as Jaguaribe counseled, with the proviso that this leadership be used to maximize the efficiency of entrepreneurship, adapt Brazilian capitalism to the requirements of social and mass democracy, reduce class privileges, and equalize opportunities. If this condition were met, there could be far worse ways of bringing the whole of Brazil into the modern world.

20. Rollie Poppino, *International Communism in Latin America* (New York, 1965), 12–13.

A large part of Brazil, led by São Paulo, has already been modernized, so that the problem facing the country's nationalists is not the one that faced them a generation ago. São Paulo, with a population of some three million in 1964, is not only the fastest-growing big city in the world, but is also one of the most modern; architecturally, it makes most cities in the United States look old-fashioned. It is also the largest industrial city in Latin America, as Volta Redonda is the area's largest steel-producing complex. Through this center and others, Brazil now accounts for almost one-fourth of the total industrial production of Latin America. In addition, the country has recently taken great strides in the production of petroleum and electric power. Reviewing such facts as these in 1963, even the ardent nationalist José Honório Rodrigues concluded that Brazil was now well on its way to achieving "a satisfactory degree of self-sufficiency, adequate for the protection of the effective exercise of national sovereignty."[21]

Consequently, in Brazil the old nationalist battle cries of imperialism and economic colonialism are obsolescent and may soon be obsolete. There still is much work for nationalist hands to do, but most of it lies on the home front. For example, as Rodrigues also notes, only south central Brazil is advancing, and as it moves ahead, the backward northeast falls further and further behind. Then there are the vast reaches of Brazil which are not even underdeveloped but simply undeveloped; it was largely to this problem that President Kubitschek addressed his heroic (or, as some Brazilians say, harebrained) decision, taken in 1957, to build the new capital, Brasília, in the wilderness. In short, the time may be at hand when Brazilians will focus their nationalism not on foreign but on domestic concerns, as others have often done throughout the history of modern nationalism.

21. *Aspirações nacionais: Interpretação histórico-política* (São Paulo, 1963).

SIX

Colombia and Peru: Defensive Nationalism and Practical Reform

SOME NATIONALISM in contemporary Latin America seems to be primarily defensive. Its leaders react to the modernization problem with reforms designed to mitigate the excessive pressures of revolutionary nationalism while it defends traditional values.

Unfortunately, there is no purely objective way to determine when reformist leaders are defensive nationalists. Usually these nationalists will be drawn from the traditional ruling groups and usually their program will be *ad hoc* or a response to a specific crisis. In Colombia there is an open agreement to maintain stability even at the cost of change; in Peru, there is a radical reform program that may be doomed because those administering it reflect traditional values. Because of these influences, reform does not basically threaten the traditional system's sources of power. On the other hand, revolutionary nationalism, even if implanted in an evolutionary way, would fundamentally change the economic, social, and political bases of power in the society. Defensive nationalists do not intend such a result.

It is not easy to make a definitive statement that the dominant nationalist appeal under Peru's current president, Fernando Belaúnde Terry, is defensive in purpose. It may well be that the nationalism embodied in Belaúnde Terry's *Acción Popular* is more pragmatic than defensive, in that it does not want to alienate the traditional power structure before it has created a power base to support long-term goals. Certainly Peru's other great reform movement, the Apristas,[1] fell into this trap.

Thus it is probable that Peru's contemporary nationalist leaders are genuinely dedicated to practical reform. The stress on community development in Belaúnde's presidency may obtain more basic change than other, more avowedly revolutionary programs. With his drive to let the people undertake their own development projects, Belaúnde may be more successful in developing a "modern" society than is now realized.

One element, however, suggests that the objective result of Belaúnde Terry's practical reforms is a highly sophisticated defensive nationalism. That is the extent of the effort that must be made to destroy traditional bases of power. Belaúnde Terry is praised for the reasonableness of his agrarian reform law, particularly that part which protects productive and efficiently run properties. To be a genuinely revolutionary nationalist, Belaúnde would have to have a little Cárdenas in him, a determination to distribute some of the productive lands in order to affect basic power relationships.

COLOMBIA

Colombia is currently governed under an agreement to alternate the presidency until 1974 between its two traditional political parties, the Conservative and the Liberal. This arrangement is a compromise initiated by the Liberal statesman Alberto Lleras Camargo to restore the country to civilian rule and to reduce the bitter conflicts between nationalist groups. The Conservative and Liberal leaders represent the traditional ruling groups of Colombian society. They offer stability, gradual modernization, and a traditional, mildly reformist nationalism. Their rule is not secure, but they do have some background of flexibility which may allow them to defend their traditional leadership.

1. APRA—the Alianza Popular Revolucionaria Americana—is the name of a movement that united students and workers to initiate social, economic, and political reforms.

A brief historical sketch may suggest how these parties have reacted to change, and the extent to which they are threatened now.

In 1819, with the battle of Boyacá, Colombia gained *de facto* independence from Spain. Like that of Mexico, Colombia's political life degenerated into divisive conflicts between Conservatives, who were supporters of a strong central government, a state church, and limited electoral participation, and Liberals, who were advocates of a federalist government, separation of church and state, and universal suffrage. Their conflicts kept Colombia in turmoil throughout most of the nineteenth century. These clashes did not take on a contemporary nationalist coloration, however, until the twentieth century.

Both the Liberals and the Conservatives were content with the traditional society they represented. Although they clashed over political ends and processes, both accepted the traditional social and economic system as natural and as subject to very slow change, if any.

The Process of Change

In the early twentieth century Colombia suffered a series of jolts that began to widen her self-awareness and to heighten her sense of national identity. The first was the loss of Panama in 1903 through a combination of Panamanian particularism and the high-handed activities of the United States. Hard on the heels of this event came the Mexican and Russian revolutions, World War I, and a significant influx of foreign capital. These events stimulated critical ideas among Colombia's intellectuals and led some to revolutionary social and economic beliefs. Gabriel Turbay, Luis Tejada, Guillermo Hernández Rodríguez, and Moisés Prieto were drawn to communism and were instrumental in organizing Colombia's Communist Party. Syndicalist ideas were advocated by Díos Romero and Mario Coro, and such well-known intellectuals as Germán Arciniegas, Armando Solaro, and Juan Lozano flirted with socialism.

Interestingly enough, the most significant intellectual criticism of Colombian society came from a man who proposed to bring change by working within Colombia's traditional political structures. This important intellectual reformer was Jorge Eliécer Gaitán. In his book *Socialist Ideas,* which appeared in 1924, Gaitán presented his basic views.

Unlike many of Mexico's intellectuals of the pre-1910 period, Gaitán contemplated reform as occurring within the system. He chose the Liberal Party as the vehicle for bringing about change. In order to capture or at least influence it, Gaitán organized The National Union of the Revolutionary Left (UNIR), through which he gradually extended his influence and pushed the Liberals toward greater reform.

High on the list of targets for criticism was Colombia's landowning system. Nevertheless, well before Gaitán and other intellectuals began their criticism of Colombia's agrarian structure, the country had been gradually moving away from a simple *latifundio* and landless peasant split. Although it was true that throughout the nineteenth century many *latifundios* expanded at the expense of Indian holdings, the growing number of mestizos and immigrants from Spain was exerting pressure on the *latifundios,* Indian communities, and the state-owned lands, and was, as a consequence, producing a growing rural middle class.

The pressure exerted by rural migrations set up new settlement patterns quite different from the extreme concentration of land in the hands of the few characteristic of late nineteenth-century Mexico. The rural middle class in Colombia grew rapidly in the late nineteenth century. In some areas, particularly where settlers opened up new lands, as in the Colombian highlands, it eased the conflicts between the great landowners and the peasants.

Colombia aided this colonization process with the rule that occupation and effective cultivation led to ownership. As a result, the landholding pattern in Colombia was not completely rigid. In many areas a quasi-feudal land system did exist but it was never exempt from criticism. There existed a legal tradition backed politically by a small but growing rural middle class which supported the reform of Colombia's agrarian structure. Thus, government support of landowners who violated rights acquired by effective cultivation and residence could fuel mass discontent.

It was just such a violation that made Gaitán a national figure in 1928 and helped to bring the Liberal Party to power under Alfonso López in 1934. In the late 1920s, rural unrest became more and more evident. Its most significant indication was the banana revolt at the port of Santa Marta in 1928. The government, controlled by the Conservatives, crushed the rural uprising by the use of federal troops. Gaitán investigated the revolt for Congress, and charged that the Conservative government had used the nation's military forces to further the economic interests of a foreign company—the American-owned United Fruit Company—at the expense of Colombia's rural workers. A potential link between economic nationalism and a changing landholding pattern was implicit in Gaitán's position.

The increasing dissatisfaction with Colombia's social and economic system that this report mirrored was stimulated by other events. The 1929 depression caused the government to cut back its spending, and when coffee income began to decline, mass unrest was intensified. President Miguel Abadía Méndez, who was also the leader of the Conservative Party's reactionary wing, was criticized by members of its moderate wing. These dissatisfied Conservatives joined forces with the Liberals under the leadership of a wealthy Liberal, Enrique Olaya Herrera. They hoped to lessen the possibility of a revolution by transferring the presidency to moderate Liberal leadership. After a three-week campaign, Olaya was able to win the 1930 elections for his Liberal-Conservative coalition, *Concentración Nacional* (National Concentration.)

The 1930 election represented another step toward cooperation among the members of the elite. Leading Conservatives and Liberals had worked together for years. Between 1910 and 1930 some Liberals had been given influential positions in return for promises not to weaken the Conservatives by supporting Liberal candidates during presidential elections. The need to maintain stability in the face of radical change reveals a tradition of compromise among Colombia's aristocrats. They were alarmed by the depression and the appearance of such radical movements as communism and socialism. To the extent this was a nationalist response, it was clearly designed to defend the traditional power structure.

As president, Olaya did undertake reforms. He distributed some land to the peasants, started low-cost housing, initiated government supervision of the oil industry, and eliminated the tariff charges on goods moving between Colombia's Departments. Nevertheless, these measures did not still the demands, particularly for land distribution, that Gaitán voiced for the rural masses. Gaitán's UNIR-led peasants clashed repeatedly with government authorities and Colombia's domestic crisis was only alleviated because of a territorial dispute with Peru.

Despite the dispute with Peru, the reformist wave continued and brought the Liberal Party candidate Alfonzo López to the presidency in 1934. López vigorously pushed reform, particularly for the rural masses.

In the late 1920s and early 1930s the great landowners made major evictions of peasants who had settled as squatters on their land. One of the first laws that López rushed through Congress gave the rural squatter rights on both public and private lands. These "rights" were clearly stated in the land law of 1936 (Law 200). Under article 4, the break-up of the large estates was authorized if there were many squatters on the land, and it was made difficult for the landowners to prove ownership. The law helped the squatters by creating a presumption of ownership in favor of those who lived on the land and made economic use of it. The great gain of this law was, as Albert O. Hirschman has observed, that it "consummated and legalized the breaking up of certain large estates and plantations which had been in process during earlier years."[2]

López undertook to provide other social legislation for the masses. He accepted, for the government, increased responsibility for the welfare of the poor. For example, Article 19 of the reform law of 1936 stated: "Public assistance is a function of the State."

2. *Journeys Toward Progress* (New York, 1963), 110.

Under this law, the government had discretion in determining what form assistance should take and to whom assistance should be given.

Besides general welfare legislation and rural reform, López attempted to support the urban working classes. His administration explicitly sought to create an independent labor movement, and in 1936 the Confederation of Colombian Workers (CTC) was formed. A López advisor, Carlos Lozano y Lozano, maintained that unions aided social progress and that the government desired to encourage and protect the unions.

López thereby blunted the populist nationalism that was growing around Gaitán and identified much of it with the reforms of the Liberal Party. Unfortunately for Colombia, reaction to López's policies grew rapidly both within and outside his party. The opposition within the party became sufficiently strong to weaken López's influence and led the party to nominate Eduardo Santos as a "moderate" Liberal for the 1938 elections. The Liberal label, however, enabled Santos to gain the presidency.

Opposition to López was most violently centered in the Conservative Party. In Laureano Gómez the opposition found a relentless and resourceful spokesman. He gathered together a group of intellectuals which included Guillermo León Valencia and José de la Vega, who propagandized right-wing views. Hispanidad and Falange ideas were initially present in their thought. Their opposition to López and the Liberals grew even though the second presidency of López (1942–1945) was a pale shadow of his first.

When López returned to the presidency in 1942 he had lost his reforming zeal. A partial explanation for his milder views is that he wished to industrialize the country and to increase agricultural production in the face of wartime inflation and acute supply shortages.

Despite this marked mellowing of the Liberal leader, the right-wing nationalist groups became increasingly strong. Gómez had not rested his appeal on landed interests any more than had right-wing nationalists in other modernizing Latin American countries. He had gained the support of the *burguesía nacional*. In particular, two organizations supported him: the National Association of Industrialists (ANDI) and the National Federation of Merchants (FENALCO). Both groups were drawn from the new class of commercial and industrial businessmen who desired to protect their interests with tariffs and other governmental help.

Because of these developments, López found himself in the embarrassing position of trying to gain the cooperation of the *hacendado* by his law 100 of 1944 to increase productivity, and of the *burguesía nacional* by his efforts to stimulate domestic industry. This put him in competition with Gómez and alienated his populist nationalist support. As López went into eclipse, Gaitán reemerged as the most militant representative of the populist nationalism of the urban and rural masses. When the Conservatives returned to power in 1946, because of Liberal splits, their victory underlined the increasing polarization of Colombian politics. One coalition of nationalist groups, traditional-rural and *burguesía nacional,* backed the Conservatives, while another coalition, the populist nationalists, backed the left-wing liberal Gaitán. When Gaitán had been minister of education in Santos' administration, he had pushed educational programs for the rural and urban masses and had reasserted himself as their champion. This unhealthy polarization of nationalist forces exploded in the famous *Bogotazo*[3] of April 9, 1948, when Gaitán was assassinated. The bloody rioting that followed Gaitán's death was a portent of the protracted conflicts which disrupted Colombian society throughout most of the 1950s.

Since the Liberal split in 1946 between Gaitán, representing populist nationalism, and Gabriel Turbay, then representing the more moderate Liberals, the Conservatives had gained power under Mariano Ospina Pérez. Following the Bogotazo, Ospina attempted some reforms but ran into stiff opposition from his fellow-Conservative, Laureano Gómez. Gradually Gómez came to dominate the Ospina government, and finally had himself

3. *Bogotazo* is the name given to the bloody rioting that occurred in Bogota following the death of Gaitán.

"elected" President in late 1949, with the support of the landed and commercial oligarchy.

During Gómez' administration the country was racked by civil war. In 1953 General Gustavo Rojas Pinilla moved against Gómez, who, he feared, wanted him assassinated. His coup ushered in a dictatorship that to many represented a Peronist-type system. Superficially it had some of the same features: a Third Position between capitalism and socialism, appeals to urban workers, and the initial support of the army and the Church. Rojas Pinilla's regime drew ideological sustenance from *Doctrina del estado nacional,* written in 1942 by Lucio Pabón Núñez. But Pinilla's edifice came tumbling down as his regime proved both corrupt and inept and was opposed by Conservatives and Liberals alike.

In order to end the divisive clashes that had racked the country and to return to civilian rule, the Conservatives and the Liberals agreed to alternate the Presidency between them until 1974. They were agreed on the importance of a stable and orderly society, but not on much else.

The Level of Change

Despite its conflicts the country has been moving steadily away from the traditional system to an urban and industrial society. Nevertheless, in 1961, the rural population remained 51 per cent of the total, and despite the "reforms" 4 per cent of the landowners controlled 64 per cent of the cultivated land. Only two years later it was estimated that the population was now 52 per cent urban.[4] Between 1938 and 1958 migration to the cities accounted for 40 per cent of the rise in the urban population, but this has only slightly eased the pressure for land reform and has brought with it staggering urban problems.

The arrangement between Conservatives and Liberals, based as it is on traditional ruling groups, can survive only if it meets

4. "El País en Cifras," Colombia, Departamento Ad. Nac. de. E. H. (DANE), Bogota, 1963, p. 4.

the extraordinary pressures generated in the rural areas and in the cities by the massive internal migrations. So far, stability has been maintained, but it shows signs of cracking.

A faction of the Liberal Party, the *Movimiento de Recuperación Liberal* (MRL),[5] led by Alfonso López Michelsen, son of the former President, rejects the Conservative-Liberal agreement and claims to be the direct political descendant of Gaitán.[6] There are some signs that the MRL is concentrating on the urban masses as the power base of the future. This situation suggests that a significant proportion of Colombia's populist nationalist leaders are dissatisfied with the present arrangement.

Furthermore, although Gómez was a party to the agreement between the Conservatives and the Liberals, he soon firmly opposed it, and it is possible that he drew a large proportion of the national bourgeoisie with him. This opposition suggests that the reformist nationalism of the coalition government will continue with ever decreasing popular support. Elections in late 1964 confirmed this unhealthy situation. There was heavy abstention among the voters, indicating, at best, widespread apathy.

The bright hope for the current defensive nationalist leaders is Carlos Lleras Restrepo of the Liberal Party. He was the principal champion of another land reform law that was recently passed by the coalition government. It should not be inferred that defensive nationalism in the hands of men like Lleras Restrepo cannot be successful. Geographic barriers, intense regional loyalties, and city-stateism make this sort of nationalist response to change both understandable and appealing. The ecological context sets certain limits on what is economically and socially possible. Other limits to more rapid change exist in the very nature of coalition rule. Thus reform-oriented nationalism is perhaps the most one could expect from the present system in Colombia. Whether or not Colombia can pass the test of adapting to modernity with a mildly reformist nationalism as the defense of her traditional ruling groups remains, as yet, uncertain.

5. It in turn is now (1965) divided in two segments.
6. Alfonso López Michelsen, *Colombia en la hora cero* (Bogotá, 1963).

PERU

Like Colombia, Peru is still highly responsive to the interests of traditional ruling classes. President Fernando Belaúnde Terry came to power in 1962 with a strongly reformist and nationalist program. He promised agrarian reform and effective measures to raise the standard of living. He may not be able to deliver on his promises because he has accepted the traditional democratic system and it is hamstrung by its sensitivity to the wishes of the traditional interests and to the pressures of his rival reformers.

Although Peru has not yet had a successful social revolution, the conditions for producing a revolution have been present for some time. For many years, Peruvian intellectuals have been criticizing the traditional social, political, and economic system, and slowly but steadily various social and ethnic groups have become increasingly conscious of their destiny and its connection with the Peruvian state.

The Process of Change

Some Peruvian intellectuals date the beginnings of the awakening of a Peruvian national consciousness with the fight for independence from Spain, but for most of them the War of the Pacific (1879–1883, in which Chile defeated both Peru and Bolivia) was the critical event that shocked Peruvians into an incipient collective awareness. Manuel González Prada gave voice to this sense of outrage with his cry that "Peru is not a nation, it is only an inhabited land."[7]

González Prada was influenced by his country's humiliation and absorbed the intellectual currents of his times. He perhaps best symbolizes the beginning of the intellectual desertion from the ruling structure of nineteenth-century Peru. This structure represented the interests of the landed oligarchy, the Church, and the military. González Prada wrote that the people had suffered too much, and that it was time they destroyed the false de-

7. Quoted by Jorge Guillermo Llosa, *En busca del Perú* (Lima, 1962), 3.

mocracy under which they lived. He denied that Peru was, or should be, represented by the *criollos* of the coast and stoutly maintained that the Indians of the sierras were the true Peruvians. He denounced the exploitation of the Indians, the indifference of the intellectuals, and the ignorance of the masses.

Some of González Prada's most biting attacks were against the clergy, whom he regarded as intellectually retarded and selfishly allied with the ignorant militarists and *latifundistas*. He gave the classic cry of a nationalist deserting an old system for the love of creating a nation: "Old men to the grave, young men to work!"

González Prada became an advocate of a revolution that would liberate all the oppressed classes of Peru. His ideas have been present ever since in much of Peru's populist nationalism. In this respect, it is significant that his views were also strongly antimilitary. Published in 1933, although written much earlier, his *Bajo el oprobio* demonstrated González Prada's hostility to the military. Shortly after this book's publication, it was suppressed by the military dictator, General Oscar R. Benavides. González Prada's negative views on the military infected most of his intellectual followers in Peru's populist nationalist tradition and are still a factor in the tendency of these leaders to clash with the military elites.

González Prada called for the workers and the intellectuals to unite. His approach was hailed by José Carlos Mariátegui, one of his most influential followers, as "the germ of the new national spirit."[8] In 1921, only three years after the death of González Prada, Víctor Raúl Haya de la Torre attempted to put into practice the unity of the workers and the intellectuals by founding "popular" universities.

There was a less radical criticism of Peru in the late nineteenth and early twentieth centuries that had influence in some reformist circles. A group of intellectuals which included Alejandro Deustua, Javier Prado, and Manuel Vicente Villarán responded to González Prada's challenge to re-examine Peruvian society. Prado stressed the nationality problem, and he encouraged the integration of the Indian. Vicente Villarán, like Sar-

8. *7 ensayos de interpretación de la realidad peruana* (Lima, 1958), 221.

miento, believed in the importance of education in the formation of man and feared Peru's backwardness in this area. These ideas seem more influential today than at the time they were first expressed.[9] In any case they failed to influence Peru's populist nationalism as embodied in APRA. González Prada, and later the *Apristas,* stimulated regional antagonism, which may well have impeded the populist nationalism they were promoting.[10]

Besides González Prada, two other intellectuals, José Carlos Mariátegui and Víctor Raúl Haya de la Torre, are primarily responsible for creating Peru's populist nationalism. Although it was Haya who developed Peru's first organized populist nationalism, the *Aprista* movement, many views of this movement were derived from González Prada. The need to incorporate the Indians into the Peruvian nationality[11] and the necessity to keep Church and State separate were partially his legacies. Neither Mariátegui nor Haya was as anti-Catholic as González Prada,[12] but they shared his hostility to the military and the great landowners.

The rise of these intellectuals corresponded to the rise of the dictator Augusto Leguía, who came to represent Peru's incipient *burguesía nacional.* As in Colombia, Peru's populist nationalism and rising middle-class industrial nationalism conflicted.

In 1919, Leguía, a member of a modest provincial family, rose to power as the champion of Peru's growing industrial middle classes. He mixed into this *burguesía nacional* a heavy dose of religion and clericalism, in addition to establishing the most severe dictatorship in recent Peruvian history. The combination of his autocratic rule with its proclerical middle-class nationalism provoked a student-worker uprising which was sparked by Leguía's dedication of Peru to the sacred heart of Jesus. Haya de la

9. Guillermo Llosa, *op. cit.,* believes that men like Vicente Villarán represent the failure of the progressive conservatives as an effective force in their generation.

10. Frederick B. Pike makes this point in "The Old and New APRA in Peru: Myth and Reality," *Inter-American Economic Affairs,* Vol. 18 No 2, 1964, 11.

11. The goal of incorporating the Indian into the nation was also influenced by Vicente Villarán and others in the moderate group.

12. In some of Haya's early writings he reveals about as strong an anti-Catholic bias as González Prada.

Torre, the revolt's most prominent and articulate student leader, was expelled from Peru.

While in exile Haya traveled widely and studied in Mexico and Europe. In 1924 he founded APRA (American Popular Revolutionary Alliance), which became the organized expression of Peru's populist nationalism despite its strong ingredient of continental Latin Americanism.[13] However, with Haya absent from Peru, the principal populist intellectual living in the country was Mariátegui. He bore most of the burden of furthering Peru's populist nationalism until his death in 1930.

José Carlos Mariátegui had a profound impact on the formation of Peru's populist nationalism. He embraced socialism and applied it to the Peruvian condition. In the process many socialist ideas became nationalized.[14] As late as 1927, however, he considered himself a socialist, not a nationalist. Nevertheless, his socialism was not even materialistic (as a matter of fact, he did not consider Marx a materialist) but a metaphysical conception of life that, in essence, sought a Peruvian national identity. It is in this role as a nationalist intellectual that he has had a lasting impact on Peru.

Although he broke with Haya in 1928 and founded the Socialist Party of Peru, he continued to argue for a mass movement based on rural workers as much as, if not more than, the urban proletariat. Also, he implanted in the populist nationalism of Peru its fundamental hostility to both the landed oligarchy and foreign capitalism.

The best conjunction of Mariátegui's socialist and nationalist thought is found in his *7 ensayos de interpretación de la realidad peruana*. He felt that twentieth-century Peru labored in three different economies. One was feudal and derived from the conquest, another was communist and inherited from the Incas, and the last, the capitalist, had developed during the Republican era. As a result of his three-fold economic analysis, Mariátegui

13. See below, Chap. Nine.
14. Shortly before Mariátegui's death he was denounced as a Trotskyite: Rollie Poppino, *International Communism in Latin America* (New York, 1964), 56.

saw Peru in a complicated exploiter-exploited relationship. The whites of European origin (*criollos*) exploited the lower classes whether the workers labored in the colonial or capitalist economies, since these economies, he believed, mutually supported each other. He felt that the great landowners had become dominated by foreign capitalists and, therefore, subordinated the general interest to foreign interests. According to him, the true Peru was to be found in the sierra, where the Indians lived.

Mariátegui argued that the Indians represented the national interest, and to prevent their exploitation foreign interests should be nationalized and socialized. He claimed that Lima, the capital of the *criollos*, should be "decapitalized" and that a new capital should be set up somewhere in the sierra. The Indians were the key to a new and better Peru. They were more national than the *criollo* aristocrats; they were the basic ethnic group of Peru, "the cement of the nationality."[15]

Mariátegui also protested the country's political forms. He considered Republican Peru a farce and maintained that Peru had betrayed her national personality by imitating forms of government that were meaningless in the Peruvian context. Although he lived for only thirty-five years, Mariátegui's imprint on Peru's populist nationalism has been indelible.

Unlike Mariátegui, Haya de la Torre developed Peru's populist nationalism along lines that led it into open opposition to international communism. He explicitly modified the Marxist argument by noting that imperialism was the first stage in the development of an underdeveloped country. In his later years, he argued that it was impossible to plan socialism until there were assets to socialize. Thus he maintained that private capital investment should be encouraged until the country was sufficiently developed so that nationalization and socialization would mean something.

By 1930 the *Aprista* movement had begun to develop momentum under Haya's inspiration. The depression had seriously hurt Leguía and opposition to the dictator had increased. As conditions further deteriorated, a revolution led by army Colonel Luis M. Sánchez Cerro broke out in Arequipa. The revolt was

15. *Ibid.,* 289.

successful and Sánchez Cerro installed himself in the presidential palace.

He ordered elections in 1931, and Haya de la Torre's *Apristas* claimed victory. Nevertheless, Sánchez Cerro announced his own victory. During the election campaign, Haya had visited many parts of the country and organized *Aprista* cells wherever he went. He had established a widespread political organization to support his populist nationalist movement, but he encountered increasingly severe military opposition. As the *Apristas* gained support they became involved in a bitter struggle with the military.[16] When Sánchez Cerro was assassinated in 1933, the military blamed the *Apristas*. Intermittent conflict between the two groups continued throughout the dictatorship of Oscar R. Benavides (1933–1939), and to this day they still oppose each other as a matter of course.

Until the 1945 elections, the *Apristas* either had been prohibited from going to the polls on their own (1939) or had witnessed the returns being annulled (1936). In 1945, however, they supported José Luis Bustamante y Rivero and he gained the presidency. Although indebted to the *Apristas,* Bustamante cracked down on them when Francisco Graña Garland, the director of the newspaper *La Prensa,* was assassinated. Because of *La Prensa*'s harsh attacks on the *Apristas,* Garland's death was attributed to the highest leaders of the party. Despite Bustamante's action, the military moved against the government and ousted him.

In the fifteen years between 1930 and 1945, the populist nationalism represented by the *Aprista* movement never was able to establish itself firmly in the presidential palace. It had always been strongly opposed by traditional landowning groups, which are still powerful, as well as by the military.

After World War II, the national bourgeoisie became increasingly influential and continued to oppose the *Apristas,* and also the landed aristocracy. They increasingly tended to represent the

16. Whether it was the military or the *Apristas* who started the conflict remains controversial in Peru. There is considerable evidence that the *Apristas* are not as blameless as has sometimes been maintained. See Pike, *op. cit.,* 25–27.

interests of the urban upper class and were supported by the influential newspaper *El Comercio*. An extreme group within this nationalist sector was the *Unión Revolucionaria*, which former dictator Sanchez Cerro had started in the early 1930s.

The conservative agrarian interests represented by the rural upper class received the backing of *La Prensa*. Their most effective organization, which was founded in 1947, was the *Alianza Nacional*, led by Pedro Beltrán. This traditional nationalist group invariably opposed the agrarian reform proposals of APRA. For this reason, the revolt against Bustamante in 1948 initially looked as if it were dominated by their interests. But the *Unión Revolucionaria* also was represented in the revolutionary junta. Despite these elements General Manuel Odría emerged as the chief figure of the new government.

Although more "moderate" than some in the *Unión Revolucionaria*, Odría favored urban interests, including the urban workers, over the landed oligarchy. His regime raised urban wages and introduced profit-sharing for the workers. He attempted to remove *Aprista* leaders from the trade unions and sought to bring labor more directly under government control. The landholding system remained unaffected, however. He represented another attempt by a military leader to link the army with urban forces and thereby establish a firm power base for the benefit of the rising industrial interests.

In 1956, the *Apristas* emerged again as the power behind the President, this time, Manuel Prado. Prado won the presidency with their help and they appeared to be set to gain power on their own in 1962. This dream never came true. Fernando Belaúnde Terry, an architect and the leader of *Acción Popular*, won the presidency when the military prevented an Odría-*Aprista* coalition from taking office and ordered new elections.

Level of Change

The process of change in Peru suggests that there had not been either a successful populist nationalist movement or a triumphant national bourgeoisie prior to the victory of Belaúnde Terry. Despite this lack of militant and reformist nationalist success, the conditions for a social upheaval are present. Peru has an entrenched landed oligarchy and an export economy. A high proportion of its people live outside the money economy, and its numerous intellectuals voice the grievances of its lower classes.

In this situation, Peru has begun to implement social reform under the leadership of Belaúnde Terry. In a country where 1.4 per cent of the population owns four-fifths of the arable land,[17] the government has finally passed a land-reform bill. Already some 900,000 acres of land have been redistributed to the restless peasants, with the exception of efficiently run farms and the highly productive sugar and cotton plantations of the coast. Nevertheless, the leader of the left wing of Belaúnde Terry's own *Acción Popular* argues that the bill prostitutes the reform program. Some believe it maintains the privileges of the oligarchy while only producing more unproductive small plots for the peasants.

Belaúnde Terry offers Peru another opportunity to modernize within the framework of her traditional institutions. There appears to be very little desire in Belaúnde's *Acción Popular* to maintain the status quo. Nevertheless, Belaúnde and AP may necessarily have to proceed somewhat more slowly than reformers in other Latin American countries. One reason for this more deliberate pace is the value judgments of many coastal Peruvians, irrespective of social class, who continue to fear rapid change on ethnic grounds. This semi-racial or cultural tension has impeded Peru's economic nationalism. The belief that the Indian is inferior has fostered the judgment that Peru needs help from abroad. Consequently, revolutionary reform, even if it is offered at an evolutionary pace, is feared both for its international and internal consequences.

On this basis a defensive nationalist may be considered genu-

17. It is estimated that 7,800 families own one-third of the land. Near the capital city of Lima six haciendas average fifteen square miles each, with the owners paying their workers an average of seventy cents for a thirteen-hour day.

inely dedicated to change. Belaúnde Terry stimulates this change by encouraging the people to act on their own initiative and to cooperate with others in their communities. This sort of emphasis may be more revolutionary than is presently believed. As a defensive nationalist leader, he offers reform and a steady, if unspectacular, commitment to modernization.

Much of the change occurring in Peru today is spontaneous, although some of it is now directed and stimulated by the country's traditional leaders. Nevertheless, the ingredients for a major social upheaval are still present. The traditional social, economic, and political structure is intact. It may break down, however, if Belaúnde Terry's moderate policies are either unsuccessful or too successful.

SEVEN

Chile, Uruguay, and Venezuela: Revolutionary Nationalism and Evolutionary Change

R EVOLUTIONARY NATIONALISTS who support evolutionary change have provided one answer to the problem of how to keep the people's support while modernizing their societies. They attempt to bring about change in the terms of their nationalism, but using the means at hand. They thereby talk revolution and practice evolution. The three countries discussed in this chapter are all, in varying degrees, struggling with nationalist values that may conflict with the most efficient, rapid, and pragmatic methods for modernizing their societies. All have different prospects.

CHILE

Currently Chile is ruled by the Christian Democratic Party. The President, Eduardo Frei, makes no bones about his determination to redistribute wealth and power in a country where two million peasants—one-quarter of the population—are still virtually outside the money economy, where 2.5 per cent of the landowners have 75 per cent of the land, and where over 300,000 children go uneducated every year because of the school shortage. Frei knows what the Chilean people want: "The Chilean people want a government capable of making rapid reforms, economic development and social justice, and I think that is the essence of our movement."[1] Unlike his Communist rivals, Frei never promised to nationalize "imperialist monopolies," meaning the American-owned copper mines. These mines represent a U.S. private investment of $750 million and account for 90 per cent of all Chilean copper production and 60 per cent of all Chilean foreign exchange income. Frei has a more evolutionary attitude toward fundamental change, for he plans to "Chilean-ize" the copper industry by having the government buy into the big American companies. Despite the promise of Frei and his Christian Democrats, Chile has had a long history of frustrated revolutionary nationalism.

The Process of Change

In Latin America, there is no country more proudly national-istic than Chile. Raúl Marín Balmaceda expresses this pride when he describes Chile: "Formed by the bravest Indians of America, and by the best soldiers that Spain had to send to the most re-bellious of its colonies; forged as a race in an incessant battle against men, against nature, and against the poverty of the soil, a natural selection of men was formed that should make us the exception of America and an example to the world."[2] Neverthe-less, since the late nineteenth century, Chile has been preparing for a social and economic revolution that to this day is still largely unfulfilled.

Between the end of the war of the Pacific (1883) and 1891 both the Army and the Navy became predominantly commanded by men of middle-class origin. This change in the social com-position of the Armed Forces began to show up on the political scene in the 1920s. In Chile's intellectual community a grow-ing concern with social problems and the ordinary man accom-panied the changes in the military.

Early in the twentieth century Chilean literature became oriented to social problems. The exploitation of native workers by the large and mostly foreign mining corporations was a favor-

1. *The Evening Bulletin* (Philadelphia), November 20, 1963.
2. *Derechas o izquierdas?* (Santiago, 1945), 7.

ite theme. Baldomero Lillo represents this trend especially well
with his *Sub-Terra* (1904) and *Sub-Sole* (1907). Literary figures
like Federico Gana and Mariano Latorre probed Chilean nationality through descriptions of the countryside and regional
customs. Others discovered the Chilean common man and his
surroundings and found them both worthy of novels and poems.

The changing social composition of the military and the
growing intellectual concern with social problems was accom-
panied by a constant increase in the urban population. In 1930,
when Chile began to articulate in a popular manner some of her
revolutionary nationalist demands, 45 per cent of the population
was urban. This urbanization trend has continued. In 1940, 52.5
per cent of the population was urban, and in 1952, it had swollen
to 60.2 per cent.

In 1920, social change was already a burning issue in Chilean
politics. Elected to the Presidency in 1920, Arturo Alessandri,
the "Lion of Tarapacá," was the first national political figure
who attempted to exploit the concern with social change and
social justice. Alessandri was hindered in his endeavors to establish constructive programs because other politicians, including
some traditional conservatives, vied with him for working class
support and did not want him to take all the credit for such
progress as occurred.[3] Alessandri's social justice program floun-
dered between the hostility of rival politicians and the fear of
taxation. In theory social justice was fine, but in practice it required the taxation of the rich, something not even Alessandri
was willing to undertake.[4]

In 1924, the military, supported by extreme conservatives, removed Alessandri from office. Then, these military leaders, a
rather small minority, were replaced by a younger junta of
middle-class officers composed of Carlos Ibáñez del Campo, Bartolomé Blanche, and Marmaduke Grove. Favoring greater state
intervention in the economy and wanting to develop ties with
the growing urban working classes, these officers invited Alessandri back to serve out the balance of his term.

3. Frederick B. Pike, *Chile and the United States* (Notre Dame, 1963), 177.
4. *Ibid.*

During this period, Alessandri pushed through a new constitution in which the power of the presidency was greatly increased vis-à-vis the legislature. The cabinet was made directly responsible to the President and church and state were separated. Nevertheless, land reform and other basic issues were generally neglected, despite the new constitutional stipulation that the government was responsible for the general welfare.

General Ibáñez, who had been instrumental in bringing Alessandri back, remained on the scene. In the national elections of May 22, 1927, he gained the presidency unopposed. With the support of the military, he did much for the masses and appeared to have the potential to lead a populist nationalist movement. He had military support and attempted to woo the trade union movement. He used the government's power to structure a labor force favorable to his regime. He created his own union and granted it legal recognition as the Republican Confederation of Civic Action (CRAC). It in turn supported Ibáñez and his vague ideas of a corporate state.

Despite the potential for a nationalist and populist support for Ibáñez, his movement collided with Chile's growing economic nationalism when he sold many of the nation's nitrate mines to the Guggenheim interests. For many Chilean nationalists, Ibáñez became the man who ruled the country at a time when United States capital seemed to be taking it over. Indeed by 1930, foreign capital investments exceeded those of domestic investments in manufacturing, industry, and mining. Such developments blurred his nationalist-populist image and made him vulnerable when the full effects of the depression were felt in Chile. Between 1929 and 1932 revenue from the sale of nitrates and copper fell from $27 million to $3.5 million, and these sales accounted for 70 per cent of the national income. As a result, the country in 1931 could buy only 12 per cent of what it had imported in 1929. In the face of this almost complete collapse, Ibáñez resigned in July 1931.

Following the fall of Ibáñez, the country went through a period of chaotic change which even included a short-lived "Socialist Republic." However, in 1932 Alessandri became President again, this time with the support of the traditional conservatives. This return to "normalcy" was briefly interrupted (1939–1941) by the popular front government of Pedro Aguirre Cerda, which was backed by the Radical, the Socialist, and the Communist parties. The Radical-led Popular Front coalition produced a great deal of social welfare legislation but it fell from grace during the war.

The Radicals continued to control the government until 1952. However, these years saw the gains made under previous administrations vanish because of inflation. Middle- and lower-class discontent rose because of inflation and helped account for the successful return of Carlos Ibáñez to the presidency in 1952. The passing years had dulled the impact of the fiasco of his first administration and once again he played his familiar reformist role.

As President, however, Ibáñez made no fundamental attack upon the nation's problems. He fell into the conservative pattern of believing that those problems that could be solved would solve themselves. He did make an attempt to halt Chile's perennial inflation. However, this symptomatic element of Chile's festering economic nationalism remained out of genuine reformist hands for one more presidential term. The failure of Ibáñez led to a revival of the traditional Conservative and Liberal parties. In 1938, Jorge Alessandri, the son of Arturo, ran on the conservative ticket and won. He called for honest government and economic austerity. However, the narrowness of Alessandri's victory underlined the shaky position of the Conservative forces. He won by a mere thirty-five thousand votes over a coalition of Socialists and Communists called Popular Action Front (Frente de Acción Popular, or FRAP) and headed by Salvador Allende.

To a dangerous degree, this group appeared to speak for Chile's lowest classes: the landless peasants and the industrial workers who represent 70 per cent of the population of eight million. In addition, the strong showing of FRAP indicated that Communists and Socialists were increasingly identified with Chile's economic nationalism. The only party that could prevent FRAP from monopolizing Chile's popular economic nationalism was now the Christian Democrats.

Chile's economic nationalism has deep and complex roots.[5] It is evident, as the quotation from Raúl Marín indicates, that Chilean national pride runs deep. Politically, militarily, and culturally the Chileans have a strong sense of national identity and great self respect. For years, however, they have struggled with an ailing economy.

In the middle of the nineteenth century, Chile adopted the habit of turning to foreign experts for the solution of economic problems. Beginning in 1855, Chile relied on a Frenchman to educate its young economists. Jean Courcelle-Seneuil imbued his students with classical economic theory, and many of Chile's current economic nationalists still complain about his influence. Some believe that the laissez-faire economic liberalism taught by Courcelle-Seneuil turned the military and political victory of the War of the Pacific into an economic defeat. This defeat occurred, they believe, when Chile returned the nitrate mines to private owners following the war. The private owners in turn sold out to foreign monopolies, thereby becoming *vendepatrias*. To this day, Chileans charge that the influence of foreign economic theory brought by foreign experts has continually harmed the economic interests of the Chilean nation.

In 1925, the Kemmerer mission came to Chile. In order to apply effective monetary control of inflation, the mission recommended that Chile go on the gold standard and establish a central bank. The government accepted these recommendations and faithfully put them into practice, but the political results were unfavorable. Many considered these monetary measures as weapons of the oligarchy. The privileged classes were to reap benefits at the expense of the masses. In other words, many people less well off than the oligarchy felt that stability would freeze a *status quo* that left a great majority of the population perpetually poor.

Chile's leaders continued to seek foreign help in managing inflationary problems. In 1949, the government invited the advice of missions from both the United Nations and the International

5. One of the best accounts is Albert O. Hirschman, *Journeys Toward Progress* (New York, 1963), 161–223.

Monetary Fund. The advice given by these two missions did not significantly alter Chile's policies and did not eradicate the continuing inflation problem.

During Ibáñez's second regime (1952–1958) inflation continued its unsettling course. By the end of 1953 it had become acute, and the government turned to a team headed by Prescott Carter from the Washington consulting firm of Klein and Saks. Undoubtedly, the recommendations of the mission prevented Chile's inflation from getting out of control. But politically, and eventually economically, the mission's policies—which were based on familiar monetary principles—were rejected. Chilean economists such as Aníbal Pinto developed what they felt were proper methods of dealing with the sources of Chile's inflation, rather than its symptoms.

The new argument was called "structural." Its principal thesis was that basic economic patterns in society must be changed in order to prevent inflation. The structuralists see the landowning pattern as completely outdated. They charge that monetary controls—credit restrictions, wage and salary freezes, or balanced budgets—only treat superficially an economically distorted society. The disease is the *latifundio* system, which they blame for agricultural inefficiency and a consequent unnecessary demand for agricultural imports.

This attitude toward the landowning system completed the picture of Chile's economic nationalism. Hostility to foreign-owned companies, opposition to the landowning patterns, and a major change in the structure of the economy were its main features. The Christian Democrats identified with this revolutionary reform program and came to power in 1964.

The Level of Change

With the triumph of the Christian Democrats in the presidential election of late 1964 and the congressional election of early 1965, all the reforms Chile needs—land, tax, constitutional —can be approached in a calm and constructive manner. That reforms will be carried out in an evolutionary manner despite the revolutionary promises of the Christian Democrats is suggested by the Party's historical and national development.

The Christian Democratic movement in Chile began in 1935 as the *Falange Conservadora*. It drew its ideas from papal encyclicals, particularly *Rerum Novarum, Quadragesimo Anno,* and *Mater et Magistra,* and the writings of Jacques Maritain. It is not a confessional party and it offers a third position between Washington and Moscow.

Even before the 1964 elections the Christian Democrats had shown great strength among the working classes. They recently claimed control of as much as one-third of the nation's labor unions. During the 1964 election campaign, the Christian Democrats stole so much of FRAP's political thunder that the Chilean Communist Party secretary-general, Senator Luis Corvalán, said: "They steal all the fruits of leftist agitation and play on the unfounded fear in parts [sic] of the Chilean people about how we would carry out those revolutionary reforms."[6]

The Christian Democrats attacked Chile's class structure and offered to bring about a social revolution. The Party platform called for higher progressive income taxes and higher import duties to support domestic industries. Foreign investment, the program maintained, must be made to operate under closer Chilean control, including an increase in Chilean representation in the management and ownership of foreign concerns operating in Chile. The Party also promised to improve education, particularly that of the lower classes.

Late in the 1964 campaign, Frei attacked as irresponsible and unrealistic FRAP's plans for nationalizing foreign concerns. He claimed that his plan of "Chileanization" was less extreme and more effective. Two other factors aided the Christian Democrats in their defeat of FRAP, the fear of international Communist control of the country and hostility to atheism. Both these aspects of communism clashed with Chile's indigenous political and cultural nationalism.

It is, of course, too early to be sure that President Eduardo Frei will effectively tackle his country's problems in an evolution-

6. *The Evening Bulletin* (Philadelphia), November 20, 1963.

ary manner. But he is imaginative and constructive and may well be Chile's last chance at evolutionary fundamental change. In his *Pensamiento y Acción,* Frei argues against both capitalism (in its unrestricted sense) and communism. He believes there is an alternative to the evils that exist in both systems. He seeks a "humanistic economy."

Frei and the Christian Democrats have identified most closely with Chile's economic nationalism. They object to unfavorable terms of trade, unrestricted foreign private investment, insufficient aid from the United States, slow industrialization, and backward agricultural conditions. The Party is committed to carrying out revolutionary nationalist reforms within the established system.

URUGUAY

José Batlle y Ordóñez was the great revolutionary leader of Uruguay during the early part of the twentieth century. He brought to Uruguay revolutionary ideas of social justice and economic reform, and the first half of the century saw most of them written into the nation's life. In recent years, many of these now traditional values have been attacked as hindering a more rapid modernization of Uruguayan society. The challenge to the national identity inspired by Batlle is coming from a historical opponent, the *Blanco* party.

Like the other Latin American republics, Uruguay was unstable when she obtained her independence. Throughout the nineteenth century her politics revolved around the intense party conflicts that developed from the rivalry of two great caudillos, Manuel Oribe and Fructuoso Rivera. The followers of Oribe wore *blanco* (white) ribbons while the followers of Rivera wore *colorado* (red) ribbons. From 1843 to 1851, Oribe's forces kept Rivera's backers bottled up in Montevideo. The *Blancos* received backing from the Argentine dictator Rosas and the *Colorados,* from the British and French navies as well as anti-Rosas

Argentines. The long years of fighting etched into the Uruguayan national profile a party division that remains to this day.

Structurally the two parties were similar; each had local chieftains, and each had followers both in the interior and in the capital city of Montevideo. Nevertheless, Montevideo is considered to be predominantly *Colorado* and the countryside, mostly *Blanco*. Until the beginning of the twentieth century, the rivalry was personal and traditional, but gradually more fundamental divisions developed, largely as the result of the work of one great *Colorado* leader—José Batlle y Ordóñez.

The Process of Change

José Batlle, sometimes known as Don Pepe, was the son of a famous *Colorado* chieftain and former president of the Republic. In his early life he demonstrated an intense interest in philosophy and was caught up in the late nineteenth-century debates in Uruguay between Idealists and Positivists. Indirectly influenced by the German Idealist K. C. F. Krause, Batlle subscribed to the view that society could be reformed if its foundations were built on the innate dignity of man. Indeed, he declared that a book written by Krause's Belgian disciple Ahrens had served as his guide in public life. Early in his career Batlle demonstrated an egalitarian interest in the masses. In 1889, when he began managing the newspaper *El Día,* it sold on the streets for two cents a copy and thus became Uruguay's first paper aimed at a mass readership.[7]

Despite these rather meager signs of Batlle's unusual interests and potential unorthodoxy, he gained the presidency in 1903, principally as the result of astute political infighting. It could not have been otherwise, because under Uruguay's complex representational system there was no other way to gain power peacefully. His reputation as a reformer was limited at this time to the political realm. He had argued for free suffrage and for a reorganized *Colorado* Party based on internal democracy rather than on

7. Milton I. Vanger, *José Batlle y Ordóñez of Uruguay: The Creator of His Times* (Cambridge, Mass., 1963), 24.

its perennial boss rule. He also urged one-party rule as against the established practice of government by pacts or deals between *Colorados* and *Blancos*. Nevertheless, he himself made deals to gain power in 1903,[8] and he attained his goal of one-party rule only after the chief *Blanco* leader, Aparicio Saravia, had been killed in the civil war of 1904. Although he was known to favor protective tariffs, he made few public statements about his economic views prior to his first election.

The most significant feature of Batlle's first term (1903–1907) was that he emerged as a *Colorado* hero. His victory over the *Blanco* forces established him both as firm party leader and as a national figure, and united the party under his leadership. The civil war of 1904, which consolidated *Colorado* control of the government, was followed by a great electoral victory in 1905 that put his followers in the key party posts all over the country. From this position of strength he was able to start the country on its spectacular reform when he returned to the presidency in 1911.

Throughout his first presidency, Batlle represented a political nationalism aimed at centralizing political power. In subsequent years, however, changing conditions in the country allowed him to identify his party and the government with social and economic reform.

By the turn of the century Uruguay was already a highly urbanized country. Thirty per cent of the developing nation's population was located in Montevideo, and heavy immigration—a quarter of the population was foreign-born—had brought with it new skills of many kinds. The country was modernizing and this fact, together with the concentration of the new population in urban areas, gave Batlle and his *Colorados* a chance to champion the new interests. His success made Uruguay for many years the envy of South America.

Perhaps Batlle was successful in his efforts at modernization because the traditional system that was so strong in other countries of Latin America was relatively weak in Uruguay.[9] Its Indian

8. *Ibid.*, 67–68.
9. Many of the ideas in the following two paragraphs are suggested by John J. Johnson, *Political Change in Latin America* (Stanford, 1958), 45–47.

population, never large, had been either killed off or rapidly absorbed into the predominantly European society. Although the rural landholding patterns were based on large estates, most of these raised cattle and did not exploit the tenant farmer to the excessive degree found elsewhere in Latin America. The fairly typical rural man was a gaucho or cowboy who was anything but downtrodden. In any case, the traditional economy and society were already changing by 1900 under the impact of foreign investments, business enterprise, and immigration. Moreover, Uruguay had a rather weak military tradition. To be sure, there were military rulers and many conflicts, but the evenness of the *Blanco-Colorado* split prevented purely military domination.

Finally, the Church's position had never been strong. In colonial times Uruguay, late and sparsely settled, had been remote from the Church's traditional South American center in Peru. The first diocese was not established in Uruguay until 1878, and at the close of the century there were only 122 parish priests in the whole country. Although the country's constitution made Roman Catholicism the official religion, it also allowed freedom of worship. Most of the country's intellectuals, including Batlle, were anticlerical. In addition, the high rate of illegitimacy—as much as one-quarter of all births—suggests the weakness of the Church's influence among the lower classes. Finally, the great number of immigrants who came to Uruguay's shores in the nineteenth century were relatively unchurched, even though they came from Catholic Spain or Italy.[10]

In short, the system that Batlle was to start changing so remarkably in his two presidential terms was not well entrenched. When he began initiating his reforms, Uruguay's social, economic, and political identity was in flux. It was Batlle who initiated what was to be Uruguay's first national identity. The reaction to this identity explains many of Uruguay's contemporary nationalist problems.

10. Arthur P. Whitaker, "Nationalism and Religion in Argentina and Uruguay," in William V. D'Antonio and Frederick B. Pike, eds., *Religion, Revolution and Reform* (New York, 1964), 76–80.

The Level of Change

Under Batlle, Uruguay embarked on many reforms. In his first term a divorce law was initiated and in his second term he encouraged constitutional reform to separate Church and State. Such measures relegated the Church to an official role commensurate with its political power in the rise of Uruguay as a secular nation-state. Whereas this anticlerical strain was strong among the *Colorados,* some factions of the *Blancos* have woven pro-Church ideas into their beliefs to oppose the *Colorado* type of nationalism.

Batlle was first and foremost a nationalist. Early in his career, in 1878, he had founded a journal devoted to emancipating "the American spirit" from Old World tutelage. As president, he strove to emancipate Uruguay from economic domination by foreigners, first, by strengthening the national economy, and second, by nationalizing its key features.

Batlle's chief means of strengthening Uruguay's economy was to diversify it. He encouraged domestic industries with protective tariffs and gave tax credits to Uruguayans who invested in the national economy. Research organizations were established to help the new national industries. The Industrial Chemicals Institute and the Fishing Institute were created to promote new industries and provide them with up-to-date technical procedures. By 1920 over one-half the nation's gross national product came from manufacturing and commerce.

Nationalizing key features of the economy began in earnest in Batlle's second administration. This meant not only transforming ownership and control from foreign to Uruguayan hands, but also transferring them from private hands to the Uruguayan government, for he noted with approval (in 1911) that "The sphere of state intervention is expanding in every civilized country." In 1911, the government entered the insurance field; in 1912 it took over the nation's light and power business; in 1915 it began to acquire (by purchase) the country's British-owned railways. Under Batlle and his successors the program was extended to other fields, such as banking, port facilities, and packing houses. Private enterprise and foreign investments were not squeezed out completely, but, in the main, the modernization of Uruguay, particularly in the manufacturing and processing industries, was encouraged and directed by the government.

When Batlle first came to the presidency in 1903 Uruguay's labor unions were weak. After the civil war of 1904, the recently formed railroad union attempted a strike for higher wages, a shorter working day, and other benefits, but Batlle did not intervene and the strike was broken. It was evident that the unions at this early stage could not help themselves. Batlle set out to change the anti-labor attitude not only of the government but of the people as well, and in most respects, the urban workers found the atmosphere congenial under his subsequent *Colorado* governments.

Batlle's attitude toward the role of government in furthering social and economic justice resulted in an excessively large bureaucracy. For example, the social security system started by him was based on separate funds for each working group. As a result, there was no single administrative system covering what is now the largest welfare-state operation per capita in South America. The cost was and continues to be staggering.

Uruguay owes another reform to Batlle. In 1907, between his presidential terms, he traveled to Switzerland and was greatly impressed by its system of a plural executive. Over strong opposition, he finally got a modified version of the Swiss model written into the Constitution of 1919. Scrapped in 1934, this still controversial reform was revived in 1952, since which time Uruguay has had a "collegiate" executive consisting of a nine-man National Council of Government, six of whose members come from the majority party and three from the minority.

Neither Batlle nor his subsequent *Colorado* followers in the presidency took much interest in furthering agricultural reform. As a consequence, the rural economy deteriorated. This came about partly because much of the interior was discriminated against as *Blanco* territory and partly because, as industrialization progressed, the farmers and ranchers found themselves subsidizing this growth through a complicated multiple exchange system which increasingly reduced their power to purchase modern equipment, fertilizers, and the like.

Under their great leader the *Colorados* established for Uruguay a modern identity that harmonized in most respects with the social and economic trends of the times. An orientation toward urban areas, a firm commitment to social welfare programs, a strong assertion of economic nationalism, and an inventive if controversial solution to the problem of the too powerful chief executive were all elements in this Uruguayan national identity.

For almost half a century this system also had strong social and political support. Most intellectuals, except the Marxist university professors, approved. Batlle's *Colorados* had adopted most of the socialists' criticisms of the inhumane capitalist system, and socialism or some variant of it was in vogue among nationalist reformers. The urban masses also approved. Their needs were given more than a sympathetic hearing and they received concrete benefits while retaining their own independent organizations. Such a situation was enviable indeed! As for the commercial and industrial classes, the *Colorado* regime gained their support and deserved it. Those people who are often identified as the national bourgeoisie had many of their interests and aims anticipated and satisfied long before they had become a highly politicized group.

Despite this impressive achievement, the national identity maintained by the *Colorados* was constantly attacked and is now seriously threatened. The principal challenge comes from the Blancos.[11]

Although the *Blancos* have often used the word "Nationalist" as a substitute name for their party, they, like the *Colorados,* are not really an ideological party. They draw on Uruguayan historical experience and represent certain enduring national interests. They are generally more conservative economically and socially than the *Colorados*. They are not as anticlerical and they tend to represent the interior or rural interest more than urban areas, though they have important city supporters.

11. For excellent material on this, see Philip B. Taylor, *Government and Politics of Uruguay* (New Orleans, 1962).

It is neither fair nor accurate, however, to equate the *Blanco* party exclusively with large business and agricultural interests. For example, a recent leader of the party, Benito Nardone, was spokesman for lower class rural interests. Formerly allied with the *Colorados,* Nardone switched in 1956. By means of his weekly newspaper, *Diario Rural,* and his twice-daily radio broadcasts, Nardone had exercised important influence over rural and conservative voters. Other *Blancos* have been influenced by fascist ideas. Luis Alberto de Herrera was the foremost *caudillo* of the party until his death in 1959. He was noted for his sympathy for Hitler and Perón and for fascism in general. His attitudes were shared by another important *Blanco* leader, Eduardo Víctor Haedo.

In 1958, a coalition of Nardone, Herrera, and Haedo led the party to victory for the first time in this century, aided by divisions within the *Colorados.* The *Colorados* were divided between two factions, mainly by personal rivalries within José Batlle's family. One faction was led by his sons, César and Lorenzo Batlle Pacheco, and the other by his nephew, Luis Batlle Berres. Personalism is still a force to be reckoned with in Uruguay.

The new *Blanco* government undertook some important reforms. Exchange controls were abolished, as were import quotas, import duties were standardized, and a mild income tax was enacted. These measures helped the interior rural economy. The *Blancos* have attacked some of the elements of the *Colorados'* social and economic system and the idea of the plural executive.

In this changing situation, Uruguay has begun to show the stresses that were already apparent in other Latin American countries. An important difference, however, is that the *Blanco* attack is on a "traditional" system that has most of the elements of the welfare state. The strong social welfare orientation which is the dominant feature of her national identity has been maintained at a cost that now exceeds her means. The supporting economy shows signs of stagnation, political wrangling blocks remedial measures, including Alliance for Progress projects, and frustration breeds extremism on both the right and the left.

Whether the resulting tensions will be resolved by moving

further to the right or to the left cannot yet be determined. Some observers fear that growing activism among the military and discontent among the masses may combine to fortify a populist and military nationalism. In any case, the revolutionary ideas so gradually accepted by Uruguay under Colorado rule are now under major attack. The ever-changing problems of modernization keep requiring adjustments in nationalism. Uruguay's flexibility, no doubt, will be tested.

VENEZUELA

Venezuela has had a long history of military dictatorship. Today, the country is ruled by the Democratic Action Party (Acción Democrática, or AD), which has revolutionary nationalist goals but is committed to carrying them out within a constitutionally established system. This commitment to evolutionary means despite revolutionary ends is criticized by the impatient. Nevertheless, it seems to have the overwhelming majority of the people behind it, for the two parties next in size to AD likewise advocate evolution. Venezuela's revolutionary and modernizing nationalism has been fermenting for a long time.

Like so many of her fellow Spanish-American countries, Venezuela fell into a long period of domestic strife following her liberation. Much of the nineteenth century was marked by contention between Liberals and Conservatives ceaselessly struggling for political power.[12]

Venezuela's modern ills are usually traced to Cipriano Castro, who ruled from 1899 to 1908. He was noted for his personal vices and misrule as well as for his cavalier attitude toward Venezuela's international obligations. In 1902 Venezuela was blockaded and bombarded by warships of Great Britain, Germany, and Italy because he refused to pay debts claimed by them on various grounds. Castro finally paid, and later traveled to Germany for

12. For a good nineteenth-century history see Guillermo Morón, *A History of Venezuela* (London, 1964). A good general modern account is Edwin Lieuwen, *Venezuela* (London, 1961).

his health. While he was there, in 1907, Vice President Juan Vicente Gómez took over the government and ruled Venezuela with an iron hand until his death in 1935.

Although Castro had discouraged foreign investors, Gómez invited them in to develop the country's resources, not so much on principle as from lack of it. Even before World War I, British and Dutch oil interests gained concessions from Venezuela. They were followed after the war by American interests. The companies were permitted to write their own code for the exploitation of Venezuelan oil, and by 1928 Venezuela was the world's second largest producer of oil and the world's largest exporter.

A genuine opposition to Gómez's political rule and economic policies quickly developed. A group of intellectuals, centered among the students at the Central University in Caracas, were inspired in their opposition by the writings of the Venezuelan novelist Rómulo Gallegos. Known as the Generation of 1928, they raised the banner of social justice, economic nationalism, and democracy. They were particularly bitter over the foreign control of Venezuelan economy.[13] Their opposition reached its first peak in February of 1928, when they revolted. The revolt failed, as did all subsequent efforts to oust Gómez.

After Gómez's death, Eleazar López Contreras ruled the country, and began to relax the dictatorship. A new constitution was adopted which prevented the President from being immediately re-elected and shortened the presidential term from seven to five years. Also, Congress under his regime granted greater rights to labor.

The law was immediately exploited by members of the Generation of '28. These leaders formed a political party, Venezuelan Organization (ORVE), which propagated their views. Rómulo Betancourt was the driving force behind its creation. Alarmed by ORVE's success in gaining support among the people, López Contreras cracked down on it and other "leftist" parties. As a

13. For a description see John D. Martz, "Venezuela's 'Generation of '28': The Genesis of Political Democracy," *Journal of Inter-American Studies,* VI:1 (January, 1964), 17–32.

result, until just before the 1940 elections, his own political following remained the only legal political group in Venezuela.

After its suppression by López, ORVE reorganized as the Democratic National Party (PDN), but this soon split into Communist and non-Communist factions. The non-Communist leaders of the PDN regrouped as the Democratic Action Party (AD), and in 1940, nominated Rómulo Gallegos, whose campaign was managed by Rómulo Betancourt.

Again López, following traditional practice, prohibited direct elections and named Isaías Medina Angarita candidate for President. Medina was of course elected. With the aid of pressure from Washington on the oil companies in the interest of the war effort, Medina's government won notable success in gaining a greater share of the oil revenues; but criticism of the overall political and economic situation of Venezuela continued to mount.

The Process of Change

The intellectual elite of AD had long been the vanguard of this criticism. AD promised reform to all the workers no matter where they worked, in the oilfield, the factory, the school, or the office. It also called for electoral reform and taxes on foreign investors and native capitalists. Important military backing was given it by some younger military officers who had formed a military lodge, the *Unión Patriótica,* led by three men, Major Carlos Delgado Chalbaud, Major Marcos Pérez Jiménez, and Captain Mario Vargas. These officers were disenchanted with the policies of the top army officials and the dominance of the traditional landed aristocracy, particularly the coffee-producers of the western states. In fact, the alliance with AD was proposed to the latter by one of the lodge's leaders, Pérez Jiménez. On October 18, 1945, the lodge spearheaded a revolt that removed Medina from office.[14]

The lodge leaders then turned the government over to the civilian leaders of AD. Rómulo Betancourt was named provi-

14. Olive Holmes, "Army Challenge in Latin America," *Foreign Policy Reports,* XXV:14 (1949).

sional president and served in that capacity for two years. The AD drive for political reform was evident from the beginning. A new electoral law gave all Venezuelan citizens over eighteen the right to vote. All restrictions on freedom of speech, press, and assembly were removed, as were restrictions on political parties.

Besides AD, several other political parties emerged. A Christian Democratic party, COPEI, was formally organized in 1946 by Rafael Caldera.[15] Like the Christian Democrats of Chile, it originated in the middle 1930s when it had been partially inspired by the Spanish Falange. It was at that time connected with the landholding interests of the Andean States of Tàchira, Mérida, and Trujillo. Caldera cooperated with the new regime and began to widen COPEI's appeal by expanding its social and economic reform program.

Another party that gained importance at this time was the Republican Democratic Union (URD) founded by Jóvito Villalba. Also a member of the famous Generation of 1928, Villalba left AD because of conflict with Betancourt for control of that party. The URD, too, was democratic and reform-minded. Although it sought working-class support, it was not considered to be as far left as AD at this time.

Late in 1947 presidential elections were held, and the AD's candidate, Rómulo Gallegos, was victorious. One of the first tasks the Gallegos government undertook was to gain a higher percentage of the oil companies' profits. It also set up plans for a state-owned oil company to exploit Venezuela's reserve fields, and launched a broad-based attack on the conditions in housing, education, and agriculture. Perhaps the most important issue facing the AD government was that of land reform. At the time of the 1945 revolution, approximately 80 per cent of the land was owned by only 5 per cent of the landowners. Furthermore, out of a population which in 1946 was two-thirds rural, a mere 10 per cent held title to any land whatever. With some three-fourths of the arable land lying fallow, AD faced a staggering reform problem.

Under Gallegos, the government attempted to remedy this

15. The full name of COPEI is Independent Committee for Political and Electoral Organization.

situation. It adopted an Agrarian Reform Law which was intended to avoid Mexico's mistakes while profiting by its examples. Although great estates were to be broken up, the owners were to be compensated and the economies of large-scale operation were to be retained by appropriate means, such as collectives or government management. Provision was also made for improving transportation, credit facilities, and farming methods, and the administration of the reform was centralized in a new National Agrarian Institute.

In 1948 this reform regime was ousted by the same young officers who had brought it to power in 1945; it was too reformist and civilian to suit them. One officer, Marcos Pérez Jiménez, was a member of the military triumvirate that ruled until 1950, when he became sole dictator.

The extent to which the AD's domestically oriented reform movement had caught on was illustrated when Pérez Jiménez attempted to legitimize his rule by holding elections in 1952.[16] Although AD was not allowed to campaign, both COPEI and URD were given free rein. The URD maintained a program that even went beyond that of AD, for it not only supported the latter's domestic reform programs but also challenged the economic penetration of the country by foreign capitalists. This won it AD endorsement and a majority of the votes, but when the early election returns indicated an URD victory by a wide margin, Pérez Jiménez stopped the publication of election results and announced the victory of his own party. Subsequently, he was named to serve as "constitutional" President for a term of five years.

During his rule, Pérez Jiménez violated many of the nationalist principles of Venezuela's reform parties. He failed to check the penetration of the foreign oil companies into new oil-producing lands. For all practical purposes he abandoned the agrarian reform program of AD and other nationalist parties and made no sustained effort to aid the industrial working classes. In addition, he ridiculed the democratic and representative political

16. José Rivas Rivas, comp., *El mundo y la época de Pérez Jiménez* (Caracas, 1961).

ideas of those parties, repeating the tired slogan that the people were not yet ready to rule themselves. His policies and corruption aroused the united opposition of the political parties, and even alienated most of the military. In a bloody coup—over 350 persons were killed—Pérez Jiménez was expelled in January, 1958.

The ruling Junta, led by Admiral Wolfgang Larrazábal, promised elections, and the leading parties promised to cooperate in restoring constitutional government. When elections were held in December 1958, Rómulo Betancourt, the leader of AD, gained the presidency with 49 per cent of the vote. He was followed in order by Larrazábal, the candidate of the URD, and Rafael Caldera, COPEI's standard bearer.

The Level of Change

Under Betancourt, who again had COPEI as a coalition partner, reform of the traditional structure really began. On March 5, 1960, an agrarian reform law was enacted which revived the National Agrarian Institute, (IAN). In late 1961 an IAN survey showed that over thirty-five thousand peasant families had been settled on slightly under a million and a half hectares; by 1963 the total had risen to some fifty-seven thousand families on a million and a half hectares.[17]

The land-distribution program was bitterly disputed between Ildegar Pérez Segrini, president of the IAN, and Ramón Quijada, president of the Peasants Federation. Pérez Segrini felt that the land given to the peasants should be government-owned land that was relatively underpopulated. Quijada voiced the Peasants Federation's position that privately held lands should be distributed to their tenants. This latter view became the official policy of the IAN in late 1961.[18]

AD's agrarian reform has been attacked by nationalists of both the left and the right. The left-wing position is well represented

17. Robert J. Alexander, *The Venezuelan Democratic Revolution* (New Brunswick, 1964), esp. chs. 11–14.
18. *Ibid.*

by the views of Domingo Alberto Rangel, formerly an AD deputy, who became a significant figure in the Castroite Movement of the Revolutionary Left (MIR).[19] He charges that the reform has proceeded too slowly and without sufficient attention to raising the productivity of the peasants, and that it has been inspired by political opportunism rather than by the real needs of the peasants.

The right-wing position magnifies the relatively infrequent seizures by the peasants of privately owned land and their effect on the development of a sense of responsibility. In the right-wing view the result has been to retard economic growth.[20]

Despite these criticisms it seems clear that AD has a solid base among the rural masses because of its land reform policies. The great majority of the peasant organizations are loyal to AD, except in the Andean states of Mérida and Táchira, where they support COPEI. As a result, Cuban type revolutionary movements have not been welcomed among the peasants.

On the other hand, AD has nowhere near the same support among the urban working classes as it enjoys in rural areas. The reasons are many. Foreign corporations still control key sectors of the economy, including the recently developed iron mines and the older petroleum industry. The cost of food is high, for such staples as eggs and corn are imported. For many among the working masses, social and economic justice is still remote, and the AD government is blamed. The stickiest issue is the dependency of the Venezuelan economy on foreign-owned oil. Betancourt realized, as must all fair-minded Venezuelans, that he could not nationalize the oil companies even if he wanted to, which he probably did.[21] As he knew, a nationalization program would have completely disrupted the economy because practically every government fiscal program was dependent on revenues from oil.

Accordingly, Betancourt left oil alone while attempting to

19. Demetrio Boersner, "El proceso electoral venezolano," *Política*, 3:27 (October, 1963).
20. *Ibid.*
21. See Rómulo Betancourt, *Venezuela: Política y petróleo* (México D. F., 1956).

build up other sectors of the economy. He instituted high protective tariffs to aid new domestic manufacturing, supported government financing of private companies engaged in manufacturing, and initiated government involvement in such fundamental areas as electricity, steel, transportation, petrochemicals, and aluminum.

Much of the criticism of Betancourt, particularly from the left, stresses that in the process of seeking an admirable goal, the government's budget has become even more dependent on oil, thereby enhancing the influence of the foreign oil companies. However, if the policies initiated under Betancourt are successful, this situation should not last indefinitely and AD may regain much support among the highly politicized urban masses.

Most of Venezuela's nationalist energies are directed toward internal problems. The important exception has been the increasing hostility against Castro's Cuba for its proved interventions in Venezuelan affairs in support of the subversive terrorist organization FALN (Armed Forces of National Liberation).[22] Thus AD's candidate for the presidency, Raúl Leoni, in 1963 ran on a program that included greater international cooperation, support for the principle of self-determination, and opposition to the totalitarian regime in Cuba.

The orientation of AD's traditional national values is both domestic and foreign, as indicated by its official goal of bringing to Venezuela a "democratic revolution, national, anti-imperialist, and antifeudal." Specifically, its long-term aims are to establish a representative government, to diversify and industrialize the economy, to eliminate the *latifundios* by agrarian reform, to free the nation from economic and political dependence on foreigners and foreign powers, and to bring its mineral and oil resources under its own control.

Since coming to power AD has proceeded cautiously in carrying out these goals. It has been careful not to antagonize the military and has cooperated with them to the extent that seemed

22. A. P. Whitaker, "Cuba's Intervention in Venezuela: A Test of the OAS," *Orbis*, VIII:3 (Fall, 1964).

necessary. AD played down its differences with other parties in order to control the antidemocratic extremes of both the right and the left.

The elections of December, 1963 continued AD in power under Leoni, although by a much-reduced margin, and attest to a substantial consensus on the main issues involved in the party's program. Among the other center-left parties the most important was URD, which came in third, with 19 per cent of the popular votes as compared with AD's 33 per cent. Led by Jóvito Villalba, a leading member of the Generation of 1928, URD has programs as radical as those of AD. They are designed to appeal to the lower middle classes, among which it has significant support.

The center-right opposition to AD came from its coalition partner, COPEI. With veteran leader Rafael Caldera as its presidential candidate, COPEI backed AD's reforms but claimed that it was better qualified to carry them out. COPEI gained second place in the party, standing behind AD with slightly over 20 per cent of the presidential vote. Thus, the three largest parties, AD, URD, and COPEI, which stood so close together on major issues, polled 71 per cent of the total popular vote. For what it may be worth, this was evidence of widespread agreement on the direction of Venezuela's internal nationalist orientation. The evidence gains support from two further considerations. The first is that although the composition of Venezuela's voting population[23] would seem to have favored left-wing extremists, the only other substantial block of votes (16 per cent) was in fact polled by a more conservative party. This was the Independent Party, headed by a noted Venezuelan author, Arturo Uslar Pietri, which urged more reliance on foreigners for economic development. The other consideration is that there was apparently no identification of the business interests in Venezuela's rapidly expanding economy with any one party. At any rate, in this election the members of the businessmen's pressure group, *Asociación Venezolana Indepen-*

23. In this election, voting was mandatory, under stiff penalties, for "all Venezuelans over 18 years of age, including illiterates and unconvicted prisoners." "Two-thirds of the population was under 25 years of age." *Hispanic American Report*, February, 1964, 1166.

diente, divided their support among AD, COPEI, and Independent.[24]

The two parties—one Communist, the other Castroite—most attractive to left-wingers were excluded from this election. Moreover, tension remained high after the election, what with continued subversive activity on the part of the FALN and constant rumors of another military coup; and the new president, Raúl Leoni, called a "political journeyman," did not seem fit to cope with this situation.

Yet Venezuela had turned a corner in that Leoni was the first constitutionally elected president in the country's history to succeed one who had filled out his term; 1964 passed without a major upset, and the economy continued to expand. Perhaps the election of December 1963 did reflect the achievement of a sufficiently broad national consensus so that Venezuela's current leadership can continue to seek revolutionary nationalist goals in an evolutionary manner.

24. *Ibid.*

EIGHT

Bolivia and Cuba:
Revolutionary Nationalism and
Revolutionary Change

REVOLUTIONARY NATIONALISTS who attempt revolutionary change have had difficulty in avoiding some form of tyranny. These leaders tend to have an inflexible image of modern society and a fixed program. They seem to believe uncritically in the ideas they use to destroy the authority of the old regime. Often, however, these values are not in accord with the most efficient methods available for modernizing society. The revolutionary leaders must meet demands for social justice and rapid economic growth in order to keep power. A frequent consequence has been either considerable frustration or dictatorship.

BOLIVIA

On November 4, 1964, Bolivia's vice president, General René Barrientos Ortuño, led a successful military coup that ended the thirteen-year rule of the Nationalist Revolutionary Movement (MNR). In 1952 the MNR had led a genuine social and economic revolution. It inaugurated such measures as nationalization of the tin mines, agrarian reform, and universal suffrage, as well as the integration of Indian peoples into the political life of the nation. Unfortunately, however, the revolution brought inflation and a decrease in productivity. The MNR had a history of sympathy with national socialism and may have been prevented from

139

turning to some form of tyranny only by massive American assistance.

Today the military, which the MNR officially reorganized on a "national" basis, openly runs the country. A review of recent history demonstrates, however, that Bolivia's contemporary nationalism is aimed mainly at legitimizing the state's entry into the modernization process.

The Process of Change

The origins of contemporary Bolivian nationalism are complex and varied. Most of it was gradually developed by critical Bolivian intellectuals as a response to indigenous conditions and calamitous events: the War of the Pacific (1879–1883), the Chaco War (1932–1935), the large Indian population, the *latifundios,* the domestic tin monopolies, the foreign control of oil, and the rule of the conservative oligarchy. These were criticized over a relatively long period of time and by 1952, had produced a successful revolutionary and nationalist ideology and movement.

Bolivia suffered severe territorial losses in the War of the Pacific and was strategically cut off from the Pacific. Intellectuals like Daniel Sánchez Bustamente voiced their concern over Bolivia's isolation from the sea, calling for a greater self-awareness among Bolivians so that such a debacle could not occur again. He argued that access to both the Atlantic and the Pacific was an abiding interest of Bolivia, a position all Bolivian governments have maintained to this day.

The loss of self-esteem caused by this war increased among nationalist writers the concern with the urgent need for coming to grips with Bolivian reality. An important example of this sort of concern was Franz Tamayo's *La creación de la pedagogía nacional* (The Creation of National Education, 1910). In 1944 it was republished under the auspices of the MNR as one of the ideological antecedents of the movement. In somewhat the same way as Argentina's Ricardo Rojas, Tamayo represented a cultural nationalism opposed to foreign intellectual influences, particularly in Bolivia, to the ideas of the Belgian Georges Rouma.

Tamayo called for "a new scale of values, as Nietzsche would say, more human, more wisely self-centered from the viewpoint of the [Bolivian] nationality."[1]

Like the Peruvian Mariátegui, Tamayo saw the Indian as fundamental in the formation of his country's nationality. He believed that the Indian was the source of national energy, a man of action who had not been destroyed by the conquest.

Many intellectuals coupled this positive cultural nationalism with attacks on the regime and the dominant political and economic ideas. Classical liberalism, which was the prevailing credo of the ruling oligarchy, was assailed. Excessive individualism was criticized from a socialist base by Ignacio Prudencio Bustillo. Gustavo A. Navarro called for a social revolution based on the social and political forms of the Incas. In *La justicia del Inca* (The Justice of the Inca), an article published in 1924 under the pen name Tristán Marof, Navarro extolled the collectivist ideas of the Incas and coined the slogan "Lands to the Indians, Mines to the State." Basic economic changes, he argued, were necessary, and foremost among these was the nationalization of the mines. Later in his career, Navarro founded the *Partido Socialista Obrero de Bolivia* (Socialist Worker's Party) to carry out the revolution.

The real source of this view was fear of foreign economic control of Bolivia's oil-producing lands. In 1922, Standard Oil of New Jersey gained a concession of a million hectares of oil-bearing land which had originally been obtained in 1920 by Richard Levering and Company. An immediate, although rather mild, economic nationalist response occurred in ruling government circles when a law was passed (1922) which limited all further concessions to 100,000 hectares. In addition, one year later taxes were imposed for the first time on the tin mines. To avoid these domestic taxes, the "tin barons," Patiño, Hochschild, and Aramayo, had their companies incorporated in foreign countries. Although this action intimidated the government, it only aggravated the intellectuals' hostility to "international" capitalism.

1. Guillermo Francovich, *El pensamiento boliviano en el siglo XX* (Mexico D.F., 1956), 55.

The crystallization of these economic nationalist ideas occurred at the first Congress of University Students held at Cochabamba in 1928. The students agreed on a program of government aid for the urban and rural working masses and condemned the policy of laissez faire on the ground that it contributed to the economic and social colonialism of the country.

The alienation of the intellectuals from the prevailing social, economic, and political system in Bolivia picked up momentum following Bolivia's humiliating defeat by Paraguay in the Chaco War. Revolutionary nationalists blossomed everywhere, and developed a strong left-wing economic orientation. Many of them attributed the war to rivalry between Standard Oil of New Jersey and Royal Dutch Shell over oil-producing lands in the Chaco.[2]

Until the end of World War II much of Bolivia's revolutionary nationalist thought showed an anticonstitutional trend. For a while it was influenced by German national socialism, despite the cultural nationalists' resistance to modernizing under foreign inspiration. The main focus of Bolivia's nationalism, however, was indigenous. Even when its intellectuals borrowed foreign ideas, they addressed them primarily to the country's own problems: economic imperialism, the integration of the Indian, the nationalization of the mines, cultural independence, and the like. This nationalist cast was given to all ideas borrowed from abroad, whether of the left wing or the right. By the 1940s the intellectuals had forged the major outlines of a nationalist ideology that was comprehensive as well as indigenous, and it was hostile to the prevailing social, political, and economic patterns.

Gradually, the intellectuals were joined in this critical nationalist outlook by other elements of Bolivian society. Their own desertion of the traditional system had started well before

2. On this question Alexander concludes that "One can only guess at the importance of the part played by the international oil companies in encouraging the two nations to push their claims in the Chaco to the point of war." Robert J. Alexander, *The Bolivian National Revolution* (New Brunswick, 1958), 23. A typical example of a Marxist statement on the question is provided by Raúl Ruiz González, *Bolivia: el prometeo de los Andes* (Buenos Aires, 1961), 87.

the Chaco War broke out in 1932. After that war they were joined by many army officers who were bitterly disillusioned with the extent and manner of their country's defeat. Some banded together and formed a secret military society which was called the Marshal Santa Cruz Lodge but later came to be known as *Razón de Patria* (Cause of the Fatherland), or RADEPA. Although the initial motive behind their organization was to plan a defense should they be accused of responsibility for the disaster, they later became involved in Bolivia's revolutionary nationalist campaign.[3] Two of their members, Colonel David Toro and Lieutenant Colonel Germán Busch, successively ran the country.

These military men were deeply alienated from the *status quo* in Bolivia. Colonel Busch claimed that while the people fought against Paraguay, the government entangled itself in endless debates and never supported the army. The disaffection of the military led them to seek a definition of Bolivian nationalism. Busch saw it in affirming Bolivian nationality and in removing foreign economic control. On June 10, 1939, he cried:

> We have a destiny to complete: the definitive affirmation of our nationality, and a mandate from our glorious dead which we must listen to, the mandate that shouts "country and liberty" and of those that only yesterday showed us how to die, and we can condense [this mandate] into these words: Gain the complete independence of Bolivia, obtain her economic independence.[4]

In May, 1936, the dictator was unseated by a junta headed by David Toro and supported by the Republican Socialist Party and the Socialist Party. Both these "socialist" groups were anything but Marxist. The Republican Socialists believed that there was "good" and "bad" capitalism—"bad" was foreign, "good" was domestic. They prized domestic private property, were anti-Marxist, and wanted to incorporate the Indians into national life. The Socialist Party also saw some capitalism as progressive, liked private property, and had a go-slowly approach toward the nationalization of domestic monopolies.

In 1936 the Republican Socialists were removed from their

3. Alberto Ostria Gutiérrez, *The Tragedy of Bolivia* (New York, 1958), 7–9.
4. Porfirio Díaz Machicao, *Historia de Bolivia*, Vol. IV (La Paz, 1957), 102.

role of cooperation with the ruling junta and the Socialist Party became the junta's only "official collaborator." This party was perhaps more strongly nationalistic than its former partner. It backed the junta's leader, Colonel Toro, when he decreed the nationalization of the Standard Oil concession in 1937.

Shortly thereafter Toro was edged out of office and replaced by Busch, but the new dictator only confirmed the nationalist trend. He incurred the enmity of the tin barons by a decree controlling mineral exports and by his threats to nationalize the mines. And he matched Toro's establishment of a state petroleum monopoly by setting up a state-controlled Central Bank. Clearly, these military leaders were moving into the mainstream of Bolivia's growing revolutionary nationalist movement. As Lieuwen has said of Toro and Busch, although "these precursors of Perón ruled less than two years, . . . in that short time they revealed the potential power of an alliance of the military with popular forces."[5]

In 1939 Busch committed suicide, or was murdered, and the conservatives regained power until another nationalist revolt overthrew them in 1943. This revolt was instigated by a coalition of RADEPA, *Estrella de Hierro,* and the MNR. In 1952 the MNR was to lead Bolivia to her first major social revolution. It was this militant party that first definitely established revolutionary nationalism in Bolivia.

The MNR was officially founded on June 7, 1941, in honor of Germán Busch's decree-law controlling mineral exports. Its chief architect, Víctor Paz Estenssoro, an economics professor, had served as one of Busch's economic advisers and shared the views of those who had asserted shortly before his mysterious death:

> If the dictator [Busch] is capable of liberating the state from its submission to imperialistic and feudal interests, is able to control exports and nationalize the banking system as a means of retaining for the country the wealth the nation produces, is successful in promoting mineral production and in finding new international markets which would free the country from its semi-colonial position, and an increased agricultural production so that the poverty of the peas-

5. Edwin Lieuwen, *Arms and Politics in Latin America* (New York, 1961), rev. ed., 79.

antry is reduced . . . [then] there can be no doubt that the whole nation—with the exception of the oligarchy—will follow and support his actions.[6]

In 1940 a campaign was under way among the restored conservatives to return the oil properties to Standard Oil. Foreign Minister Alberto Ostria Gutiérrez was charged with initiating it. Paz Estenssoro cried out against it and maintained that Bolivia rested "on an economic field of black gold, wealth that ought to benefit the people of Bolivia and nobody else."[7]

In the face of this and other threats to revolutionary nationalism, Paz Estenssoro, Hernán Siles, and several others formed the MNR. Joining forces with Major Gualberto Villarroel of the junior officers' RADEPA, they seized the government in December 1943. The new regime combined terrorism with incompetence and in July, 1946 it was overthrown by a bloody revolt led by senior officers. Villarroel was hanged from a lamp post.

Finally, in 1951 early election returns indicated another victory for the MNR, but it was balked by a military junta. The MNR leaders responded by hatching a revolutionary plot for which they obtained the support of the junta's own minister of the interior, who was also chief of the Military Police, by promising him the presidency. In April, 1952, the three-day rebellion succeeded, but the promise was not kept and the presidency went to Paz Estenssoro.

Once in power, the MNR began its reform program. By the time it was ousted a dozen years later, it had revolutionized key aspects of Bolivian life. Understanding this revolution requires a knowledge of the mass base of the MNR. While it was out of power between 1946 and 1952, the MNR had broadened its original base in the labor movement, particularly among miners and factory workers. In order to appeal to the recently organized rural Indians, the MNR leaders turned their rather vague pro-Indianism of earlier years into a specific commitment to gradual agrarian reform, including distribution of land to the Indians.

6. Pamphlet, *Víctor Paz Estenssoro Adalid de la Revolución Nacional* (n.d.) 15.

7. José Fellman Velarde, *Víctor Paz Estenssoro: El hombre y la Revolución* (La Paz, 1955), 7.

This appeal was ultimately successful and immensely significant. The Chaco War had shocked the Bolivian Indians into a more general awareness of their exploitation than the Indians in any other Andean country. Thousands of them had been conscripted into the army, in which they fought side by side with townsmen and were taught that they all were citizens of a "nation" and had rights as well as duties. Yet, after the war, as Richard Patch has written, these Indian veterans "returned to the *latifundios* as serfs, on land which was theirs only at the pleasure of the *patrón,* for which land they labored three days each week without pay, and for which the entire family owed many other obligations . . ."[8] The Chaco veterans formed an agrarian syndicate to aid them in escaping from these obligations by attacking the *latifundio* system. Independent of the government and led only by Indians, it had become powerful by the time the revolution of 1952 occurred. They took no direct part in the war, for it was confined largely to the capital city of La Paz, but their hostility to the existing order aided the revolutionists.

The Level of Change

By 1952, the nationalist movement that the MNR represented and attempted to direct was inward-looking. Its focus on integrating the various elements within the Bolivian masses was heralded by one of the government's first decrees, universal suffrage. Up to this time the right to vote had been limited to those who could read and write Spanish; now Indians as well as many mestizos were given the right to vote.

The MNR leaders also moved to nationalize the mines. This measure was a matter of principle as well as of political necessity. Nevertheless, the new government offered to pay for the mines on the basis of international law and the rights of property. The MNR leaders wanted to develop the business spirit among Bolivians and to attract foreign capital for future development. A decree-law of October 31, 1952, nationalized the tin mines belonging to the Patiño, Aramayo, and Hochschild companies,

8. R. W. Patch, "Bolivia: The Restrained Revolution," *American Academy of Social and Political Science, Annals* (March, 1961), 128.

and a government-owned institution was established to run them. To date the operation has been financially unprofitable, mainly because of the companies' wholesale removal of their experts and records needed for running the mines efficiently. In addition, the unions made demands that seriously cut productivity, thereby weakening the already marginal position of Bolivian tin in the world market.

Of even greater long-term importance to the country, and perhaps the only irreversible measure introduced by the MNR, was the agrarian reform. Pressure from the Indians precipitated quicker and more sweeping action than the MNR had planned. Proclaimed on August 2, 1953, the Agrarian Reform Law had six major objectives: to redistribute the land, to develop the traditional Indian communes, to improve the status of the farm worker, to increase productivity, to conserve national resources, and to promote internal migration and settlement. Control was centralized in a National Agrarian Reform Institute. The land distribution proceeded fairly rapidly, and by January, 1962, more than three and one-quarter million hectares of land had been distributed. On the other hand, the promotion of the Indian communes had little success. Also, as in Mexico, the immediate result of the reform was a decline in productivity. The effort was respected, however, and in national elections the rural areas gave the MNR solid support.

Nevertheless, on November 4, 1964, the rule of the MNR was ended. Víctor Paz Estenssoro, who had just begun his second term as President, was ousted by the military and his Vice President, Air Force General René Barrientos Ortuño. The MNR had never been hostile to the army as an institution. It had cooperated with a large group of officers in 1943, and although the armed forces were broken up in 1952, they were reconstituted a year later. In fact, the MNR's proclaimed policy was not to dissolve them but merely to reorganize them on a national basis. Officers who were deemed loyal to the MNR were brought back and soldiers were formed into working battalions. The military academies were opened to men of all social classes. This cooperation between the party and the army helped push the revolution's objectives along rapidly, but because the army was rebuilt, it remained an important power group.

The potential of the military was augmented by constant and bitter strife within the MNR. The two main factions were the *Rabanitos* (later to be called Trotskyites) and the *Derechistas* (Rightists). The *Rabanitos* or left wing were led by self-styled Trotskyite Juan Lechín, and their position was propagandized by *Rebelión,* the official paper of the labor organization COB (Bolivian Workers' Center). At one time, *Rebelión* took the position that the MNR was the party of the nationalistic middle class and should be supported only so long as its programs were "anti-capitalist and anti-imperialist." It opposed the government's attitude toward the mine owners because it wanted the mines nationalized "without indemnification and under the control of the workers."[9]

On September 12, 1952, *Rebelión* published an ideological program for the workers of Bolivia that provoked a counterblast from the "moderate" leaders of the MNR. The latter branded COB's leaders international Communists and its ideology as "contrary to national sentiments," declared that the MNR "is in its essence a national party and as a consequence is against international communism," and claimed that 90 per cent of the Bolivian workers were "nationalists, with a profound Christian religious sentiment and, clearly, the enemies of materialistic and atheistic communism."[10] Denying that this revolution was a stage in the process of implanting a dictatorship of the proletariat, they maintained that "the problem of Bolivia is one of a national character and not exclusively of social classes, which is a communist principle."[11]

This position was maintained by the CPN (*Comité Político Nacional*), the only group authorized to speak for the MNR, which was controlled by Víctor Paz Estenssoro, Hermán Siles Zuazo and Federico Alvarez Plata. The leaders of COB, Juan Lechín and Germán Butron, bowed to this pressure, at least

9. Lydia Gueiler Tejada, *La mujer y la revolución* (La Paz, 1949).
10. *Ibid.,* 78.
11. *Ibid.,* 86.

officially, and thus retained important influence within the party. Nevertheless, this ideological conflict for the direction of the MNR weakened its position.

The Party was also racked by personal feuds among the moderates, and its position was undermined by several factors. These included the government's dependence on aid from the United States; its acceptance, as the price of that aid, of the International Monetary Fund's stabilization plan; and the failure, despite both, either to stabilize or to develop the economy. Inflation continued, but its effects were felt mainly in the towns and cities. Paradoxically, this contributed to another revolt. By 1964 substantial progress had been made towards the goal of creating a united Bolivian nation, in the sense that the sharpest class distinctions had been erased by the elevation of the lowest class and the destruction of the old oligarchy, and that, in what remained, social mobility was greater than before 1952. Yet, at the same time, so sharp a rift developed between town and country that by 1964 this seemed a probable line of division in the next civil war. In fact, after his overthrow, Paz Estenssoro was reported from his city of refuge, Lima, to claim that he could have defeated the urban rebels if he had only had time to mobilize his rural militia. His explanation of his failure to mobilize them throws an interesting sidelight on bucolic life in Bolivia: When the coup started, he said, a fiesta was in progress throughout the countryside, and most of the *campesinos* were drunk.

Did the military coup of 1964 that ended the MNR's twelve-year rule mark a break in the development of Bolivian nationalism? The answer at the present writing is no. General Barrientos, the new ruler, has shown some signs of developing a nationalist movement of the Nasserist type, and he may succeed, what with his backing by the Christian Democrats, the Social Christians, and the right-wing Falange, the military, and even the peasants. But that might mean only a change in the balance of power from civilian to military, without a change in basic nationalist principles and policies. Barrientos and his fellow officers still bear the imprint of the MNR's nationalization of the armed forces. Barring a massive resort to a more radical, left-wing nationalism by the frustrated townspeople of Bolivia, the changes and direction imposed by the MNR seem likely to endure. In any case, Bolovian nationalism will probably continue to be oriented primarily towards its own domestic problems.

CUBA

For the student of nationalism, the Cuban revolution, led by the charismatic Fidel Castro, is the most perplexing movement in present-day Latin America. The causes of this revolution are fairly clear, and so are its defects and achievements and its identification with communism. What is perplexing is that, although at the outset it seemed to be a bona fide nationalist movement, it very soon became closely identified with communism. We believe, on the basis of the information now available, that nationalism and communism have been united in a marriage of convenience. If so, the most significant feature of the Cuban revolution is its demonstration that international communism can be successfully grafted onto an indigenous nationalist movement and can become the justifying ideology for that movement. This conclusion will give little comfort to those who believe that nationalism is necessarily incompatible with communism.

Early in Cuban history political nationalism became identified with anti-Americanism. After the War of 1898, the United States maintained military rule over the island until Cuba signed the permanent treaty of 1903, which gave the United States the right to intervene in the affairs of the country for the preservation of Cuban independence and for the protection of life, property, and individual liberty. This severe limitation on Cuban political sovereignty was occasionally exercised in subsequent years and it was only in 1934, during the administration of Franklin Delano Roosevelt, that the United States gave up this right. Even then it retained the Guantánamo naval base, which it had acquired under the treaty of 1903. This American policy has created and maintained a strong current of anti-Americanism in Cuba's political nationalism.

Another important factor in its growth has been the extensive control of the island's economy by United States nationals. Between 1913 and 1928 American investments in Cuba rose 536 per cent. In 1928 more than 70 per cent of Cuba's main export crop, sugar, was owned by Americans. This American control of Cuban sugar began to wane in the late 1930s, but in 1956 United States-owned companies still controlled 40 per cent of the country's sugar.[12]

Other areas of the Cuban economy were almost completely dominated by Americans. They owned 90 per cent of Cuba's utilities, mines, and cattle ranches and controlled 50 per cent of the public railways. American-owned banks contained 25 per cent of all bank deposits. This control of the Cuban economy was maintained through the middle 1950s even though the rate of American direct investments in Cuba since World War II had been the lowest in any important Latin American country.[13] Cuba was also largely dependent on the United States for her imports and as a market for her exports.

Dependency on American-owned companies for production, and dependency on American products for consumption created the strong economic nationalism demonstrated by all Cuban reform movements. The first major movement of this kind was represented by Dr. Ramón Grau San Martín and his Party of the Cuban Revolution, commonly called the *Auténtico* Party.[14] Its general objectives were the economic and political independence of Cuba, and its economic reforms included the distribution of foreign-owned *latifundios*. It also championed democratic reforms such as women's suffrage and civil liberties.

The *Auténticos* emerged in 1934, just after the brutal dictatorship of Gerardo Machado was overthrown. Grau San Martín served briefly as President before he was forced to resign by

12. See Robert F. Smith, *The United States and Cuba* (New Haven, 1960), 24, 166; also see U.S. Department of Commerce, *U.S. Investments in the Latin American Economy* (Washington, 1957), 175.

13. The chief reason for this decline has been that most direct American investments in Latin America since 1946 have gone into oil and Cuba produces very little oil.

14. *Partido Revolucionario Cubano Auténtico.*

pressure from the United States and the army's new strong-man, ex-army sergeant Fulgencio Batista, whom the United States favored as less "radical." Batista ruled behind the scenes until 1940, when he became President himself. Between 1944 and 1952 the *Auténticos* were allowed to rule, but their reformist zeal was gone and they attacked none of the nation's basic problems. Batista returned in 1952 through a bloodless coup, and ruled until 1959.

It is clear that Cuba's political and economic nationalism was frustrated most of the time until Castro's success in 1959. The explanation lies only partly in United States interference, which continued in the form of pressure even after the right of intervention was canceled. American interference might have been taken as a reason for establishing a stable government rather than as an excuse for the continued disorder that frustrated national aspirations. However that may be, Cuba's efforts at political stability have usually led to authoritarian regimes, and Cuban nationalism has never been consistently identified with democratic forms of government.

Cuba also suffered from a severe urban-rural imbalance. Nearly one-fourth of her population lived in Havana, where living standards were much higher than in the rural areas. This imbalance, though not peculiar to Cuba, was so marked there that it sharply reduces the social and political significance of the fact that the Cuba of the late 1950s ranked high among Latin American countries in per capita income. Income was not evenly distributed, and the city dwellers, especially in Havana, had all the best of it. For example, 90 per cent of the homes in Havana had electricity, compared to only 10 per cent in rural Cuba. Just under 8 per cent of the rural families owned 71 per cent of the land, while 70 per cent of them owned only 11 per cent of it. The migrants who worked the many sugar mills scattered around the countryside owned no land at all. The seasonal nature of the sugar industry created an annual average unemployment rate of 25 per cent.

Many Cubans felt their country's *latifundio* system was even worse than that in other Latin American countries for the very reason that it had been modernized and was operated on a commercial basis. As we have already noted, this and other sectors of the economy were controlled by a minority, many of whom were foreigners, and this situation of monopoly capitalism seemed to be backed up by the United States.

As a result, some observers have noted that by the 1950s many Cubans had accepted fundamental Marxist ideas without being sectarian Communists. The economic and military hegemony of the United States made these values "natural" for Cubans. Nevertheless, there was no consistent body of national ideas, and no mass desertion from this monopoly capitalist-feudal system. There was not even an intellectual consensus on the ills of Cuban society and what should be done about them. There was a rural mass, but it was largely inert; there was a Communist party, but it was highly urban and frequently cooperated with Cuba's dictators; and there was no traditional political party—including the *Auténticos*—that adhered uncompromisingly to a reform ideology aimed at national goals. Nevertheless, a revolution did occur and it fell into the hands of a Communist party and a Communist ideology.

The Process of Change

In 1953, on the now famous 26th of July, the Moncada barracks in Santiago, near the eastern end of Cuba, were attacked. The raid was unsuccessful, and the leader, Fidel Castro, was jailed. Freed in 1955, he went to Mexico, where he organized and trained a group of his followers in guerrilla tactics. He returned to Cuba in December 1956 and began a campaign of harassment that ended in total victory on January 1, 1959.

The goals of Castro's 26th of July Movement were vague. He was surrounded by individuals who represented a variety of political and economic beliefs. Some were anti-Communists, some had democratic-socialist beliefs, and some had personal and other informal ties with Communists. Fidel's brother Raúl had been in a Communist group while a university student,[15] and his trusted

15. This is a frequent occurrence among university students in Latin America.

advisor and friend Che Guevara was openly a Communist, with Marxist connections that ranged from his native Argentina to Guatemala, where he had supported the Communist-infected Arbenz regime.

There was always an element of class consciousness in Castro's ideology. This attitude was clearly present in his speech, "History Will Absolve Me," which he delivered at his trial in 1953 for the attack on the Moncada barracks. He directed his appeal to the Cuban masses—both urban and rural—and to the lower middle classes. At this time he favored a democratic-reformist revolution, calling for the restoration of the Constitution of 1940 and a government based on popular elections. In the middle of 1957, he promised to hold elections within one year of obtaining power. He always implied, however, that reforms were an integral part of his movement. He stressed agrarian reform and various welfare schemes, which included public housing and rural health programs.

Although Castro's military force remained small almost to the eve of victory, he nevertheless developed a strong rural base in Oriente province, by his denunciations of wealthy Havana and his promises of land distribution. Also, it seemed at this time that he planned to carry out his reforms through his indigenous 26th of July Movement, which could have become the core of a national party organization.

Batista's opposition was so inept, and soon developed into a campaign of terrorism so indiscriminate, that most of his supporters deserted. At the end of 1958 it simply disintegrated and Castro won without ever having fought a major battle.

When Castro rode to triumph on New Year's Day, 1959, he was hailed throughout the hemisphere as "the soldier-scholar" who had brought down the corrupt and cruel Batista regime. But he had come to power in a manner strikingly different from that of Batlle, Betancourt, or even Paz Estenssoro. His ideology for reform was a patchwork, and his movement was not associated with any historical national party or movement. In short, his movement triumphed while still in the embryo stage. To be sure, it had some rural backing, but up to this time its main support had come from the middle class. Moreover, the 26th of July Movement was far more clearly identified with Castro's charisma than it was with anything promising stability. As such it had no core of long-time supporters who were trained in party politics and loyal to party goals. All this made Castro's goals and rules accessible to destruction or co-option.

The Level of Change

One way for Castro to strengthen his position was to identify the revolution with Cuban nationalism. This he did. In early 1960, for example, he said: "To be a traitor to the Revolution is to be a traitor to the country. The destiny of our sovereignty is at stake. . . . We have decided that either we are or we are not a free country. And we are and want to be a free country."[16] But identification by oratory was not enough; action was needed. This raises the most controversial question regarding the change imposed by Castro, the reasons for his identification of Cuba's national interests with international communism.

There are a variety of conflicting answers to this question. The Machiavelli thesis is that Castro always was a Communist and merely concealed his views in order to deceive the Cuban people, the United States, and everyone else until he had gained absolute power. Then there is the persuasive thesis developed by Theodore Draper that Cuba suffered two revolutions under Castro. It is consistent with the indefiniteness of the early goals of the 26th of July Movement and allows for the revolution's high nationalist potential. At the same time it explains why the revolution could not be given an exclusively nationalist orientation. Draper has written of the second Revolution: "Only the ingenuous can still believe that Fidel Castro walked into a Communist trap or that he gave up the democratic road because the United States did not give him enough support in his early months of power. The Communists and Fidel walked toward

16. Quoted by James O'Connor, "On Cuba's Political Economy," *Political Science Quarterly*, 79:2 (June, 1964), 240.

each other, each with his eyes open, each filling a need in the other.[17]

Finally, there is the eclectic thesis, which is that both of the first two theses are partially true. Various combinations of the two have been made by the eclectics.

On the basis of the evidence now available, we believe that the question still remains open, but that Draper's thesis is the most probable.

When Castro came to power in January, 1959, he was faced with staggering problems. Marxism, as distinguished from Soviet communism, was a part of Cuban nationalist doctrine for bringing about social change. This fact, along with the traditional animosity of Cuban nationalists and reformers toward the United States, predisposed Castro to lively suspicion of American reactions to his course.

Much has been made of the American willingness to tolerate his reforms. Thus, Draper has noted the fact that the oil companies were willing to extend a credit of $16 million to the new Cuban government.[18] On January 26, 1960, President Eisenhower made a conciliatory statement to Castro in which he promised, in effect, not to interfere in Cuba's domestic affairs and offered to negotiate all disputes, including those arising from Cuban seizure of American properties and alleged acts of United States aggression. To give only one more example, even after the recall of the American ambassador from Havana, Argentina's ambassador there, who acted for the United States, was requested by it to offer Castro its "aid and cooperation."[19]

The Argentine's mediation was interrupted, however, by the arrival of Anastas I. Mikoyan, First Deputy Premier of the Soviet Union, whose visit led to a trade agreement on February 13, 1960, and a credit of $100 million to Castro's government. The fact of the matter is that the United States could only tolerate Castro's "reforms," whereas the Soviet Union could identify with them. The United States would have to do more than tolerate; it would

17. *Castro's Revolution* (New York, 1962), 107.
18. *Ibid.*
19. *The New York Times,* April 19, 1964.

have to woo, in order to overcome the ingrained hostility of
Cuba's nationalism.

As for the Cuban Communists, until a few months before
Castro's victory they not only opposed him, denouncing him as
a "bourgeois opportunist," but also gave positive support to
Batista. But they deserted the sinking ship in time and then
moved ever closer to Castro. It was easy for them to do so since
they shared many of his reformist goals. On his part, he needed
them, for they brought him what he lacked: a trained and disciplined party. Even so, his government was at first made up of
moderates and he sponsored a campaign to attract American
tourists and offered to pay with bonds for the lands taken by his
agrarian reform law.

The United States responded with friendly gestures. On
March 2, 1959, Philip Bonsal, the new U.S. ambassador to Cuba,
upon presenting his credentials to the Cuban President,[20] stated
that the United States supported the objective of raising the
country's standard of living. A month later, Castro visited the
United States. The Assistant Secretary of State for Latin American Affairs, Roy Rubottom, invited Castro's aides to discuss
Cuba's financial needs and offered help. Although he was turned
down, Washington later expressed its sympathy with Castro's
agrarian reform law so long as there was "prompt, adequate and
effective compensation."

This "sympathetic" stance was maintained in the face of continuing seizures of American-owned land and despite Castro's
announcement in March, 1959, that Cuba would no longer support the United States in the Cold War. The American government remained outwardly calm when Cuba signed an agreement
in September, 1959, to sell Communist China 50,000 tons of sugar.
As mentioned previously, the United States continued to try to
keep contacts open through the Argentine ambassador even after
its own Ambassador had been recalled (January 23, 1960). By all
normal standards the United States had behaved reasonably toward Castro. Clearly, he was moving with his eyes open toward

20. Manuel Urrutia, a moderate, was President at this time. He resigned
on July 17, 1959.

the Communist Party and the Communist bloc. What we can never know is whether his entrance into the Communist orbit might have been prevented if the United States had given him strong support, as it did Bolivia's left-wing government after the revolution of 1952.

In the first half of 1960, relations between the United States and Cuba deteriorated and by summer, all possibility of accommodation ended. The United States then cut Cuba's sugar quota, following the seizure of the Esso and Texaco oil refineries, which had refused to refine Soviet crude oil. The rift had now become unbridgeable, and the United States began giving secret aid to Cuban exiles for an invasion of Cuba. This ended in the Bay of Pigs fiasco of April, 1961, which greatly enhanced Castro's prestige in both Cuba and Latin America at large. But he still faced the unabated hostility of the far stronger United States, only ninety miles away. Apparently feeling the need of stronger Soviet aid and firmer assurance that it would continue, he forced the Kremlin's hand by publicly announcing, in December, 1961, that he was a Marxist-Leninist and always had been one. The Cuban Communists, on their part, had already proclaimed their complete solidarity with the Castro revolution, in August, 1960.[21] From December, 1961 on, the nationalist reforms of his "Socialist Republic" were explicitly identified with the Communist Party and Communist ideology.

As the missile crisis of October, 1962, demonstrated most strikingly, tightening ties with the Soviet Union could be a serious liability to Castro as a nationalist leader. In the end, however, he came out of the crisis rather well. His regime appeared to have been reduced to the status of a Soviet satellite when missile bases were established in Cuba, and still more when, yielding to the heaviest kind of pressure from President Kennedy, Khrushchev ordered their removal without consulting Castro. But Castro regained his nationalist lustre by upsetting one of the prime conditions of the settlement between Washing-

21. Rollie Poppino, *International Communism in Latin America* (New York, 1964) 182.

ton and Moscow: verification of the removal by on-the-spot inspection. The inspection never took place.

Since then Castro has continued to assert Cuba's independence in various ways, as, for example, by having Cuba participate as a full-fledged member in the conference of nonaligned nations at Cairo in 1964. Several factors favored its successful assertion, despite the heavy pull of Cuba's economic dependence on Soviet aid, among them the rift between Peking and Moscow. In early 1965 it appeared that the rift had been healed, at least momentarily, so far as Cuba was concerned, for the two Communist giants were cooperating in stepping up their aid to the island. But one thing was certain: Cuba could not be a satellite to both these rivals at the same time. A second factor favored its escape from domination by either. This was the rapid increase, after 1963, of Cuba's trade with Western Europe, despite strong protests from the United States to its European allies.

Thus, by 1965 Cuba was moving along a line that converged with one followed by Rumania in the last few years, for both had developed strong Communist regimes that were also strongly nationalist. While Cuba was successfully resisting Soviet domination, Rumania was freeing herself from it. Cuba, as well as Rumania, represented the new pattern of Communist polycentrism, which has made communism quite compatible with nationalism. This development aggravates the danger from Castro's persistent efforts to export his revolution to the rest of Latin America.

Castro has changed Cuba. A nationwide effort to wipe out illiteracy is well under way and an emphasis on technical education has replaced the former domination of Cuba's university curriculum by the liberal arts. The social and economic structure of the nation has been altered. The Law of Agrarian Reform has brought about a massive redistribution of land. Cooperatives have been organized and great private landholdings broken up. New industries have been established. The rural areas are gaining new housing, electricity, medical services, and roads. A rural minimum wage, and state farms providing year-round employment have improved the lot of the peasants and made them loyal to Castro. The urban worker has benefited too. His change has not been as pronounced as the rural worker's, but he has been aided by a reduction in rents and the promise of owning his home.

Castro's reforms seem to be based on a solid power position. He has the support of the urban and rural masses. His upper- and middle-class enemies, overt or potential, have been eliminated, mainly by emigration. He has accepted the Communist ideology and has thereby acquired a coherent philosophy for mobilizing his mass supporters and for controlling them. Yet, at the same time, he has maintained his role as champion of Cuban nationalism with a substantial degree of success. He has the support of Cuban intellectuals like Juan Marinello, Alejo Carpentier, and Nicolás Guillén. Far from deserting his regime, these intellectuals lend it moral support by agreeing with its goals. Like Castro, they do not have the bourgeois attitude that the ends do not justify the means. The United States' economic embargo provides an excuse for every economic difficulty his people suffer and additional grounds for connecting his Communist goals with traditional anti-American nationalist feelings.

Cuba's economy is still vulnerable. Sugar is still its basis, and since 1961 the sugar output has shrunk sharply, and Cuba has been unable to meet her sugar export quotas to the Soviet Union. But a good sugar harvest was in prospect for 1965, with the aid of cane-cutting combines sent by the Soviet Union. This could speed Cuba's economic reorientation toward the Communist bloc, now being promoted for example, by a large-scale shift from American to Soviet factory equipment.

This process of "Sovietizing" Cuba has its dangers for Castro and his lieutenants. As already noted, they have been seeking with some success to avoid exchanging dependence on the United States for dependence on the Communist powers, but their ultimate success is still in doubt. If they fail, the result may be a new cycle of explosive nationalism in Cuba. If they succeed, their fusion of nationalism with communism could make more trouble for the United States in Latin America than it has ever known before.

NINE

Continental Nationalism

As APPLIED to Latin America, "continental nationalism" seems a contradiction in terms, for the continent in question is in fact an aggregation of seventeen continental and three insular countries, all of which are independent and highly diversified, and each of which has its own separate nationalism in the conventional sense. What is more, even if we consider this continental nationalism merely as an aspiration, the achievement of its presumptive goal, the economic and political unification of the area, seems too remote and doubtful a contingency to warrant discussion in the present work.

Yet these considerations are overborne by others that give the theme a strong claim on our attention. For one thing, it has long been taken seriously by Latin Americans, and increasingly so in recent decades.[1] As the noted Peruvian Aprista leader, Víctor Raúl Haya de la Torre, said in 1959, "Latin America is the *Patria Grande* [Great Fatherland], of which each of its component states is an inseparable and interdependent part."[2] In other words, continental nationalism is a significant factor in the psychological

1. An early example is the Chilean Joaquín Edwards Bello's *El nacionalismo continental* (Santiago, 1935), with a prologue by Gabriela Mistral, Nobel Prize winner for literature, 1945, and a letter to the author from Haya de la Torre, dated London, May 23, 1926. The first part (of three) had first been published in Madrid in 1926, under the same title.

2. Cited in Whitaker, *Nationalism in Latin America, Past and Present,* (Gainesville, 1962), 63.

161

environment in which conventional nationalism has developed in Latin America.

Second, although even the flexible term nationalism may seem to be strained to the breaking-point by its use in this continental sense, that use has been justified on much the same grounds as most of the conventional nationalisms in Latin America, Europe, and elsewhere, such as a common history, common culture, and common interests. In recent years, various pressures have sharpened this Latin American community sense. Third, no matter how remote the goal of unification may be, continental nationalism has already produced a variety of significant side effects. It has aided in the formation of the Latin American Free Trade Association (LAFTA), has introduced a strong note of ambiguity into the Latin Americans' relations with the West, the Communist world, and the nonaligned nations, and has served as a whetstone for conventional nationalism in individual Latin American countries. Finally, continental nationalism in Latin America offers interesting points of comparison with continentalism in other areas, such as Europe and Africa.

At all times, needless to say, the student of continental nationalism must keep in mind its competition or interplay with other ideas, including Pan Americanism, "Westernism," and various universal or cosmopolitan concepts, as well as conventional nationalism.

THE DEVELOPMENT OF
CONTINENTAL NATIONALISM

The term "continental nationalism" seems to be of recent origin, but the underlying idea found support among Latin American leaders from the beginning of the struggle for independence, about 1810. These included the two chief liberators of Spanish America, the Venezuelan Simón Bolívar and the Argentine José de San Martín, and the author of Chile's first constitution, Juan Egaña. Typically, Egaña reserved "nation" for Spanish America at large and referred to Chile not as a nation but as a "people" (*pueblo*). "Americanism" was the ecumenical label then in vogue, in literary as well as political circles, but, unless otherwise indicated, the America in question was often (as it still is) only "our America" (*nuestra América*), that is, Spanish or Latin America. To be sure, the broader Western Hemisphere idea found some acceptance in Latin America at that time, but much less than in the United States. Although both ideas were projections of the New World concept, Latin Americans felt from the start that certain basic factors set "our America" apart from the other America, which then meant only the United States (no one bothered his head then about Canada and the other European possessions in America). The factors that differentiated the two Americas and bound "our America" together were stated in familiar nationalist terms by Juan Egaña: "blood, language, interrelations, laws, customs, and religion."[3]

As Bolívar regretfully foresaw, the hope of welding "our America" into a single nation was defeated by distance and the clash of rival particularisms and personal ambitions. Instead, a variety of more or less primitive conventional nationalisms prevailed, producing first a dozen and finally a score of independent states. As the next best thing, Bolívar and those who followed him in the next six decades sought to bind these succession states together as closely as possible through a series of three political conferences at Panama and Lima and, finally, a juridical conference at Montevideo. The conferences failed, however, and by the time the last was held (1888) it was clear that the progressive incorporation of Latin America into the world economy was pulling the countries of that area still further apart.

This process, begun by Great Britain and its European neighbors in the third quarter of the nineteenth century, and later accelerated by the United States, was characterized by the rapid development of Latin America as a source of foodstuffs and raw materials and also as a market, mainly through investments of private capital and the introduction of modern technology. Although the pace of change varied substantially from one part of Latin America to another, by 1900 all the principal countries ex-

3. *Ibid.*, 56–58.

cept Colombia, and some of the smaller ones, had been profoundly affected. For our purposes, the two chief results were: (1) In each country the economic and cultural relations of the ruling classes were oriented away from the rest of Latin America and towards Europe (later, towards the United States as well). (2) Continentalism, which seemed out of place in this situation, was largely supplanted by a conventional nationalism focused on the internal growth and consolidation of each country and on maintaining beneficial relations with the more advanced countries. This attitude was perfectly illustrated by Argentina as early as the 1860s and still maintained a half century later by revolutionary Mexico to the extent that, although Mexican nationalism had now become xenophobe and left-wing, it remained cool to continentalism.

By that time, however, a resurgence of continental nationalism was under way in other parts of Latin America, notably Argentina. The outstanding pioneer of the movement appears to have been the Argentine Manuel Ugarte, indefatigable writer, speaker, and traveler, who, beginning about 1910, first gave currency to the term *Patria Grande*. After 1918, systematic support for the propagation of the idea was provided by the University Reform movement which started at Córdoba, Argentina, in that year and soon spread throughout Latin America. As its chief exponent, Gabriel del Mazo, later wrote, the University Reform was "a vast undertaking aimed at organizing and unifying Indo-Spanish America on ethical-social bases, transforming its states through the inspiration and effort of the genius of its soil and people." Among the many influential converts were the versatile Argentine *pensador,* José Ingenieros, said to have been the most widely read writer in Spanish in those years, who in 1925 founded the Latin American Union (*Unión Latino Americana*), and the Peruvian Haya de la Torre, whose APRA, also founded in the 1920s, was designed to unite all Latin America in a revolutionary alliance and who was still preaching the *Patria Grande* idea in the 1960s.

Why the resurgence of continental nationalism took place at this time is a question that cannot yet be answered with any certainty. With our present knowledge, we can only suggest the hypothesis that its revival was due to the convergence of various political, economic, social, and intellectual factors in an area already in the state of flux which has become so pronounced today; and that continentalism became attractive to different people for different and sometimes conflicting reasons.

To begin with the most obvious factor of all, from the turn of the century Latin American apprehensions were aroused by the rise of the United States to world power, its expansion into the Caribbean, and its assumption of the role of policeman of the Western Hemisphere. Yankeephobia throve, and this has always been one of the strongest motivations for Latin American union. But the United States was not the only source of apprehension. Latin Americans were beginning to complain that the recent rapid incorporation of their area into the world economy had subjected them to a new form of imperialism, and in most of Latin America prior to World War I this had been the work of Europeans, not the United States. In addition, continental nationalism began to be identified in some quarters with political and social revolution, for it was maintained that the new imperialism had been riveted on Latin America by an unholy alliance of its own oligarchies with the foreign imperialists, and that the only way to shake off this yoke was to form a counteralliance of the popular elements in Latin America at large. This was the thesis both of the University Reform as interpreted by Gabriel del Mazo and also of Haya de la Torre's APRA. Yet conservatives too were continentalists on occasion, especially after two world wars shook their faith in Europe; a striking illustration is the clarion call to Latin American union sounded in the book *Hispano-América en Guerra?* (*Hispanic America at War?*) written in 1941 by a Peruvian oligarch, Felipe Barreda Laos, and warmly applauded by his congeners in other Latin American countries.

Finally, from the early years of the century, Latin American thinkers engaged in an almost frantic quest for what Pedro Henríquez Ureña called the identity of Latin America; and one should never underestimate the power of intellectuals in Latin

America. The rationale of their quest could be summed up in a proposition and a question: We Latin Americans are different from other people, but what are we? In Spanish America the question was particularly difficult to answer in the nineteenth century because of the widespread Hispanophobia and rejection of the Spanish heritage. (No comparable difficulty existed in Brazil, where the struggle for independence from Portugal had left fewer scars.) Yet even after this obstacle had been removed by the passage of time and the sympathy for Spain evoked by the Spanish American War of 1898, no generally acceptable answer was found.

One that has delighted many Latin Americans for many years was provided in 1900 by José Enrique Rodó in his essay *Ariel,* which identified Latin America by differentiating it from the United States as Ariel from Caliban and by linking it with the humane tradition of Europe and the Greco-Roman world. But, though the essay is still widely admired, increasing numbers of Latin Americans complain that it omitted the most distinctive features of Latin America, those variously referred to as autochthonous or telluric or the genius of the soil and people; specifically, it took no proper account of the area's great mass of Indians, mestizos, and Negroes. In a way, this deficiency was made good a quarter of a century later by the Mexican José Vasconcelos in another classic, *The Cosmic Race.* Yet this too failed to satisfy, for it added up to little more than the identification of Latin America as the melting pot par excellence—a proposition that failed either to please the many Latin Americans who are still conscious and even proud of ethnic differences, or to tell much about the product of the melting pot. The quest has been continued in recent years by Leopoldo Zea and others, who have sought not only to identify Latin America but even to produce a distinctively Latin American philosophy.

Since World War II the question has become more practical and urgent as a result of material and psychological pressures on Latin America. The heaviest pressures have had their source in the Latin Americans' great postwar obsession: development in a broad sense, beginning with the economy. The connection is clear

and direct. While this obsession with development and betterment has grown, Latin Americans have seen their relative position in the world deteriorate, individually and collectively, and
in both the economic and the political fields. In the former they
note bitterly that after nearly a century and a half of political
independence they are still in varying degrees underdeveloped
and that in recent decades they have been outstripped by nations both old and new, most strikingly by the United States and
the Soviet Union. In the political field their relative decline has
been most obvious in the United Nations General Assembly: in
1945 they accounted for nearly 40 per cent of its membership and
formed its largest voting bloc, but by 1964 the figure had dropped
to less than 20 per cent through the admission of a host of new
Asian and African states. These had replaced Latin America as
the principal voting bloc and were threatening its tenure of
prestigious posts in the Security Council and other organs. Moreover, the Latin Americans were impressed by evidences of continentalism in other areas. First and foremost was the European
Common Market, which not only set them an example but constituted a serious threat to their export trade, much of which
was still geared to Europe. Even the new African states, though
individually weak and unstable and far less developed than most
of Latin America, had formed a more effective political union
than any ever achieved by the latter.

All these disagreeable facts were brought home to the Latin
Americans more poignantly than any set of facts in all their previous history. The information was assembled and made available by new agencies, both national and international, such as
the United Nations Economic Commission for Latin America
(ECLA), founded in 1949. It was disseminated not only by the
older mass media of newspapers and periodicals, but also by radio
and television, which began to operate in Latin America on a
large scale in the 1930s and 1950s respectively, and which reached
even the illiterate 50 per cent of Latin America's population.
Finally, the impact was intensified by the rapid urbanization of
Latin America in the postwar period. One of the most persistent
and misleading myths about that area is that its society is pre-

ponderantly rural. Actually, in most of it all kinds of power—political, economic, cultural—are concentrated to a high degree in the cities, and that is where the mass media are most effective.

As a result, the conviction that "united we stand, divided we fall" has made substantial headway among Latin Americans since 1945. Sometimes the preferred solution has been less than Pan Latin American. In 1963, for example, a noted Bolivian, Fernando Díez de Medina—diplomat, cabinet minister, historian, and publicist—proposed a unification confined to South America.[4] Starting from the premise that the irresistible trend of our age is towards the formation of regional or continental blocs, he examined the question of what Latin America should do in "this grand awakening." Various alternatives were first considered and rejected. The idea of a union of all Latin America was dismissed as "utopian" since its "20 countries behave, in general, like separate cells, not like parts of a continental body . . . Latin America does not exist." As for the Organization of American States, it not only suffers from "bureaucratic paralysis" but also "reflects the thinking in Washington rather than in Latin America" as well as "our [Latin American] classical divisionism, the absence of a philosophy of self-defense"; and the Alliance for Progress, though "noble in purpose," "does not accurately reflect or effectively serve either the United States or the South Americans."

On the other hand, continued Díez de Medina, "South America should be one of the world's great regional blocs." "United in solidarity," it could "bring into focus the main lines of hemispheric development," including, among other things, the Alliance for Progress, technical aid from Europe, and defense against Communist penetration, and at the same time "resist better the pressure-forces which come from the United States, from the Soviet Union, from Europe, and from the Orient." Why the author thought his idea less utopian than the one of Pan Latin America, he did not explain; perhaps it was because fewer states in a more compact area were involved. At any rate, even he concluded by describing his projected South American bloc

4. "A South American Bloc," *Atlas* (July 1963) 79–81.

as "an inevitable step in the advance to a Confederation of the South," that is, a confederation of all Latin America.

Other recent Latin American writers have held that continental union can be achieved without any such intervening step. Their views of the nature and function of a united Latin America cover a wide range. One of the broadest visions was offered in 1961 in an article by a leading Uruguayan intellectual, the essayist and poet Emilio Oribe. Referring to Latin America as "our America," he gave his article the title, "Unity of Our America in History and Thought."[5] According to Oribe, there had always been a "Latin American community" and its unity was both "self-willed" and also based upon "the linguistic unity of our race [*raza*]."[6] After reviewing the earlier forms assumed by this "self-willed unity," he assigned Latin America no less a role than that of "integrator of the future civilization of the West." And in the performance of its role, it was destined to supply the too-practical, over-mechanized, and morally "deaf" West with the sorely needed "dynamism of a mystique."

If such notions strike non-Latin Americans as somewhat fanciful, more mundane expressions of the underlying thought by spokesmen of the area can be cited in abundance. Sometimes they take its unity for granted; more often they speak of it as something still to be achieved; but, in either case, they almost always treat it as indispensable. If the wish is father to the thought, at least the wish is there. A few examples must suffice.

The rising Christian Democratic movement in Latin America is committed to the unification of the area. In 1963 a general statement on behalf of the movement declared that if the area was to meet the enormous problems facing it, revolutionary changes in its existing structure would have to be made, and that for this purpose "the primordial [requirement] is for an increase in mutual cooperation among the Latin American states." A much stronger statement to the same effect was incorporated that same year in the platform of the Chilean Christian Democratic

5. "Sobre la unidad de nuestra América," *Cuadernos,* 49 (June, 1961), 3–8.
6. In Spanish, *raza* generally has a cultural rather than a biological significance.

Party (*Partido Demócrata Cristiano de Chile*), whose candidate for the presidency of Chile, Eduardo Frei Montalva, won the election of 1964 by a substantial majority of the popular vote. Because we are anti-imperialist and wish to strengthen Latin America against all kinds of pressure from abroad, said the platform, "we are deeply devoted to the economic and political integration of Latin America."[7] The reasoning behind this position was more fully stated by Emilio Máspero, a leader of the Latin American Confederation of Christian Trade Unionists from Venezuela, another country in which Christian Democracy has developed substantial strength. " . . . Christian trade unionism," said Máspero, "is Latin American trade unionism. One of the most profoundly significant goals of the revolution in our continent is the unification of our countries. . . . If Latin America is to opt for solidarity, it must employ original instruments that are products of its own culture and experience." Later, he added: "Each [Latin American] country on its own has its contradictions and deficiencies; it cannot overcome these unless there is unity in Latin America. That is why we insist upon the political, social, and economic integration of Latin America."[8]

To be sure, the Christian Democrats, though apparently on the upgrade, are still minor groups in most of Latin America, but similar statements have come from leaders of other groups, including heads of governments. Even in Chile and Venezuela, where the Christian Democrats are strongest, they have no monopoly of the continental doctrine. In March, 1964, President Raúl Leoni of Venezuela, a member of the Democratic Action Party [*Acción Democrática*], told the National Congress in his inaugural address that "since Venezuela is integrated into the Latin American cultural community [and] linked to it by historic roots, our relations with Latin American countries will be guided by the desire to attain identity of thought and action in everything related to international policy." This, he continued,

7. *Boletín informativo demócrata cristiano*, March 1963.
8. "Latin America's Labor Movement of Christian Democratic Orientation . . . ," in D'Antonio and Pike, eds., *Religion, Revolution, and Reform* (New York, 1964), 180, 236.

will enable us to make our voices heard in the world and safe-guard our interests. A month earlier, the presidential candidate of Chile's conservative Democratic Front (*Frente Democrático*), Julio Durán, had said in a radio broadcast: "I think that the common markets of Africa, Europe, and the Soviet countries are impelling our nations in Latin America to constitute a solid continental bloc. . . . The only way to answer our problem is to create unity and consolidate the economic process in Latin America."[9]

A strong pronouncement to the same effect was made in November, 1963, by João Goulart, a member of the left-wing Social Democratic Party and then President of Brazil. Addressing a meeting called to review the Alliance for Progress, Goulart gave its supporters cold comfort. Asserting that the time had passed for palliatives and "superficial concessions" by the advanced, capital-exporting countries, he called on the Latin Americans to unite for self-defense in their own way.

> Reality can no longer tolerate that Latin America remain an archi-pelago of nations. . . . Today, and each day more so, Latin America should present to the world a united, solid, and cohesive front in the collective defense of our common interests. Our objectives must be the establishment of a new international division of labor, just and remunerative prices for our exports of raw materials, expansion of our exports of manufactures and semimanufactures.[10]

To conclude our exhibit with a sample from a middle-of-the road source, there is the following from a radio address on May 1, 1964, by the President of Argentina, Arturo Illia, a member of the not-at-all radical People's Radical Party (*Unión Cívica Radical del Pueblo*): "Latin America must cease being just a mere geographic and historical accident and become an international force in each one of our nations and constitute a natural unity for the development of our economies." Such unity, he said, is "one of our main concerns," for in it "lie the greatest possibilities for defense and the complementation of market and state."[11]

9. Monitored radio broadcast, Feb. 10, 1964.
10. *New York Times*, November 12, 1963, report by Juan de Onís.
11. Monitored radio broadcast.

These were fine words; they came from a rather impressive spread of sources, ranging from right to left, in a large part of Latin America; and they could be strongly reinforced from earlier sources, such as the declarations of the Mexican Vicente Lombardo Toledano and the Argentine Juan Perón in support of their respective efforts to develop Latin America-wide organizations of labor. But were these professions of continental faith anything more than fine words? This question will be examined in the next section.

SIDE-EFFECTS OF CONTINENTAL NATIONALISM

Since the nineteenth-century congresses of Panama, Lima, and Montevideo, Latin American continentalism has found no direct expression of great consequence, in institutions or otherwise. Perhaps its most important expression has been the Latin American bloc in the United Nations, but, far from being monolithic, that has shown less consistency in its voting record than some of the other blocs. In the Inter-American System, too, Latin American unity breaks down on crucial questions. It made a brief show of strength at the Punta del Este conference of 1962 when a group led by the Big Three—Mexico, Brazil, and Argentina—stood shoulder to shoulder against imposing certain sanctions on Cuba, and ultimately carried the other nations with them. In July, 1964, however, a similar meeting in Washington ended with Mexico and three other Latin American countries on one side of a high fence, still opposing sanctions, and Argentina, Brazil and all the rest on the other side.

Nevertheless, Latin American continentalism has recently produced some significant side-effects, principally by contributing to three developments: the formation of the free-trade association, LAFTA; the growth of ambiguity in Latin America's relations with the West, the Communist world, and the nonaligned nations; and the sharpening of conventional nationalism in individual Latin American countries. Each of those developments requires some explanation.

The precise relation of LAFTA to continentalism is not easy to determine for LAFTA means different things to different people in Latin America and, although it was established as recently as 1960, its character has already shown signs of changing. Intended ultimately to become Pan Latin American, actually it included at the outset only Mexico and six South American countries, and only two more were added in the next four years. Moreover, Cuba, whose application for membership, though supported by some LAFTA members, was rejected, is apparently excluded for the duration of its Castro-Communist regime. As for LAFTA's purposes, these were nominally not political, but economic, and even in the economic field its functions were narrowly limited. It was not a common market arrangement, but an association for lowering trade barriers among its members and gradually working towards the establishment of free trade. Strongly influenced by recent European precedents, it resembled the loose European Free Trade Association of the "outer seven" headed by Great Britain, rather than the much more cohesive European Common Market of the "inner six" headed by France.

We cannot review LAFTA's history here, but it should be noted that, despite strong dissatisfaction with it in other quarters, its record in its first four years won an encomium from the head of one of its principal member states, Mexico. In his farewell address to the Mexican National Congress on September 1, 1964, President Adolfo López Mateos declared that LAFTA had "contributed greatly to . . . encouraging a spirit of solidarity and mutual understanding among member countries." His enthusiasm for it may have been increased by the fact that, as he also noted, it had likewise "contributed greatly to improving our foreign trade [and] encouraging our industrial development," but that too was one of its functions.

Yet, from the start it had been felt that LAFTA must some day grow into something more than a free-trade association. In the long run, some hoped, it would become a force for political as well as economic unification, as the German Zollverein or customs union had done in the nineteenth century. More immediately, an expansion of LAFTA's economic functions was contemplated. In 1958, even before it was founded, President-elect Frondizi of Argentina, one of its chief sponsors, told an audience in Chile that Latin American economic cooperation must be aimed not only at promoting trade among the members but also at defending the prices of their products in the world market. In 1964, at a LAFTA meeting in Bogotá, supporters of the association began to realize that even in its assigned field of intra-Latin American trade, it could not do its job until it took on some of the functions of a customs union.[12] And in the same year, President Illia of Argentina advocated the creation of a labor organization which would "facilitate the economic complementation being carried out by LAFTA."

Illia denied that the proposed labor organization would be detrimental to the existing Inter-American labor organization, ORIT, which includes the United States as well as Latin America; but he did not give a reasoned statement of the grounds for his denial. The same possibility of conflict exists between LAFTA and the Alliance for Progress, that is, between Pan Latin Americanism, on the one hand, and the existing hemisphere arrangement, on the other. As we have noted, Brazilian President Goulart in 1963 held that the conflict was already under way and took a strong stand for Pan Latin Americanism as against the Alliance for Progress.

Interestingly enough, the Alliance's basic document, the Charter of Punta del Este (1961), not only gives its blessing to the economic integration of Latin America but also specifically declares the Montevideo Treaty (which founded LAFTA) and the much less ambitious Central American Customs Union "appropriate instruments" to attain such integration. Yet, other provisions of the Charter of Punta del Este had the opposite effect by assigning a key role to national planning by each individual country. This, together with the necessarily great influence of Washington as the chief dispenser of funds, gave the operation of the Alliance the appearance of a series of bilateral arrangements between the United States and each of the disunited Latin American states.

12. *New York Times,* Oct. 25, 1964, report by Richard Eder.

Partly in order to meet complaints on this score, though for other reasons as well, the machinery of the Alliance was modified in 1964 by the creation of a new chief organ, a kind of board of directors called the Inter-American Committee for the Alliance for Progress, which was dominated by Latin Americans. One of them, the Colombian Carlos Sanz de Santamaría, was its chairman. This new departure might aid in giving substance to the charter's verbal encouragement of LAFTA and thus ultimately establishing the dualism United States-Latin America in place of the old polycentrism dominated by one great center, Washington. That, at any rate, was the consummation hoped for by the more moderate Pan Latin Americanists, who still thought of Latin America as belonging to the West and more particularly to the Western Hemisphere.

This brings us to the second side-effect of Latin American continentalism: its stimulus to ambiguity regarding Latin America's relation to the West. In the nineteenth century there had been no such ambiguity, at least so far as the literate and politically active members of society were concerned: almost as a matter of course they identified "our America" with the West, and rather with its heartland, Europe, than with the United States. Their attitude is perfectly illustrated by Rodó's Europeanist *Ariel* of 1900, of which we have already spoken; but that famous essay marks the beginning of the end of an era. The next decade was marked by the rapid rise of *indigenismo* in Spanish America, a many-faceted movement which in English means both "Indianism" and "native Americanism." As Indianism, it flourished most in countries such as Mexico and Peru which had had high Indian cultures in pre-conquest times and in which the majority of the population was still made up of Indians and mestizos. But even in countries where neither condition existed a rough equivalent was provided by a native Americanism based on such concepts as that of the "genius of the soil and people"; examples are *gauchismo* in Argentina and *sertanismo* in Brazil, which we have already discussed in other chapters.[13] Next came recognition of

13. See Chapters Four (Argentina) and Five (Brazil).

the role of Negroes and African culture in Latin American life, particularly in Brazil and the Caribbean area.

Surely no less important than this intellectual change was the political change involved in the emergence of the great mass of Indians, mestizos, and Negroes as a significant factor in the public life of Latin America; the latter change may be dated from the Mexican Revolution of 1910. Two world wars and the disastrous depression decade of the 1930s further weakened Latin America's traditional Europeanism. Finally, since 1945 the cold war, obsession with the urge for development, and the growing conviction that development could not be achieved until Latin America had emancipated itself from control by the great capitalist-industrial nations all combined to complete the alienation of a host of Latin Americans from the West—from the United States and Europe. The result was not necessarily hostility to the West, but rather the conviction that Latin America had become something different: "Eurindia," the Argentine Ricardo Rojas had called it earlier; "a cosmic race," according to the Mexican José Vasconcelos; or, more broadly, a product of a "meeting of East and West" in Northrop's summation of Mexico. In any case, there can be no question that the Latin Americans' traditional continentalism has intensified this sense of difference.

The difference sets Latin America apart not only from the rest of the West, but also from the rest of the world. None but a handful of its people would identify it with either the Communist or the nonaligned nations. Early in the Castro regime many of them applauded Castro's program of social revolution and envied his success in tweaking Uncle Sam's beard, but his stock plummeted with the Soviet missile crisis of 1962 and has never fully recovered. And there is no sense of identity with the nonaligned nations. When they held a conference at Cairo in 1964, seven Latin American states sent observers, and only Cuba sent a full-fledged delegate. Only Brazil has shown a positive interest in the new nations of Africa, and that for reasons of prestige and national interest. No Latin American country has shown a comparable interest in the new nations of Asia. In the

United Nations, Latin America's cooperation with the Asian-African bloc, never more than spotty, has recently tended to change into rivalry. Thus, on September 22, 1963, the *New York Times* reported that the challenge from the more numerous African and Asian countries had "spurred the 19 Latin American members to seek greater policy unity to achieve greater impact on the rapidly changing world situation." This is only one illustration of the way in which events since 1945 have combined to stimulate Pan-Latin Americanism by differentiating Latin America as a bloc from the rest of the world.

Yet the effective unification of Latin America is so unlikely to be achieved in the near future, and this fact is so well understood by its people, that one of the chief practical consequences of the propagation of continentalism has been to strengthen nationalism in each country of the area. The reason is obvious, for the difference between "us" and "them" is basic to the whole concept of nationalism, and differentiation in continental terms provided a broader and firmer base for the development of nationalism in each country by investing its peculiarities with the dignity of widely shared group traits. In other words, continental nationalism has served in Latin America as a whetstone for conventional nationalism.

Two illustrations, both from Argentine sources, make this clear. One comes from the pen of Gabriel del Mazo, chief spokesman for the University Reform. In 1938, after speaking with approval of the projection of that reform in political terms and on a continental scale by APRA, del Mazo declared that the proper defense against "international plutocracy" and "imperialism as a system" is the organization of an "emancipating union," by which he meant the unification of Latin America. But he stipulated that this should be an "effectively national" association which would permit the quest for independence under the banner of complete democracy. The rest of his discussion continued in the same vein: each state would "nationalize public power and organize the economy in the service of the Nation. . . . We must make ourselves nationally masters of all things in America. . . .

The Nation is simply and solely the life of the People; its life and its dreams."[14]

Twenty years later, in 1958, President Arturo Frondizi, one of the original sponsors of LAFTA, spoke in similar terms in his inaugural address. On the one hand, he advocated the "complete identification" of Argentina with her "sister countries of Latin America," with a view to developing Latin America into "a powerful community of nations." On the other hand, he not only called for "the economic development and integration of each one of these countries," but roundly declared it "indispensable that each one of them attain the greatest prosperity possible, since the development of each Latin American nation will make it possible to accelerate the development of the rest."[15] Reminiscent of the old laissez-faire proposition that every man enriches the nation by enriching himself, this is a clear case of using tomorrow's Pan Latin Americanism to justify and strengthen today's nationalism.

Among the Latin American nationalists who use it in this way are the Communists. They exploit it to weaken the United States and the Inter-American System, and to this end they seek alliances with nonproletarian nationalists, including the national bourgeoisie. But for the Communists, we may be reasonably sure, this is only an intermediate goal and heaven lies beyond it.

In conclusion, despite its manifest weaknesses and handicaps, continental nationalism is a by no means negligible force in present-day Latin America. It has already produced significant side-effects, and in the long run it may prove one of the world's most effective expressions of continentalism. It is more firmly based in every way than Africa's, and in some ways than Western Europe's. It lags far behind the latter in the development of integrating institutions, technical and political skills, and economic and social cohesion; but its internal dissensions are less sharp and less deeply rooted in history, and its cultural bases may turn out to be firmer if only because they are less diverse. In

14. *Reforma universitaria y cultura nacional* (Buenos Aires, 1955), 26, 28.
15. *La política exterior argentina* (Buenos Aires, 1962), 27–29.

recent years Latin American parliamentary meetings have begun to take place and there have been repeated efforts to form a Latin American block in the OAS as well as the United Nations.

Yet, at the present time, Latin America's political and cultural development is not far enough advanced for effective union. Intra-Latin American economic ties are too weak to provide a material base for union, as witness the fact that even in 1965, after five years of LAFTA, only 10 per cent of Latin America's total trade was carried on among Latin American nations. The area's economic orientation is still directed overwhelmingly towards other parts of the world, and above all towards Europe and the United States, as has been the case ever since the beginning of independence. The same thing is true of its cultural relations; and, even with the best will in the world for unification, these centrifugal forces will be hard to overcome. For a long time to come, the major emphasis in Latin America is likely to remain on conventional nationalism, which continental nationalism will serve mainly to sharpen.

TEN

Summary and Prospect

TWENTIETH-CENTURY LATIN AMERICA has shared fully in the worldwide development of nationalism. It has also provided abundant illustrations for each of the four general categories into which, as Silvert suggests,[1] all studies of the phenomenon can be fitted, namely, nationalism as a juridical concept, as a symbolic concept, as ideology, and as social value. As we have tried to show, the diversity of Latin America is reflected in the distinctive character of the unfolding nationalist process in each country. At the same time, its numerous factors of unity have also been reflected in certain general features of the process that have been common to most if not all the countries of the area. The two chief common factors have been the escalation of nationalism and the trend towards its identification with modernization and social justice.

ESCALATION, MODERNIZATION, AND SOCIAL JUSTICE

Gino Germani applies the term "inflation" of nationalism[2] to a process which we prefer to call "escalation," since "inflation"

1. K. H. Silvert, ed., *Expectant Peoples. Nationalism and Development* (New York, 1963), 18.
2. *Política y sociedad en una época de transición* (Buenos Aires, 1962), 162.

is a loaded word and tends to obscure the fact that nationalism is both socially and politically apparently an essential part of the development process in the less advanced countries of the world. But whether one speaks of escalation or inflation, they both refer to the same thing: the rising bids, as in an auction, of rival groups seeking to win popular support by appeals to nationalist sentiment.

How the auction has been conducted in Latin America can be best indicated by a comparison with Western Europe. At first glance, the two seem more alike than different in recent years, for in Western Europe, too, the nationalist tide has risen rapidly. This fact has already been noted, but we return to it here in one more effort to disabuse the reader of the delusion that nationalism is a thing of the past in the advanced countries, with the sole exception of General de Gaulle's France. In 1960 a conference of scholars at Berlin noted the "rehabilitation of nationalism."[3] Within the next few years recognition of its resurgence in Europe became widespread. A few examples from 1964 will suffice. James Reston, writing in the *New York Times* of September 6, said, "Each of the [United States'] major allies has turned its attention [in the last two years] to internal problems and has become almost as nationalistic as de Gaulle's France." In an article in *Foreign Affairs* for July, Henry Kissinger warned against the danger of the rise in Western Europe of "a new and more virulent form of nationalism, perhaps even more intense than the nationalism of the *patries.*" And in December, Knut Hammerskjold, deputy secretary general of the European Free Trade Association, made the following perceptive observation in a speech to a New York audience:

> A struggle for power in a fluid Europe is now fully engaged. It is a struggle essentially between the old, but immensely strong, concept of nationalism and national sovereignty, and the newer concept of political integration and the pooling of sovereignty. The newer idea has many ardent and dedicated supporters and has already caught the imagination of men's minds on an enormous scale, but it still lacks the strong institutions which make nationalism so powerful.

3. *Democracia, nacionalismo y militarismo,* supplement to *Cuadernos* (November–December, 1960).

Yet despite the resemblance as regards the recent intensification of nationalism, the European situation differs from the Latin American in two important ways. First, in Europe this intensification represents a rather sudden—and, to many persons, a quite unexpected—resurgence from the low point to which nationalism had dropped in nontotalitarian Europe before World War II and in all of Europe for more than a decade thereafter. In Latin America there was no such break, but, on the contrary, a steady escalation of nationalism from the 1920s on. These facts suggest that nationalism is less firmly rooted in contemporary Europe than in Latin America; and certainly its European opponents can now count on integrating institutions, such as the European Coal and Steel Community and Euratom, that have no counterpart in Latin America.

The second important difference has to do with the popular base of nationalism and bears directly on its escalation. In Europe the masses were integrated into the national society and inculcated with nationalism under the leadership of a truly national bourgeoisie, that is, one clearly identified with the fatherland, the *patrie*. In Latin America, however, the elites during the rise of nationalist sentiment have for the most part been made up of persons tied to the export economy and to foreign capital and enterprise—great landlords, urban bankers and merchants, and, until quite recently, the leading members of the emergent middle sectors or middle class. As a result, the incorporation of the masses into society in Latin America has combined with the inculcation of nationalism to produce a phenomenon quite different from its European counterpart. Latin American targets of nationalist attacks are quite often the area's own so-called *vendepatria* elites as well as the foreign "imperialists," hence the charge, so frequently noted in the preceding pages, that the two had entered into a corrupt alliance for the exploitation of the nation. And here is where escalation enters, for Latin America's elites have often sought to refute the charge by proving themselves superpatriots and out-Hectoring the Hectors of populist nationalism.

More briefly, we may note that Latin America also differs

from the underdeveloped countries of Asia and Africa as regards the escalation of nationalism. The difference lies in conditions peculiar to Latin America that tend to contain its escalation there. For one thing, Latin America has democratic traditions and institutions, which though often more honored in the breach than the observance, are still strong; and nationalism in the world at large has been given its most extreme expression under authoritarian regimes—Hitler's is the classic example. Latin America likewise has a strong tradition of internationalism, which may be a part of its Catholic and Iberian heritage. In the same connection one thinks also of Pan Latin Americanism, but this is a less reliable brake; indeed, as was pointed out in the preceding chapter, Latin America's continental nationalism can be used just as well to intensify the conventional nationalism of individual Latin American countries.

The second major feature of nationalism in contemporary Latin America, the trend towards its identification with modernization and social justice, has been most apparent in the more advanced countries. These are the ones that have achieved or are approaching an intermediate stage of development. It is not necessary that the whole country shall have achieved that stage, but only that a substantial part shall have done so, for the rest is then spurred on to emulate it. Brazil is the most striking example, with the dramatic contrast between the booming industrial area of São Paulo and the stricken agrarian Northeast. Other examples are Mexico, Chile, Venezuela, and Castro's Cuba. The Argentina of Juan Perón and the Uruguay of José Batlle y Ordóñez once fell in this category and they may rejoin it, but for some years past both countries have experienced a kind of stasis.

The strength of this trend has different causes from one country to another, but in the main it seems to lie in a combination of the following factors, which exist in some degree in all of them. First, there are rising aspirations and growing participation in public affairs on the part of the masses. Thus, in Argentina the ratio of voters to adult male population rose from 9 per cent in 1910 to 41 per cent in 1928 and 56 per cent in 1946 (the year of Perón's first election to the presidency). Next, greatly improved means of transportation and communication fostered a growing sense of national unity and, especially among the less fortunate, contributed to the rise of aspirations. In some countries the rate of illiteracy was greatly reduced; in Mexico, from 80 per cent in 1900 to less than 30 per cent in 1965. But since about half the people of Latin America at large are still illiterate, radio broadcasting has been immensely important in alerting and mobilizing masses; and radios are found even in remote villages of the Andes. Along with all this there has been a growing conviction among Latin Americans on three related points: that modernization and social justice are necessary and inseparable; that they can be achieved only by freeing one's country from foreign control of all kinds; and that this in turn can be achieved only by action on a national scale.

As will appear below, however, there has been a wide diversity of opinion on the definition of national objectives and on the question of priorities, method, and timing in pursuit of them. Consequently, the varieties of nationalism in Latin America still persist.

OBJECTIVES OF NATIONALISM

Foremost among the objectives of nationalism in most of Latin America today are the two just mentioned, modernization and social justice, but these need to be particularized and qualified and several other and older ones must be added.

Modernization

This owes its importance to the fact that it is both an end in itself and an aid to the older objective of independence. Both cases involve not only material but also psychological considerations (national pride; the desire to catch up with the advanced countries, to realize the potential of one's own country, to bring it out of the "peripheral" world into the main stream of history;

and the like). Modernization connotes development and betterment on a broad front, cultural, social, and political as well as
economic, but its central theme has been economic nationalism,
first in Mexico, Uruguay, and Argentina between 1910 and 1930
and then in the other countries. It has developed special symbols,
such as national petroleum agencies in oil-producing countries
(e.g., Pemex in Mexico, Petrobrás in Brazil, Y.P.F. in Argentina),
and steel mills in most countries. So far as oil is concerned,
Venezuela is a notable exception, for reasons suggested in an
earlier chapter.

Social Justice

This, too, is a broad term interpreted in many ways. At one
extreme it signifies merely an improvement in the lot of the
masses; at the other, unmitigated egalitarianism; and there are
many gradations in between. In political terms, the concept
draws its main support from the left, but the escalation of
nationalism has gained support for it on the right as well. Of
course, no one could take a stand against social justice any more
than he could take a stand in favor of sin, so that the question is
simply one of the application of the idea. But for our purposes
the important thing is that the achievement of social justice,
however defined, has been increasingly identified with action by
the national governments. This not only involves an encroach-
ment on particularism and localism; it is also a sign of the growing secularization of Latin American society, since it embraces
many activities and concepts formerly associated with the Roman
Catholic Church, ranging from administering hospitals and
schools to the just wage. Recently, the Church in Latin America,
as elsewhere, has vigorously reasserted its role in social questions,
in accordance with papal encyclicals such as *Mater et Magistra*.
Yet most Catholic laymen in Latin America, with the blessing of
many of the clergy, are funneling their activities along this line
through secular political parties, notably the nonconfessional
Christian Democratic parties of Chile and Venezuela.

Independence and Sovereignty

This is an old objective, which has been pursued since 1810, but in the present century it has been broadened to include cultural and economic independence. Today, it is widely believed that political independence is a frail and worthless fabric unless reinforced by economic independence. This was the thought that inspired the Perón government's formal "Declaration of Economic Independence" in 1947. Economic independence is taken to mean national control of at least the country's natural resources and their exploitation; and since many of Latin America's new leaders regard its free enterprise system as the construction of an oligarchy bound by a corrupt alliance to foreign imperialists, national control is widely interpreted as requiring a large measure of control by the national government. Of the many expressions of cultural nationalism in the last half century, one of the most recent and most characteristic is the Mexican government's adoption of the *texto único*, school texts which are written by Mexicans and are the same in all schools throughout the country. The purpose of this device is not only to free Mexico from domination by foreign ideas, but also to unify the nation by instilling the same nationalist ideas into all members of the rising generation of Mexicans. France and other European countries anticipated Mexico in this respect in the nineteenth century, but Mexico has gone them one better, if only because its government's monopoly of education is virtually complete.

Territorial Integrity

This, too, is an old objective in Latin America. Though no longer a leading issue in most of the area, it is still alive in several cases. Some of these involve disputes within the Latin American family, as between Argentina and Chile over a part of their common boundary, between Bolivia and Chile over the former's outlet to the Pacific, and between Ecuador and Peru over disputed territory awarded to Peru in 1942. Other cases involve controversies between Latin Americans and non-Americans: the long-standing claims of Guatemala to British Honduras and of Argentina to the British-held Falkland Islands (the Malvinas); Venezuela's recent revival of its boundary dispute with Great Britain over the boundary of British Guiana; and the claims of Argentina and Chile against the field in Antarctica.

Effective Occupation of National Territory

Except as a pipe-dream, this objective is of rather recent origin. It is partly a measure of national defense, taken as the great waste spaces of Latin America are beginning to be occupied. It is also partly a product of the urge for economic development. The most dramatic example is Brazil's construction of a new national capital, Brasília, far back in its underdeveloped interior. Other examples are the efforts of Bolivia and Peru to develop their lowlands east of the Andes; Mexico, its northern states and Baja California; and Chile and Argentina, their southern lands down to Tierra del Fuego.

National Unity

Always a major objective, this has been pursued in the present century with increasing zeal and on an ever-broadening front. In the nineteenth century its significance was mainly political and it generally meant little more than subordinating local caudillos and other particularists to central authority. Today, it has come to have an economic, cultural, social, ethnic, and psychological meaning as well. The aim is now to incorporate all the people of a country as active participants in the national life, to develop in them a national conscience or sense of national self-identity, and to organize them in the pursuit of specific national goals. This involves not only a vast improvement in means of transportation, communication, and education, but also the assimilation of immigrants and the reduction of class and ethnic barriers. The last is a major task in all countries and a gigantic task in some, particularly in the Andean countries and Guatemala, where great masses of Indians have never been assimilated to the dominant Spanish-creole culture.

National Defense

Effective occupation of the national territory is only one aspect of this objective, which in its full scope extends to the nation's very existence. In this sense national defense has been a minor concern of the Latin American countries in the present era, for two reasons. First, their existence has never been seriously threatened since the nineteenth century. The nearest approximation came from armed interventions by the United States in a few of the small Caribbean countries, but even when these were total they were temporary. Second, even the strongest Latin American countries are so weak on the world power-scale that their ultimate security depends not on themselves but others, as Fidel Castro showed when he sought the protection of Soviet missiles. A British scholar, R. P. Dore, comparing this situation with the very different one in which Japan's nationalism developed vigorously in response to a protracted series of military threats, questions whether a similar development is to be expected in Latin America, where no comparable danger exists. Can a sense of national purpose, he asks, be as effective when defined in terms of economic growth rates and social welfare as when the definition comes in the military terms of national defense?[4]

The question is a poser, and yet it may be that in the twentieth century Japan's real peril has had its moral equivalent in the Latin American image of the Yankee peril. A major ingredient of Latin American nationalism in this century has unquestionably been anti-Americanism or Yankeephobia. Dore himself seems to recognize this when he goes on to ask, with regard to Fidel Castro's domain, whether "Cuba Sí!" will be as strong when "Yanqui No!" fades. At any rate, somehow the armed forces in most of Latin America have long succeeded in identifying themselves with national defense in running, or greatly helping to run, the countries they serve. They have also played a leading role in the development of nationalism.

4. "Latin America and Japan Compared," in John J. Johnson, ed., *Continuity and Change in Latin America* (Stanford, 1958), 249.

CONTROVERSIAL PROBLEMS

All the foregoing objectives are present in some degree in almost all nationalist movements in contemporary Latin America, but how to achieve them has been a fruitful subject of controversy. For there are wide variations in those movements with regard to basic issues, depending on such questions as whether the main focus is on domestic affairs or foreign relations, whether nostalgic or dynamic values prevail, and which power group calls the tune. In recent years the chief subjects of controversy, all interrelated, have been as follows:

RATE OF CHANGE

All Latin American nationalists, of the right wing as well as the left, agree that the scope of change must be extensive, but they disagree profoundly both on specific changes and still more on the rate of change. Pushed to extremes, this question becomes one of reform versus revolution. Each extreme has advocates on both right and left. In Chile, for example, both Frei's Christian Democrats and Allende's FRAP are left-wing nationalists, but compared with revolutionary FRAP, the Christian Democrats are moderate reformers. Again, in Argentina, revolutionary nationalism is represented both by the left-wing Peronist group and by its worst enemies, a right-wing military group; and the two have diametrically opposite programs.

Priorities

Ideologues of all schools of nationalist thought talk as if everything could be done immediately, but once in a position of responsibility the most ardent nationalist has to put off some things so that others may be done. In the present era, the most inflammable issue of this kind is the one involving the rival claims of economic development and social welfare. Although in the long run the two are not mutually exclusive, but inter-dependent, the present underdeveloped situation of Latin America is such that what is given to one must be taken from the other. Some argue that the most urgent problem is not how to slice the pie, but how to make it bigger. But this is an unpopular view with the impatient masses, as President Frondizi of Argentina found to his cost when he espoused it at the end of 1958, for the hostile popular reaction to it contributed greatly to his overthrow some three years later. The difficulty, as Latin Americans such as Jaguaribe have pointed out, is that the rapid economic development of developing countries requires a rate of capital investment, savings, and austerity incompatible with the increased worker benefits demanded in the name of social justice. Even left-wing nationalists split on this issue. In Mexico since 1940, for example, the regime, heir to the Revolution of 1910, has concentrated on economic development and this has proceeded apace; but the regime's critics, also continuators of that revolution, complain that most of the Mexican people have not shared in the benefits.

Authoritarianism vs. Representative Democracy

Under regimes of representative, constitutional democracy, political fragmentation and other factors act as a brake on change. Impatient nationalists of all shades therefore tend to prefer an authoritarian system of one kind or another. Among right-wing elements this tendency is nourished by tradition and by fascist ideas of more recent origin; among left-wingers, by the widespread popular conviction that in Latin America representative democracy has always been a façade behind which the upper classes have ruled and exploited the country. More recently the left-wing sector has been reinforced by admiration for the rapid economic and scientific development achieved under authoritarian regimes in the Soviet Union and Communist China. Latin Americans have been much impressed by these examples of what can be accomplished by forced-draft national development. Their response may not have gained many recruits for communism in Latin America, but apparently it has given aid and comfort to the advocates of an authoritarian nationalism of a non-Communist character.

Statism vs. Capitalist Free Enterprise

This is obviously related to the foregoing topic, and many of the considerations just stated apply here too. Latin American experience, for example, has given capitalism and private enterprise as bad a name with the poorer classes as it has representative, constitutional democracy. Likewise, the Soviet Union's rapid economic and scientific development has stirred many Latin Americans to emulate its statism as well as its authoritarianism. But the former has much stronger support in Latin America than the latter, for many Latin Americans of the right and center who remain loyal to representative democracy have been converted to national planning and direction of the economy. This trend was already apparent in the depression decade of the 1930s and has been strengthened since World War II. The truth is that, as the noted Colombian Alberto Lleras Camargo observed shortly after that war, the laissez-faire, free enterprise system has always been an exotic plant in Latin America, where the tradition of government control was rooted in the three hundred years of Spanish and Portuguese rule. In the present century circumstances have combined to reinvigorate this tradition. For one thing, many of the problems of modernization are too big to be handled by anyone except the national government. Another stimulus has come, paradoxically, from the new international organizations and arrangements, for in most cases these deal only with national governments and, among other things, make them the exclusive channels and the responsible agents in all matters relating to aid and development. The most recent example, as noted in an earlier chapter, is the Punta del Este Charter of the Alliance for Progress.

Yet statism has not by any means monopolized Latin American thought. Exotic though laissez faire may have been in those parts, free enterprise and capitalism took such deep root there in the nineteenth and twentieth centuries that they too became, to many Latin Americans, a part of the national tradition. As a result, the issue between statism and free enterprise has been highly controversial and remains open. Most nationalists accept a mixed system, with elements of both; and there is, of course, further controversy over how much of each the mixture should contain. One point on which Latin American nationalists of almost all kinds agree is the inclusion of a strong ingredient of what passes for socialism in the United States.

The Role of the Armed Forces

In most of Latin America the role of the armed forces in public affairs has always been important and in recent decades it has become more so, but today it is being sharply challenged. From the start it was sustained by a variety of circumstances: the armed forces were a chief symbol of national unity and independence, in most cases they were designated guardians of the constitution as well as the country, and they were usually the principal power group in a loose-knit and unstable society. From about 1920 to 1950 their power grew as they acquired professionalization, technical skills, and modern arms. More recently, however, their position has been weakened by the growth of other power groups, such as organized labor and the national bourgeoisie; by the increasing complexity of the problems of national development, especially its economic problems, with which the armed forces were not competent to deal; and by their own disunity on the objectives of nationalism, which may reflect the fact that the officers came increasingly from the disunited middle sectors of society. Argentina, Chile, Peru, and Colombia are all cases in point, but probably the best illustration of all this is Mexico. There, the army ruled until 1940, but it has been replaced by a combination of politicians, businessmen, and technocrats. Also, although the armed forces are still the principal power group everywhere except in Mexico, Costa Rica, Chile, and Uruguay, they are no longer wedded to the oligarchy, as they once were, nor are they identified with any one variety of nationalism, as they were before the 1930s with the liberal nationalism of regimes based on a laissez-faire export economy.

Foreign Relations

In bilateral relations, contemporary Latin American nationalism has expressed itself less in chauvinism and aggression against neighboring countries than in drawing apart from the great powers. This tendency, illustrated by Perón's Third Position in the 1940s, became widespread from the late 1950s on, under such other labels as nonalignment and independent foreign policy. Its principal display in verbal pyrotechnics was provided by President Goulart of Brazil in the early 1960s, but Mexico since 1945 has been its leading practitioner. The only clear-cut exception is Castro Cuba's formation of a close tie with the Soviet Union, but that was probably imposed by strategic and economic necessity. The nonalignment trend is obviously a matter of concern to the United States, since it undermines Western Hemisphere solidarity and the quasi-alliance of the Rio Defense Treaty of 1947.

Multilateral relations can be considered mainly under the rubric of international organizations since the exceptions to this rule are relatively few and unimportant. The first point to be noted is that, as already stated, nationalism and internationalism are not necessarily incompatible; on the contrary, the latter may express and reinforce the former, as in the case of continental nationalism. Second, the attitudes of Latin American nationalists towards internationalism differ widely according to both the kind of nationalism and the kind of international organization concerned. Latin American nationalists of whatever kind look with more favor on international cooperation for peaceful purposes than for military. Thus, although they accepted the Rio Defense Treaty and its sanctions, they have never been willing to apply the sanction of armed force, and even the milder enforcement measures have been widely denounced as a violation of the Inter-American rule of nonintervention adopted in 1936 and strengthened in the OAS Charter of 1948, despite the explicit declaration in the same charter that such enforcement measures do not constitute intervention. Latin American devotion to the absolute rule of nonintervention is a clear expression of nationalism. It is also a formidable bar to effective international cooperation in the field of security. As regards economic cooperation, Latin American attitudes vary according to their real or fancied interests and their prepossessions, and in most cases nationalism is today a major factor. On the one hand, there is widespread antagonism to the International Monetary Fund, which is regarded as unduly limiting national freedom of action in financial and economic policy. On the other hand, most countries look with affection on the Inter-American Development Bank, which is more permissive and helpful for national purposes.

VARIETIES OF NATIONALISM

In preceding pages we have had occasion to discuss many different varieties of nationalism in Latin America: benign or aggressive, nostalgic or dynamic, right-wing or left-wing, bourgeois or Nasserist, and so on. These still exist, but in recent years there has been an apparent trend towards their merger in four main categories. These can be grouped in two opposing pairs, which are interrelated, *viz:* ideological vs. pragmatic, and populist vs. comprehensive.

Ideological or doctrinaire nationalism is revolutionary. It has a blueprint that it hurries to impose, that deals in absolutes and scorns compromise. Pragmatic nationalism proceeds more slowly and prides itself on its realism in, for example, recognizing the necessarily slow pace of social change and the need to build on the past and with the materials at hand. The first of these contrasting positions is illustrated by Cándido Mendes of Brazil, who would reject all foreign aid, public as well as private, and from international organizations as well as national governments. The second position is illustrated by another Brazilian, Hélio Jaguaribe, whose nationalism is realistic enough to welcome foreign aid even from "capitalistic monopolies" such as Standard

Oil, provided they could be expected to develop Brazil's economy more rapidly than the Brazilians themselves could.

Populist nationalism identifies the masses as the "real" nation, as Eva Perón did when she assured the "suffering, sweating" *descamisados* that they were the only true Argentines. It also makes the masses the primary or sole beneficiary of the nationalist program. By contrast, comprehensive or general-welfare nationalism takes the whole nation into account and would have the national government be a father to all its people. Obviously this involves some defense of the haves against the have-nots, of the status quo against revolutionary change, so that this form of nationalism can also be called defensive. President Belaúnde Terry's policy in Peru after 1963 is a case in point.

It should be clear by now that these two pairs of nationalist forms are interrelated and that the tie is likely to be closest between ideological and populist and between pragmatic and comprehensive. What is likely does not always occur. Populism can be quite devoid of ideology. Also, ideology can be violently antipopulist, as when the Argentine military extremists called gorillas tried to read the Peronist masses (one third of all adult Argentines) out of the nation.

But the likely correlation does occur frequently, and perhaps the best illustration is provided by the conflicting approaches to the basic question of agrarian reform. At one extreme is the Cárdenas approach in Mexico in the 1930s. Combining nationalist ideology and populism, this was aimed at effecting a revolution in power relationships by a quick and sweeping redistribution of land in favor of the rural masses, with little or no regard for the consequences to the rest of the nation or to the national economy. At the other extreme is the evolutionary nationalism of Betancourt in Venezuela and Belaúnde Terry in Peru, who have tried to regulate the pace of agrarian reform with a view to promoting the general welfare of the nation at the same time that it moves towards social justice and economic independence, even though this means tolerating for a time survivals of the old "colonial-oligarchic" order.

A no less striking illustration, of wider scope, is provided by the contrast between two periods in the history of the same country, Mexico. Formerly the paladin of revolutionary national-ism of the xenophobe, damn-the-torpedoes variety, Mexico since 1940 has shifted to a gradual, carefully calculated method of achieving nationalist objectives, to which it is still devoted. It has, among other things, welcomed foreign private capital and private enterprise—under proper controls of course; has had second thoughts about agrarian reform; and has given priority to increasing national wealth rather than to an egalitarian distribu-tion of it. Moreover, as in the Japan of two or three generations ago described by R. P. Dore (see note 4), Mexico, along with Brazil, Argentina, and Chile, has developed a substantial num-ber of young economists and other specialists, many of them trained abroad, who might be called scientific nationalists and who are increasingly influential in shaping public policy. If the analogy with Japan is worth anything, their emergence is a hope-ful sign for their countries. Their pragmatic-comprehensive type of nationalism is not new in Latin America, but they are bring-ing to it a new body of knowledge and skills.

MODERNIZATION AND COMMUNISM

The relationship of nationalism to modernization is complex. Modernization cannot occur without disrupting old patterns of behavior. Nationalism may justify this disruption by rationaliz-ing painful changes on the basis of collective aspirations. When it does so, nationalism plays an important role in upsetting traditional political, social, and economic systems. Revolutionary nationalism, whether of the populist or some other variety, is disruptive, and the upheaval inspired by it may be extreme if the barriers to change are great. Yet there is no rule that it must always be violent. It is revolutionary in the sense that it delib-erately undercuts the power relationships sustaining the tradi-tional order and sets up new ones in their place. Frequently this modernization by destruction of the old produces great social dislocations and, again, nationalism is useful for the reintegration of society.

One of the most perplexing problems presented by revolutionary, modernizing nationalist movements is how to estimate their vulnerability to Communist capture. Cuba has made this problem a crucial one. Usually contemporary movements of this kind express themselves in terms of an outdated anticolonialism. Western observers often respond with hasty misinterpretations leading to hostile actions that may prove counterproductive by facilitating Communist capture of what was initially a bona-fide nationalist movement.

To be sure, misinterpretation is only too easy, for there is no error-free test for evaluating a revolutionary movement while it is in progress. For example, the alleged past ideas and associations of its leaders are not a reliable guide. Betancourt illustrates the point, for in his youth he was a Communist but today he is a staunch supporter of democracy. Nor is the fact that a movement has a mass following any insurance against Communist capture.

There are, however, some guidelines that may be helpful. For one thing, if the revolutionary movement's nationalist ideology has been formed over a relatively long period of time by native critics of the traditional order, it will probably offer stout resistance to foreign capture. Mexico's eclectic and pragmatic ideology reflects this indigenous strength, although it should be borne in mind that Mexico's revolution occurred before Russia's and thus has never labored under as heavy pressure from Marxism as have subsequent nationalist movements in Latin America. Again, support of the ideology by a traditional national organization, such as a political party or the army, provides added barriers to foreign cooption. Thus, when strongly anticolonial attitudes are taken by Illia's People's Radicals or Betancourt's Democratic Action, they are less disturbing than similar ideas in such a relatively recent political creation as Castro's 26th of July Movement. The People's Radicals and Democratic Action have a history of struggle and participation that extends beyond one decade, and their followers may be actually more loyal to the party than to a particular leader. It follows that a movement led by such an organization is more immune to capture than its ideas might lead one to suppose. Nevertheless, such general guidelines as these do not free us of the responsibility for investigating each movement, new or old, on its own merits.

Another unresolved problem involves the inhibiting influence nationalism sometimes has on modernization. After successfully disrupting the traditional order, nationalism may then hold development back, for the values used to disrupt it may hinder the viability of the new order in competition with the modern world. Uruguay and Mexico, to mention only two examples, have had to struggle with this problem. How then can triumphant revolutionary nationalism be led to greater rationality? So far there is no answer, but Mexico's experience since 1940 suggests one path, for as she became more autonomous, her leaders became more rational in their methods of development. Nevertheless, there are too many examples of the reverse, of irrationality increasing with autonomy, to warrant taking Mexico's case as typical. There remains no certainty that development will bring greater rationality and a less narrow nationalism.

SOCIETY AND NATION

There are many pertinent questions about the relation between society and nation that the student of Latin American nationalism can answer only with qualified approximations or impressionistic estimates, if at all. Among such questions are: In which social sectors do the several varieties of nationalism have their main support? How widespread is the sense of nationality in any form? From which social sectors does resistance to nationalism come? And what is the correlation between, on the one hand, a given stage of economic and social development, and, on the other, nationalism, either general or specific? Obviously, until satisfactory answers to such questions are forthcoming, it will be quite impossible to move on to the next and more interesting task of explaining why these things are so and what they portend.

The roots of the difficulty lie mainly in the inadequacy of the relevant data and the retarded state of social studies in Latin America. An extreme example of the first point is the fact that Uruguay, one of the most advanced countries of Latin America, has not taken a national census since 1908. Although other countries have taken censuses quite recently, such relevant and reliable data as they contain have very seldom been analyzed with our questions in mind. Supplementary sources, such as studies of public opinion, are likewise rare.

Testimony to the retarded development of social studies in Latin America, and to the unfavorable climate for promoting them, has quite recently been provided by one of the area's leading social scientists, Gino Germani. Speaking of sociology, which in Latin America is the social science most concerned with the questions that interest us here, Germani writes with tactful restraint that "the level achieved [in Latin America] by investigation in sociology must be regarded, both quantitatively and qualitatively, as lower than one might be justified in expecting in view of the degree of development observable in other intellectual activities and scientific disciplines."[5] Elsewhere he speaks more strongly, describing the present situation as "discouraging" as regards the investigation of the "structures and transformations" of society in Latin America.[6] To a considerable extent, he holds, the sociologists themselves are responsible, for until the counter-reaction of the 1940s against the anti-positivism of the preceding generation, they showed almost no interest in scientific sociology and many of them are still indifferent, if not hostile, to it.

In this situation it is difficult to speak with precision about the social aspects of nationalism in Latin America. Thus, Germani's own statement that Latin American student movements have "in general" been characterized by nationalism, while probably true, could hardly be documented. His further assertion that the nationalism of these student movements has "almost invariably" been democratic not only lacks documentation but seems on its face far too sweeping. One thinks immediately of

5. *La sociología en la América Latina* (Buenos Aires, 1964). 67.
6. *Ibid.*, 12.

Fidel Castro, and other evidence of the same kind could be added, some from the present writers' personal experience in Latin America.

The same sort of difficulty exists in regard to organized labor. It would not be possible to document for Latin America the major findings about the tie between nationalism and political unionism contained in a recent study of the developing countries of Africa and Asia.[7] Its conclusions that nationalism led to the incorporation of labor groups into "broad-front political movements" and that labor unions promoted modernization and countered the forces of traditionalism, are probably applicable to Latin America; but nothing like conclusive proof is available for the whole area. More doubtful is the applicability to Latin America of the same study's conclusion that political unionism and the commitment to nationalism limited the economic bargaining functions of the unions and the growth of job-conscious unionism. In Latin America, where this question is highly complex, there is evidence both pro and con. The case of Brazil, for example, seems to support it, but the Argentine labor movement, which is probably the strongest and most independent in Latin America today, has been increasingly divided in the last few years over precisely this question of political versus job-oriented unionism.

To give one more example, the business-entrepreneurial group in Brazil is divided over the question of nationalism, but there is some doubt as to the identity of the contending factions and more as to their motivations. The most nationalistic members of this group, the core of the national bourgeoisie, champion high tariff protection as the only means of expediting national economic development and modernization, but critics allege that their real purpose is to protect their antiquated establishments from the competition that would be promoted by true modernization under an open economy. Again, other members of this group profess a temperate, pragmatic nationalism aimed at accelerating development with the aid of foreign capital and enter-

7. Bruce H. Millen, *The Political Role of Labor in Developing Countries* (Washington, D. C., 1963).

prise, and their motives too are questioned. The charge is that they are in fact anti-nationalists who are seeking to enrich themselves by serving foreign economic imperialists; that they are, in short, modern exemplars of the long-familiar *vendepatria* type.

What are the facts in these cases? We do not know for sure, and can only draw inferences from fragments of the truth revealed by occasional flashes of political lightning. In the absence of impartial studies by experts, we have little to go on except polemical literature and one of its specialized Latin American branches, reports of congressional investigations. Brazil has provided many of these reports, but to sort out the truth in them is a herculean task which no one so far has been bold or foolhardy enough to perform.

Despite such difficulties, some interesting essays have been made at producing typologies that relate nation to society in Latin America. One, by Seymour Martin Lipset,[8] focused on the relation between economic development and democracy. Lipset divided the Latin American countries into two groups, one comprising democracies and unstable dictatorships, the other stable dictatorships. In the first group he placed Argentina, Brazil, Chile, Colombia, Costa Rica, Mexico, and Uruguay, which tended constantly to lead the second group in per capita incomes, education, and the like. Shortly thereafter, K. H. Silvert re-examined the question. Stressing occupational differentiation as an indicator of development, he too divided the Latin American countries into two groups, but his top group consisted of Argentina, Brazil, Chile, Colombia, Costa Rica, Cuba, Mexico, and Venezuela (the order is only alphabetical). These eight countries, he concluded, "have a greater capacity and social need for national coordination" than the rest.[9]

Neither author discussed the peculiar development of nationalism in Cuba since the beginning of 1959, and neither correlated the available data with the various forms that nationalism has taken in Latin America at large. Silvert did, however, state that "democracy . . . correlates positively with nationalism in the

8. *Political Man* (Garden City, 1960).
9. Silvert, *op. cit.,* 8.

sense that the latter is a necessary but insufficient condition for the former, at least as democracy has developed in the West." One may have reservations about this proposition, but hardly about the frank avowal with which he concludes his statistical inquiry: "Such statistics are still so rudimentary for our purposes as to gain significance only through such other research as historical analysis, case studies of power distribution, attitude testing, and careful assessment of ideological currents."

We agree; and since the relevant statistics are still rudimentary, and case studies of power distribution and tests of attitudes are still as scarce as hens' teeth, the present study has perforce been based mainly upon historical analysis and assessment of ideological currents.

In the course of this study we have stressed the diversity of both Latin America and nationalism, but at the same time we have tried to bring out the common features that run through Latin American nationalism. Because of the great attraction of total modernization for so many Latin American nationalists, we have sought to give economic, social, and cultural factors their full due. Nevertheless, we have made politics the central theme, in so far as it is possible to separate politics from the other categories. For nationalism is an essentially political concept, and, although it is important for the uses that are made of it, the common denominator of all these is political.

As we have tried to show, the main trend in contemporary Latin American nationalism has been toward identity with a modernization that has broad implications for every aspect of national life, and has economic development as its core. Yet political development has remained the principal task of nationalists and all others in Latin America, as is most strikingly illustrated by Argentina's unhappy experience ever since 1930. This political theme, more than anything else, gives unity to the study of Latin American nationalism in the twentieth century. The task of political development is one they have shared with developing countries in other parts of the world, but Latin America's record is unique in important ways.

Political development has many common features in all developing countries. Foremost among these is nationalism, and, to repeat a point made in the opening chapter, nationalism is not necessarily a pathological phenomenon. Rather, it is a normal and essential feature of development. As one recent writer has said, it is necessary to modernism as a social value,[10] and according to another "nationalism is only a necessary but far from sufficient condition to ensure political development."[11] Obviously, as the latter explains, political development is necessary so that the community concerned can operate successfully not only within its own boundaries, but also as a member of a system of nation-states; and the nation-building to which political development is addressed has two main aspects: institution-building and citizenship development.

Whatever success the Latin American states may have achieved in this task in recent decades, it is clear that in general their national institutions have been greatly strengthened. As we have already noted, the existence of such institutions has buttressed nationalism even in postwar Europe, where nationalism had been thought to be on its way out at the close of World War II. Finally, let us note again that, in addition to all its internal sources and uses, nationalism in the Latin American states has also been fostered by the external pressure of their need to function as members of a world-wide system of nation-states. This pressure operates in some measure on all developing states, but it reaches maximum force in the Latin American states because of their long and exceptionally intimate ties with most of the leading members of the international community in the twentieth century, those in the North Atlantic area.

10. K. H. Silvert, *op. cit.*, 26, 31.
11. Lucian W. Pye, "The Concept of Political Development," *American Academy of Political and Social Science, Annals,* 358 (March, 1965), 7.

Selected Bibliography

THE FOLLOWING LIST is arranged by chapters in the belief that this is the most convenient form for the reader. In addition to titles cited in the footnotes, the list contains others deemed to be of special interest, but it is highly selective; a comprehensive list of all relevant works would be many times longer and probably less useful. With rare exceptions, titles are listed only once, though they may have been cited in more than one chapter. The lists for Chapters One and Two may be the most useful for the majority of readers since they include works on nationalism in Latin America at large, and in other parts of the world as well.

ONE: NATIONALISM IN LATIN AMERICA

Alexander, Robert J. *Today's Latin America*. New York, 1962.

Barker, Ernest, *National Character*. London, 1948, rev. ed.

Burr, Robert N., ed. *Latin America's Nationalistic Revolutions, American Academy of Political and Social Science, Annals*, 334 (March, 1961).

Carr, E. H. *Nationalism and After*. London, 1945.

Carrillo Flores, Antonio. "El nacionalismo de los países latinoamericanos en la postguerra," *Jornadas*, No. 28, 1945.

Cosío Villegas, Daniel. *American Extremes*. Translated by Americo Paredes. Austin, Texas, 1964.

Deutsch, Karl W. *Nationalism and Social Communication*. New York, 1953.

Hayes, Carlton J. H. *Nationalism: A Religion*. New York, 1964.

Hirschman, Albert O. *Journeys Toward Progress. Studies of Economic Policy-Making in Latin America*. New York, 1963.

Johnson, John J. *Political Change in Latin America: The Emergence of the Middle Sectors*. Stanford, 1958.

────── ed., *Continuity and Change in Latin America*. Stanford, 1964.

────── "The New Latin American Nationalism," *Yale Review* (Winter, 1965).

Kedourie, Elie. *Nationalism*. New York, 1961.

Kohn, Hans. *The Idea of Nationalism*. New York, 1960.

────── *The Age of Nationalism. The First Era of Global History*. New York, 1962.

Poppino, Rollie. *International Communism in Latin America: A History of the Movement, 1917–1963*. New York, 1964.

Schmitt, Karl M., and David D. Burks. *Evolution or Chaos. Dynamics of Latin American Government and Politics*. New York, 1963.

Silvert, K. H. "Nationalism in Latin America," in Snyder, *The Dynamics of Nationalism*.

────── *The Conflict Society: Reaction and Revolution in Latin America*. New Orleans, 1961.

──────, ed. *Expectant Peoples: Nationalism and Development*. New York, 1963.

Snyder, Louis J., ed. *The Dynamics of Nationalism*. Princeton, 1964.

Whitaker, Arthur P. *Nationalism in Latin America, Past and Present*. Gainesville, 1962.

Zea, Leopoldo. *The Latin American Mind*. Translated by James H. Abbot and Lowell Dunham. Norman, Okla., 1963.

TWO: MODERNIZATION AND CONTEMPORARY NATIONALISM

Almond, Gabriel A., and James Coleman. *The Politics of the Developing Areas*. Princeton, 1960.

Friedrich, Carl J. *Constitutional Government and Democracy.* Boston, 1941.

Janowitz, Morris. *The Military in the Political Development of New Societies.* Chicago, 1964.

—— *The Professional Soldier.* New York, 1960.

Johnson, John J. *The Military and Society in Latin America.* Stanford, 1964.

——, ed. *The Role of the Military in Underdeveloped Countries.* Princeton, 1962.

Kornhauser, William. *The Politics of Mass Society.* New York, 1959.

Lasswell, Harold D. *Who Gets What, When, How.* New York, 1936.

Lieuwen, Edwin. *Arms and Politics in Latin America.* New York, 1961, rev. ed.

—— *Generals vs. Presidents.* New York, 1964.

Lipset, Seymour Martin. *Political Man.* New York, 1960.

Needler, Martin. *Latin American Politics in Perspective.* Princeton, 1963.

Mills, C. Wright. *The Power Elite.* New York, 1956.

Powelson, John P. *Latin America: Today's Economic and Social Revolution.* New York, 1964.

THREE: MEXICO

Alba, Víctor, *Las ideas sociales contemporáneas en México.* Mexico, D.F., 1960.

Brenner, Anita. *The Wind that Swept Mexico: The History of the Mexican Revolution, 1910–1942.* New York, 1943.

Casasola, Gustavo. *Historia gráfica de la revolución mexicana, 1906–1960.* Mexico, D.F., 1960, 4 vols.

Chapoy Bonifaz, Dolores Beatriz. *El movimiento obrero y el sindicato en México.* Mexico, D.F., 1961.

Cline, Howard F. *The United States and Mexico.* Cambridge, Mass., 1961. 2nd ed.

—— "Mexico: A Matured Latin American Revolution, 1910–

1960," in *American Academy of Political and Social Science, Annals,* 334 (March, 1961), 84–94.

—— *Mexico: Revolution to Evolution (1940–1960).* New York, 1962.

Cosío Villegas, Daniel. *Change in Latin America: The Mexican and Cuban Revolutions.* Lincoln, Nebr., 1961.

Cumberland, Charles C. *The Mexican Revolution: Genesis Under Madero.* Austin, Texas, 1952.

Gamio, Manuel. *Forjando patria (pro nacionalismo).* Mexico, D.F., 1916.

González Navarro, Moisés. "La ideología de la revolución mexicana," *Historia Mexicana* (April–June, 1961).

Hafter, Rudolph P. "The New Mexico," *Swiss Review of World Affairs* (June, 1962).

James, Daniel. *Mexico and the Americans.* New York, 1963.

Kling, Merle. *A Mexican Interest Group in Action.* Englewood Cliffs, N.J., 1961.

Lewis, Oscar. "Mexico Since Cárdenas," in Richard N. Adams, *et al., Social Change in Latin America Today.* New York, 1960.

McBride, George M. *The Land Systems of Mexico.* New York, 1923.

Molina Enríquez, Andrés. *Los grandes problemas nacionales.* Mexico, D.F., 1909.

—— *Esbozo de la historia de los primeros diez años de la revolución agraria de México (1910–1920).* Mexico, D.F., 1937.

Ramos, Samuel. *Profile of Man and Culture in Mexico.* Austin, Texas, 1962.

Sáenz, Aaron. *La política internacional de la Revolución.* Mexico, D.F., 1961.

Sierra, Justo. *Obras completas del maestro Justo Sierra.* Mexico, D.F., 1956.

Silva Herzog, Jesús. *El pensamiento económico de México.* Mexico, D.F., 1947

Simpson, Eyler N. *The Ejido: Mexico's Way Out.* Chapel Hill, 1937.

Solís Quiroga, Héctor. *Una visión sociológica de la revolución mexicana.* Mexico, D.F., 1959.

Tannenbaum, Frank. *Mexico: The Struggle for Peace and Bread.* New York, 1952.

――― "Lázaro Cárdenas," *Historia Mexicana,* Oct.–Dec. 1960.

Tavera Alfaro, Xavier. *El nacionalismo en la prensa mexicana del siglo XVIII.* Mexico, D.F., 1963.

Vasconcelos, José. *Breve historia de México.* Mexico, D.F., 1932.

――― *Hispanoamérica frente a los nacionalismos agresivos de Europa y Norteamérica.* Buenos Aires, 1934.

Vernon, Raymond. *The Dilemma of Mexico's Development.* Cambridge, Mass., 1963.

Villegas, Abelardo. "Sentido e ideología de la revolución mexicana," *Política* (April 1960).

Whetten, Nathaniel. *Rural Mexico.* Chicago, 1948.

FOUR: ARGENTINA

Astesano, Eduardo B. *Rosas, bases del nacionalismo popular.* Buenos Aires, 1960.

Astudillo, Alberto. *La revolución y las clases.* Buenos Aires, 1963.

Bunge, Alejandro E. *La economía argentina.* Vol. I, Buenos Aires, 1928.

Cúneo, Dardo. *Las nuevas fronteras.* Buenos Aires, 1963.

Del Carril, Bonifacio. *Problemas de la revolución y la democracia.* Buenos Aires, 1957.

Fillol, Tomás Roberto. *Social Factors in Economic Development. The Argentine Case.* Cambridge, Mass., 1961.

Florit, Carlos A. *Política exterior nacional.* Buenos Aires, 1960.

Frigerio, Rogelio. *Unidad nacional o lucha de facciones.* Buenos Aires, 1961.

Frondizi, Arturo. *Política y petróleo.* Buenos Aires, 1954.

Germani, Gino. *Política y sociedad en una época de transición.* Buenos Aires, 1962.

Glauert, Earl T. "Ricardo Rojas and Cultural Nationalism." Ph.D. dissertation, 1962, University of Pennsylvania Library.

Hernández Arregui, Juan José. *La formación de la conciencia nacional (1930–1960)*. Buenos Aires, 1960.

Ibarguren, Carlos. *La inquietud de esta hora. Liberalismo, corporativismo, nacionalismo*. Buenos Aires, 1934.

Kennedy, John J. *Catholicism, Nationalism, and Democracy in Argentina*. Notre Dame, Indiana, 1958.

Meinvielle, Julio. *Concepción católica de la política*. Buenos Aires, 1961.

Methol Ferré, Alberto. *La izquierda nacional en la Argentina*. Buenos Aires, n.d.

Mosquera, Ricardo. *Yrigoyen y el mundo nuevo*. Buenos Aires, 1951.

Noble, Roberto. *Argentina, A World Power*. Buenos Aires, 1961.

Perón, Juan D. *El trabajo al través del pensamiento de Perón*. Buenos Aires, 1955.

Peterson, Harold F. *Argentina and the United States, 1810–1960*. New York, 1964.

Ramos, Jorge Abelardo. *América Latina: un país*. Buenos Aires, 1949.

——— *Historia política del ejército argentino*. Buenos Aires, 1959.

——— *De Octubre a Setiembre*. Buenos Aires, 1959.

Río, Manuel. "Las actuales tendencias social-políticas en la República Argentina." 1956. Unpublished; kindly lent by the author to the present writers.

Romero, José Luis. *A History of Argentine Political Thought*. Introduction and translation by Thomas F. McGann. Stanford, 1963.

Silvert, K. H., "The Costs of Anti-Nationalism," in *Expectant Peoples*, cited above, Chap. One.

Spilimbergo, Jorge E. *Juan B. Justo o el socialismo cipayo*, Buenos Aires, n.d.

———*Nacionalismo oligárquico o nacionalismo revolucionario*. Buenos Aires, 1958.

Troncoso, Oscar A. *Los nacionalistas argentinos. Antecedentes y trayectoria*. Buenos Aires, 1957.

Whitaker, Arthur P. *The United States and Argentina.* Cambridge, Mass., 1954.

—— *Argentina.* Englewood Cliffs, N. J., 1964.

FIVE: BRAZIL

Amoroso Lima, Alceu. *Revolução, reação, ou reforma.* Rio de Janeiro, 1964.

Bonilla, Frank. "A Nationalist Ideology for Development: Brazil," in Silvert, ed., *Expectant Peoples,* cited above, Chap. One.

Costa, Dagoberto, *et al. Sopram os ventos da liberdade. Antologia nacionalista.* São Paulo, 1959.

Cruz Costa, João. *Contribuição à história das idéais no Brasil.* Rio de Janeiro, 1956. Translated by Suzette Macedo as *A History of Ideas in Brazil.* Berkeley and Los Angeles, 1964.

—— "Nationalism and the Evolution of Brazilian Thought in the Twentieth Century." Mimeographed, Mexico City, 1962.

Faust, Jean Jacques. "Brésil 1963: La 'bossa nova' ou la mort," *Preuves* 148 (July, 1963).

Free, Lloyd A. *Some Implications of the Political Psychology of Brazilians.* Princeton, 1961.

Furtado, Celso. *The Economic Growth of Brazil.* Berkeley, 1963.

Guilhermo, Olympio. *O nacionalismo e a política internacional do Brasil.* São Paulo, 1957.

Horowitz, Irving Louis. *Revolution in Brazil. Politics and Society in a Developing Nation.* New York, 1964.

Ianni, Octávio. *Industrialização e desenvolvimento no Brasil.* Rio de Janeiro, 1963.

Jaguaribe, Hélio. *O nacionalismo na atualidade brasileira.* Rio de Janeiro, 1958.

—— *Burguesía y proletariado en el nacionalismo brasileño.* Buenos Aires, 1961.

Lieuwen, Edwin. *Arms and Politics in Latin America.* New York, 1961, rev. ed.

Luz, Nicia Vilela. *A luta pela industrialização do Brasil (1808 a 1930).* São Paulo, 1961.

Mendes de Almeida, Cándido Antônio. *Nacionalismo e desenvolvimento.* Rio de Janeiro, 1963.

Oliveira Torres, João Camillo de. *Razão e destino da revolução.* Petropolis, 1964.

Pinto, Alvaro Vieira. *Consciência e realidade nacional.* Rio de Janeiro, 1961.

Quadros, Jânio. "Brazil's New Foreign Policy," *Foreign Affairs* (October, 1961).

Rodrigues, José Honório. *Aspirações nacionais. Interpretação histórico-política.* São Paulo, 1963.

——— *Brasil e Africa: outro horizonte.* Rio de Janeiro, 1961.

Salles, Dagoberto. *As razões do nacionalismo.* São Paulo, 1959.

Schmidt, Augusto Frederico. *Prelúdio à revolução.* Rio de Janeiro, 1964.

Stein, Stanley J. *Vassouras, A Brazilian Coffee Country, 1850–1900.* Cambridge, Mass., 1957.

Werneck Sodré, Nelson. *Raizes históricas do nacionalismo brasileiro.* Rio de Janeiro, 1959.

——— *Introdução à revolução brasileira.* Rio de Janeiro, 1963, 2nd ed.

SIX: COLOMBIA AND PERU

Colombia

Azula Barrera, Rafael. *De la revolución al orden nuevo. Proceso y drama de un pueblo.* Bogotá, 1956.

Fluharty, Vernon Lee. *Dance of the Millions: Military Rule and the Social Revolution in Colombia, 1930–1956.* Pittsburgh, 1957.

Forero Morales, Néstor. *Laureano Gómez: un hombre, un partido, una nación.* Bogotá, 1956.

Galbraith, W. O. *Colombia: A General Survey.* London, 1953.

Gaitán, Jorge Eliécer. *Las ideas socialistas en Colombia.* Bogotá, 1924.

García, Antonio. *Gaitán y el problema de la revolución colombiana.* Bogotá, n.d.

Iregorri V., José M. *Evolución demográfica de Colombia.* Bogotá, 1959.

Jaramillo Uribe, Jaime. *El pensamiento colombiano en el siglo XIX.* Bogotá, 1964.

López de Mesa, Luis. *De cómo se ha formado el pueblo colombiano.* Bogotá, 1943.

López Michelsen, Alfonso. *Los últimos días de López, y otras íntimas de tres campañas políticas, 1929–1948–1958.* Bogotá, 1961.

———— *Colombia en la hora cero.* Begotá, 1963.

Martz, John D. *Colombia: A Contemporary Political Survey.* Chapel Hill, 1962.

Uribe Escobar, Ricardo. *Política centrífuga.* Medellín, 1960.

Villareces, Jorge. *La derrota: 25 años de historia.* Bogotá, 1963.

Whitaker, Arthur P. *The United States and South America: The Northern Republics.* Cambridge, Mass., 1948.

Peru

Alarco, Luis Felipe. *Pensadores peruanos.* Lima, 1915.

Basadre, Jorge. *Meditaciones sobre el destino histórico del Perú.* Lima, 1947.

Belaúnde Terry, Fernando. *La conquista del Perú por los peruanos.* Lima, 1959.

———— *Pueblo por pueblo.* Lima, 1960.

Carey, James C. *Peru and the United States, 1900–1962.* Notre Dame, Indiana, 1964.

Chang-Rodríguez, Eugenio. *La literatura política de González Prada, Mariátegui, y Haya de la Torre.* Mexico, D.F., 1958.

Delgado, Luis Humberto. *Drama del Perú.* Lima, n.d.

González Prada, Manuel. *Horas de lucha.* Callao, 1924, 2nd ed.

Haya de la Torre, Víctor Raúl. *Treinta años de Aprismo.* Mexico, D.F., 1963.

Holmberg, Allan R. "Changing Community Attitudes and Values in Peru: A Case Study in Guided Change," in Richard

N. Adams, *et al.*, *Social Change in Latin America Today*. New York, 1960.

Holmes, Olive. "Army Challenge in Latin America," *Foreign Policy Reports*, 25, 14 (1949).

Kantor, Harry. *The Ideology and Program of the Peruvian Aprista Movement*. Berkeley, 1953.

Llosa, Jorge Guillermo. *En busca del Perú*. Lima, 1962.

Martín, César. *Dichos y hechos de la política peruana*. Lima, 1963.

McNicoll, R. E. "Intellectual Origins of Aprismo," *Hispanic American Historical Review*, XXIII (1943).

Miró Quesada Laos, Carlos. *Radiografía de la política peruana*. Lima, 1959, 2nd ed.

Owens, R. J., *Peru*. New York, 1963.

Patch, Richard W. "The Peruvian Agrarian Reform Bill," *American University Field Staff, Report Service*, West Coast South American Series, XI. 3 (1964).

Pike, Fredrick B. "The Old and the New APRA in Peru: Myth and Reality," *Inter-American Economic Affairs*, 18:2 (1964).

Ravines, Eudocio. *The Yenan Way*. New York, 1951.

Revoredo, Alejandro. *La obra nacionalista y democrática del Partido Civil*. Lima, 1931.

SEVEN: CHILE, URUGUAY, AND VENEZUELA

Chile

Barria Serón, Jorge I. *Los movimientos sociales de Chile desde 1910 hasta 1926: aspecto político y social*. Santiago, 1960.

Becket, James. "Land Reform in Chile," *Journal of Inter-American Studies*, April 1963.

Butland, G. J. *Chile: An Outline of Its Geography, Economics, and Politics*. London, 1956, 3rd ed.

Donoso, Ricardo. *Desarrollo político y social de Chile desde la Constitución de 1833*. Buenos Aires, 1942.

——— *Las ideas políticas en Chile*. Santiago, 1946.

—— *Alessandri, agitador y demoledor: cincuenta años de historia política de Chile,* 2 vols. Mexico, D.F., 1953–1954.

Edwards, Alberto, and Eduardo Frei. *Historia de los partidos políticos chilenos.* Santiago, 1949.

Ellsworth, P. T. *Chile: An Economy in Transition.* New York, 1945.

Eyzaguirre, Jaime. *Fisionomía histórica de Chile.* Santiago, 1948.

Fetter, Frank, W. *Monetary Inflation in Chile.* Princeton, N.J., 1931.

Frei, Eduardo. *Pensamiento y acción.* Santiago, 1958.

Galdames, Luis. *A History of Chile.* Translated and edited by Isaac Joslin Cox. Chapel Hill, 1941.

Heise González, Julio. *150 años de evolución institucional.* Santiago, 1960.

Martner, Daniel. *Economía política.* Santiago, 1934.

Iglesias, Augusto. *Alessandri, una etapa de la democracia en América: tiempo, vida, acción.* Santiago, 1959.

Olavaría Bravo, Arturo. *Chile entre dos Alessandri.* Santiago, 1962.

Pendle, George. *The Land and People of Chile.* London, 1960.

Pike, Fredrick B. *Chile and the United States, 1880–1962.* Notre Dame, Indiana, 1963.

Stevenson, J. R. *The Chilean Popular Front.* Philadelphia, 1942.

Uruguay

Fabragat, Julio F. *Ensayo para una sociología del votante.* Montevideo, 1962.

Fitzgibbon, Russell H. *Uruguay: Portrait of a Democracy.* New Brunswick, N.J., 1954.

—— "Uruguay: A model for Freedom and Reform in Latin America?" in Fredrick B. Pike, ed., *Freedom and Reform in Latin America.* Notre Dame, Indiana, 1959.

Hanson, Simon G. *Utopia in Uruguay.* New York, 1938.

Martin, Percy A. "The Career of José Batlle y Ordóñez," *Hispanic American Historical Review,* X. 4 (Nov., 1930).

Pendle, George. *Uruguay, South America's First Welfare State.* London, 1952.

Rama, Carlos M. *Las clases sociales en el Uruguay.* Montevideo, 1960.

Raineri, Mario Andrés. *Oribe y el estado nacional.* Montevideo, 1960.

Solari, Aldo E. *Sociología rural nacional.* Montevideo, 1958, 2nd ed.

Taylor, Philip B. *Government and Politics in Uruguay.* New Orleans, 1962.

Vanger, Milton I. *José Batlle y Ordóñez of Uruguay: The Creator of His Time, 1902–1907.* Cambridge, Mass., 1963.

Venezuela

Alexander, Robert J. *The Venezuelan Democratic Revolution.* New Brunswick, N.J., 1964.

Betancourt, Rómulo. *Venezuela: política y petróleo. Mexico,* D.F., 1956.

Boersner, Demetrio. "El proceso electoral venezolano," *Política,* 3:27 (Oct. 1963).

Caldera Rodríguez, Rafael. *Moldes para la fragua.* Buenos Aires, 1962.

Grases, Pedro, and Manuel Pérez Vila, eds. *Documentos que hicieron historia.* 2 vols., Caracas, 1962.

Lieuwen, Edwin. *Petroleum in Venezuela: A History.* Berkeley, 1954.

———— *Venezuela. London,* 1962.

Luzardo, Rodolfo. *Notas histórico-económicas, 1928–1963.* Caracas, 1963.

Martz, John D. "Venezuela's 'Generation of '28': The Genesis of Political Democracy," *Journal of Inter-American Studies,* VI: 1 (1964).

Picón Salas, Mariano, *et al. Venezuela independiente, 1810–1960.* Caracas, 1962.

Rivas Rivas, José, ed. *El mundo y la época de Pérez Jiménez.* Caracas, 1961.

—— ed. *Un año con el gobierno de Wolfgang Larrazábal*. Caracas, 1962.

EIGHT: BOLIVIA AND CUBA

Bolivia

Alexander, Robert J. *The Bolivian National Revolution*. New Brunswick, N.J., 1958.

Bedregal Gutiérrez, Guillermo. *La revolución boliviana. Sus realidades y perspectivas dentro del ciclo de liberación de los pueblos latino-americanos*. La Paz, 1962.

Díaz Machicao, Porfirio. *Historia de Bolivia*. 5 vols., La Paz, 1957.

Fellman Velarde, José. *Víctor Paz Estenssoro: El hombre y la revolución*. La Paz, 1955.

Francovich, Guillermo. *El pensamiento boliviano en el siglo XX*. Mexico, D.F., 1956.

Gueiler Tejada, Lydia. *La mujer y la revolución*. La Paz, 1959.

Ostria Gutiérrez, Alberto. *The Tragedy of Bolivia*. New York, 1958.

Patch, Richard W. "Bolivia, The Restrained Revolution," American Academy of Political and Social Science, *Annals*, 334 (March, 1961).

—— "Peasantry and National Revolution: Bolivia," in Silvert, ed., *Expectant Peoples*, cited above, Chap. One.

Pérez Patón, Roberto. *Los partidos y la democracia; sociología del partido único*. La Paz, 1961.

Ruiz González, Raúl. *Bolivia: el prometeo de los Andes*. Buenos Aires, 1961.

Cuba

Alvarez Díaz, J., *et al. Cuba: geopolítica y pensamiento*. Miami, 1964.

American Universities Field Staff, Reports Service. "Castro Cuba in Mid-1960: Fidel of Cuba, by Voice and Violence." New York, 1960.

Berle, A. A., Jr. "Cuban Crisis," *Foreign Affairs*, XXXIX: 1 (October, 1960).

Castro, Fidel. *History Will Absolve Me*. New York, 1959.

Chester, Edmund A. *A Sergeant Named Batista*. New York, 1954.

Corbitt, D. C. "Cuban Revisionist Interpretations of Cuba's Struggle for Independence," *Hispanic American Historical Review*, XLIII, 3 (August, 1963).

Draper, Theodore. *Castro's Revolution: Myths and Realities*. New York, 1962.

Grupo Cubano de Investigaciones Económicas de University of Miami: *Un estudio sobre Cuba: colonia, república, experimento socialista*. Miami, 1963.

Huberman, Leo, and Paul M. Sweezy. *Cuba: Anatomy of a Revolution*. New York, 1960.

James, Daniel. *Cuba, The First Soviet Satellite in the Americas*. New York, 1961.

MacGaffey, Watt, and Clifford R. Barnett. *Twentieth Century Cuba*. New York, 1965.

Mañach, Jorge. *Evolución de las ideas y el pensamiento político en Cuba*. Havana, 1957.

Matthews, Herbert. *The Cuban Story*. New York, 1961.

―――― *Return to Cuba*. Stanford, 1964.

Mills, C. Wright, *Listen, Yankee*. New York, 1960.

O'Connor, James. "On Cuba's Political Economy," *Political Science Quarterly*, 79:2 (June, 1964).

Pflaum, Irving Peter. *Tragic Island: How Communism Came to Cuba*. Englewood Cliffs, N.J., 1961.

Seers, Dudley, ed. *Cuba: The Economic and Social Revolution*. Chapel Hill, 1964.

Smith, Robert F. *The United States and Cuba: Business and Diplomacy, 1917–1960*. New York, 1960.

Tannenbaum, Frank. "The Political Dilemma in Latin America," *Foreign Affairs*, XXXVIII:3 (August, 1960).

Weyl, Nathaniel. *Red Star Over Cuba*. New York, 1960.

NINE: CONTINENTAL NATIONALISM

Barreda Laos, Felipe. *Hispano-América en Guerra?* Buenos Aires, 1941.

Castañeda, Jorge. *Mexico and the United Nations.* New York, 1958.

Correa, Gustavo. "El nacionalismo cultural en la literatura hispanamericana," *Cuadernos Americanos,* XCVIII (1958).

D'Antonio, William V., and Fredrick B. Pike, eds. *Religion, Revolution, and Reform. New Forces for Change in Latin America.* New York, 1964.

Del Mazo, Gabriel. *Reforma universitaria y cultura nacional.* Buenos Aires, 1955.

Díez de Medina, Fernando. "A South American Bloc," *Atlas* (July, 1963).

Edwards Bello, Joaquín. *El nacionalismo continental.* Santiago de Chile, 1935. See note 1, Chap. Nine.

Ellison, Fred P. "The Writer," in Johnson, ed., *Continuity and Change in Latin America.* Cited above, Chap. One.

Frondizi, Arturo. *La política exterior argentina.* Buenos Aires, 1962.

Gómez Robledo, Antonio. *Idea y experiencia de América.* Mexico, D.F., 1958.

Haya de la Torre, Víctor Raúl. "Problemas de la América Latina," *Cuadernos* (July–August, 1959).

Hirschman, Albert O., ed. *Latin American Issues.* New York, 1961.

Máspero, Emilio. "Latin America's Labor Movement of Christian Democratic Orientation. . ." in D'Antonio and Pike, eds., *Religion, Revolution, and Reform.* Cited above.

Oribe, Emilio. "Sobre la unidad de nuestra América," *Cuadernos* No. 49 (June, 1961).

Rodó, José Enrique. *Rodó. Prólogo y selección de Samuel Ramos.* Mexico, D.F., 1943.

Ugarte, Manuel. *La patria grande.* Madrid, 1924.

Zea, Leopoldo. *América en la historia.* Mexico, D.F., 1957.

TEN: SUMMARY AND PROSPECT

Alexander, Robert J. *Communism in Latin America.* New Brunswick, N.J., 1957.

Democracia, nacionalismo y militarismo. Cuadernos, Supplement (November–December 1960).

Dore, R. P. "Latin America and Japan Compared," in Johnson, ed., *Continuity and Change in Latin America.* Cited above, Chap. One.

Germani, Gino, *Política y sociedad.* Cited above, Chap. One.

—— *La sociología en la América Latina.* Buenos Aires, 1964.

Imaz, José Luis de. *Los que mandan.* Buenos Aires, 1963.

Lipset, Seymour Martin. *Political Man.* Cited above, Chap. Two.

Miller, Bruce H. *The Political Role of Labor in Developing Countries.* Washington, D.C., 1963.

Poppino, Rollie. *International Communism in Latin America.* Cited above, Chap. One.

Pye, Lucian W. "The Concept of Political Development," *American Academy of Political and Social Science, Annals,* 358 (March, 1965).

Silvert, K. H. *Expectant Peoples.* Cited above, Chap. One.

—— *The Conflict Society.* Cited above, Chap. One.

Smith, Robert F., ed. *Background to Revolution. The Development of Modern Cuba.* New York, 1966.

Whitaker, Arthur P. *The Western Hemisphere Idea.* Ithaca, 1954; paperback, 1965.

Index

Acción Argentina, 66
Acción Democrática. See Democratic Action Party
Acción Popular, 110, 111
Acton, Lord, 4, 5
AD. *See* Democratic Action Party
Africa, new states of, 1, 2, 7, 8, 11, 13, 86, 162, 167, 171, 176, 177, 178, 183, 200
Aguirre Cerda, Pedro, 117
Alba, Victor, 17, 46
Alessandri, Arturo, 115–17
Alessandri, Jorge, 117
Alianza Popular Revolucionaria Americana. *See* APRA; *Apristas*
Allende, Salvador, 117, 189
Alliance for Progress, 12, 90, 128, 168, 171, 174, 175
Alvear, Marcelo T. de, 63
Americanism, 163, 175
American Popular Revolutionary Alliance. *See* APRA; *Apristas;* Haya de la Torre, Víctor Raúl
Anarchism, 61. *See also* Anarcho-syndicalism
Anarcho-syndicalism, 42, 45
Andrea, Miguel de, 60
Antarctica, 187
Anti-Americanism, 10, 150, 160, 188
Anticolonialism. *See* Colonialism
Anti-imperialism. *See* Imperialism

APRA, 95, 106, 107, 177
Apristas, 25, 95, 108–10
Aramburu, Pedro, 72
Arbenz Guzmán, Jacobo, 154
Argentina, 6, 9, 12, 26, 30, 77, 78, 83, 91, 92, 154, 156, 164, 172, 183, 186, 187, 189, 195, 196
Ariel, 166, 175
Armed forces, 11, 15, 16, 24–26, 40–44, 47, 49, 57, 59, 65–67, 68, 70, 72, 81, 91, 92, 98, 102, 104, 105, 109, 114, 115, 116, 124, 129, 131, 133, 134, 143, 145, 147, 188, 189, 192, 195, 197
Armed Forces of National Liberation, 136
Asia, new states of, 1, 2, 7, 8, 11, 13, 167, 183, 200
Atomic energy, 82
Auténtico, 151, 152
Authoritarianism, 13, 15, 31, 47, 56, 60, 66, 67, 150, 190
Avila Camacho, Manuel, 47, 48

Baily, Samuel L., 71
Bajo el oprobio, 105
Barker, Ernest, 5, 7, 8
Barreda Laos, Filipe, 165
Barrientos Ortuño, René, 147
Batista, Fulgencio, 152, 154, 157
Batlle family, 128

221

Batlle y Ordóñez, José, 25, 121–28, 154, 183
Bay of Pigs, 158
Belaúnde Terry, Fernando, 94, 95, 104, 110–12, 195
Beltrán, Pedro, 110
Benavides, Oscar R., 105, 109
Betancourt, Rómulo, 25, 130–32, 154, 195, 197
Blanco party, 121, 122, 125–28
Bogotazo, 101
Bolívar, Simón, 162, 163
Bolivia, 25, 78, 104, 158, 186, 187
Bolivian Workers' Center, 148
Bonilla, Frank, 80, 82, 89, 92
Bonsal, Philip, 157
Borlenghi, Angel, 69, 70
Bourgeoisie, old, 14; new, 14, 15, 57, 58, 59, 68, 83, 84, 85, 92, 103, 109, 110, 127, 178, 182, 192. See also Burguesía nacional; Middle class
"Bourgeoisie and Proletariat in Brazilian Nationalism," 83
Brasília, 93, 187
Brazil, 9, 11, 12, 30, 77–79, 172, 176, 183, 196
Brazilian Labor Party, 89
Brinton, Crane, 36
Bunge, Alejandro, 58, 59, 73
Bureaucracies, 11, 23, 84, 168
Burguesía nacional, 14, 15, 101, 106. See also Bourgeoisie, new
Busch, Germán, 143, 144
Bustamente y Rivero, José Luis, 109

Cabrera, Luis, 41
Caldera, Rafael, 132, 137
Calles, Plutarco Elías, 32, 43, 44
Camacho. See Avila Camacho, Manuel
Canada, 163
Capital, foreign, 35, 41, 47, 54, 82, 83, 85, 87, 96, 107, 108, 114, 116, 118, 120, 125, 130, 133, 135, 151, 158, 163, 196
Capitalism, 69, 71, 73, 88, 143, 153. See also Free enterprise
Cárdenas, Lázaro, 32, 44–48, 95, 195
Carr, E. H., 18

Carranza, Venustiano, 41, 42
Caso, Antonio, 37
Castelo Branco, Humberto de Alencar, 91
Castro, Cipriano, 129, 130
Castro, Fidel, 8, 15, 18, 87, 88, 90, 135, 138, 150, 153–60, 176, 188, 193, 199
Castro, Raúl, 153
Catholic Action, Argentine, 62
CGT. See General Confederation of Workers, Mexican
C.G.T. See General Confederation of Labor, Argentine
Chauvinism, 1
Chile, 12, 30, 104, 132, 162, 183, 186, 187, 196
China, Republic of, 90, 157, 159, 190
Church, Roman Catholic, 2, 7, 8, 34, 35, 43, 46, 47, 59–63, 68, 72, 73, 92, 96, 104–106, 124, 125, 185
Científicos, 35
Cipayo, 64
Cline, Howard, 34, 49
CNC. See National Peasant Confederation
Coffee economy, 78
Colombia, 12, 30, 94, 95, 163
Colonialism, economic, 2, 9, 10, 55, 57, 64, 87, 89, 93, 142, 197
Colorado party, 122–28
Comercio, El, 110
Common Market, European, 167, 171, 173
Communication, mass media of, 2, 10, 24, 29, 167, 168, 184
Communism, 7, 8, 16, 61, 71, 81, 89, 90, 92, 96, 108, 114, 117, 138, 148, 153, 155–58, 162, 168, 172, 178, 190, 197–98
COB. See Bolivian Workers' Center
Concepción católica de la política, 62
Confederation, of Colombian Workers, 100; of Industrial Chambers of Mexico, 46; of Mexican Workers, 46
Conferences, Inter-American: Buenos Aires (1936), 12; Cairo, 159, 176; Punta del Este (1961), 86, (1962), 172; Spanish American, 163, 172

Constitutions: Argentina, 54, 69, 71; Brazil, 81; Cuba, 154; Chile, 116; Mexico, 34, 38, 41, 42; Uruguay, 126; Venezuela, 130
COPEI, 132–35, 137–38
Copper, 114, 116
Corvalán, Luis, 120
Cosmic Race, The, 116
Courcelle-Seneuil, Jean, 118
Creación de la pedagogía nacional, La, 140
Criollo, 33, 34, 35, 37, 105, 108
Cristero Rebellion, 43
Criterio, 62
CROM. *See* Regional Confederation of Mexican Labor
Cruz Costa, João, 79, 80
CTC. *See* Confederation of Colombian Workers
CTM. *See* Confederation of Mexican Workers
Cuba, 12, 30, 74, 91, 135, 136, 150, 172, 173, 183, 197, 201
Cunha, Euclides da, 79
Cursos de Cultura Católica, 62
Customs Union, Central American, 11, 174; Latin American, 173, 174

Declaration of Economic Independence, Argentine, 69, 186
De Gaulle, Charles, 1, 13, 75, 181
Dellepiane, Luis, 64
Del Mazo, Gabriel, 164, 165, 177
Democracy, representative, 21, 54, 190, 191, 201, 202
Democratic Action Party, 131–38
Democrats, Christian, in Bolivia, 149; in Chile, 60, 113, 114, 117, 119–21, 169, 170, 185, 189; in Latin America, 169, 170; in Venezuela, 170, 185 (*See also* COPEI)
Descamisado, 67, 68, 195
Deutsch, Karl, 9
Development, economic and social, 2, 9, 10, 13, 19, 36, 38, 46, 50, 73, 75, 79, 82, 84, 85, 87, 88, 108, 113, 137, 146, 166, 167, 171, 176, 181, 187, 189, 190, 201
Development, political, 21, 39, 40, 202, 203. *See also* Leadership; names of parties and leaders; Parties, political
Día, El, 122
Díaz, Porfirio, 34–41
Díaz Defoo, 46
Didapp, Juan Pedro, 38, 39
Díez de Medina, Fernando, 168
Doctrina del estado nacional, 102
Dore, R. P., 188, 196
Draper, Theodore, 155, 156
Durán, Julio, 171

ECLA. *See* United Nations Economic Commission for Latin America
Ecuador, 186
Education, 54, 74, 112, 113, 120, 201
Edwards Bello, Joaquín, 161
Egaña, Juan, 162, 163
Eisenhower, Dwight D., 156
Elite, new, 3, 15, 21, 24, 25, 31, 40, 41, 47, 48, 79; old, 14, 18, 34, 35, 61, 77, 98, 182
Emerson, Rupert, 4, 15
Entrepreneurship, 15, 17, 84, 85, 92, 200, 201. *See also* Bourgeoisie, new
Estanciero, 58
Etchepareborda, Roberto, 63
Ethnic factors, 2, 23, 36, 78, 79, 86, 104, 108, 111, 166, 175, 176, 187
Europe, 7, 8, 159, 162, 163, 164, 165, 166, 175, 178, 181, 182; Latin American views of, 11, 35, 77, 176
European Free Trade Association, 173, 181
Explotadores Políticos de México, 38

Facundo, 56
Falangism, Spanish, 12, 132
Falkland Islands, 187
FALN. *See* Armed Forces of National Liberation
Fascism, 12, 47, 61
Fidelismo, 87
Flores Magón, Ricardo, 37
Foreign Affairs, 181
FORJA. *See* Fuerza de Orientación Radical de la Joven Argentina
France, 3, 7, 77, 121, 173, 186

Franceschi, Gustavo, 62
FRAP. *See Frente de Acción Popular.*
Free, Lloyd, 89
Free enterprise, 54, 66, 81, 118, 126, 142, 186, 191, 193
Frei Montalva, Eduardo, 113, 120, 121, 170, 189
Frente de Acción Popular, 117, 120, 189
Frías, Heriberto, 36
Frigerio, Rogelio, 73
Frondizi, Arturo, 72, 87, 88, 174, 178, 190
Frondizismo, 87
Fuerza de Orientación Radical de la Joven Argentina, 63–66, 68, 72

Gachupín, 33
Gaitán, Jorge Eliécer, 25, 97, 98, 99, 101, 103
Gallegos, Rómulo, 130–32
Gaucho, 55, 71, 78, 124, 175
General Confederation of Labor, Argentine, 17, 67, 71, 72, 74
General Confederation of Workers, Mexican, 45
Generation of 1928, 130, 132, 137
Germani, Gino, 21, 180, 199
Germany, 129
Gómez, Juan Vicente, 130
Gómez, Laureano, 100–102, 103
Gómez Morín, 46
González Prada, Manuel, 104–106
G.O.U. *See* Group of United Officers
Goulart, João, 15, 76, 89, 90, 91, 171, 174, 193
Graña Garland, Francisco, 109
Grau San Martín, Ramón, 151
Great Britain, 54, 55, 58, 65, 77, 121, 129, 130, 163, 173
Group of United Officers, 66, 67
Guantánamo, 150
Guatemala, 154, 187
Guevara, Ernesto, "Che," 154
Guiana, British, 187

Hacendados. *See* Hacienda.
Hacienda, 23, 28, 33, 34, 38, 47, 101
Haedo, Eduardo Víctor, 128

Hammerskjold, Knut, 181
Haya de la Torre, Víctor, Raúl, 25, 105–109, 161, 164, 165
Hayes, Carlton J. H., 14
Henríquez Ureña, Pedro, 165
Hernández Arregui, Juan José, 64
Herrera, Luis Alberto de, 128
Hirschman, Albert O., 99
Hispanidad, 100
Hispanism, 67. *See also* Hispanidad
Hispano-América en Guerra?, 165
Hispanophobia, 165
Hitler, Adolph, 1, 63, 70, 128, 183

IAN. *See* National Agrarian Institute
Ibáñez del Campo, Carlos, 24, 115, 116, 117
Ibarguren, Carlos, 61, 67
Ideology, 26, 27, 73, 194, 195
Illia, Arturo, 72, 74, 171, 174, 197
Illiteracy. *See* Literacy
Immigration, 54, 55, 81, 97, 123, 124, 187
Imperialism, 3, 7, 53, 57, 58, 65, 74, 80, 90, 93, 108, 136, 142, 165, 177, 182
Income, 2, 51, 201
Indians, 2, 34–37, 105–108, 111, 114, 123–24, 140, 141, 142, 145, 146, 166, 175, 176, 187
Indigenismo, 175
Industry, 46, 49, 50, 59, 78, 93, 101, 110, 125, 136, 159
Inflation, 88, 117, 118, 119, 149
Ingenieros, José, 164
Instituto de Estudos Afro-Asiáticos, 86
Instituto de Estudos Brasileiros, 82, 83
Intellectuals, 16, 17, 25, 35, 36, 37, 38, 40, 41, 47, 84, 96, 97, 104, 111, 114, 115, 124, 127, 130, 140, 141, 142, 160
Inter-American Development Bank, 194
Inter-American System, 172, 178
Internationalism, 7, 183, 193
International Monetary Fund, 87, 88, 118–19, 149, 194

Intervention, 43, 152, 188. *See also* Nonintervention
Irigoyen, Hipólito, 25, 56, 57, 63, 64, 68
ISEB. *See* Instituto Superior de Estudos Brasileiros
Italy, 61, 129

Jaguaribe, Hélio, 83–85, 87, 190, 194
Japan, 188, 196
Jauretche, Arturo, 64
Johnson, John J., 48
Juárez, Benito, 33
July 26 movement, 153, 154, 155
Justice, social, 31, 32, 60, 68, 69, 79, 115, 121, 184, 185, 190, 195
Justicia del Inca, La, 141
Justicialism, 69

Kemmerer mission, 118
Kennedy, John F., 158
Kennedy, John J., 60
Kissinger, Henry, 181
Klein and Saks, 119
Kohn, Hans, 1, 5
Kornhouser, William, 22
Krause, K. C. F., 122
Krushchev, Nikita, 158
Kubitschek, Juscelino, 93

Labor, organized, 16, 17, 23, 42, 43, 44, 47, 60, 61, 67, 74, 84, 92, 100, 116, 126, 145, 147, 148, 170, 172, 174, 192, 200
LAFTA. *See* Latin American Free Trade Association
Laissez-faire policy. *See* Free enterprise
Land ownership, 23, 33, 34, 44, 45, 97, 99, 102, 103, 111, 113, 119, 132, 152
Larrazábal, Wolfgang, 134
Lasswell, Harold, 24
Latifundio, 20, 33, 97, 105, 119, 146, 151, 152
Latin America, changes in, 9–14, 189, 190; diversity of, 1, 2, 168, 180, 202; identity, 165, 166, 187
Latin American Free Trade Association, 11, 162, 172–75, 178, 179

Latin Americanism. *See* Pan Latin Americanism
Leadership, 24–26, 29, 30, 31, 40, 50, 70, 83, 84, 92, 102, 112, 119–21
League of Nations, 78, 86
Lechín, Juan, 15, 148
Leguía, Augusto, 106, 109
Lenin, Nikolai, 8
León Valencia, Guillermo, 100
Leoni, Raúl, 136, 138, 170
Lillo, Baldomero, 115
Lima, Alceu Amoroso, 90
Limantour, José Ives, 36, 39
Lipset, Seymour Martin, 26, 201
Literacy, 13, 184
Lleras Camargo, Alberto, 95
Lleras Restrepo, Carlos, 103
Lombardo Toledano, Vicente, 46, 172
Lonardi, Eduardo, 72
López, Alfonso, 98–101
López Contreras, Eleazar, 130
López Mateos, Adolfo, 51, 173
López Michelsen, Alfonso, 103
Lozano y Lozano, Carlos, 100
Lüthy, Herbert, 4
Lugones, Leopoldo, 61
Luz, Nicia Vilela, 78

Machado, Gerardo, 151
Madero, Francisco, 38–40, 48
Mariátegui, José Carlos, 105–108, 141
Marín Balmaceda, Raúl, 114, 118
Maritain, Jacques, 120
Martínez Estrada, Ezequiel, 55
Martínez Zuviría, Gustavo, 67
Martín Fierro, 55, 58, 70
Marxism, 8, 83, 127, 153, 156, 197
Máspero, Emilio, 170
Masses, 10, 18, 22–24, 26, 39, 48, 65, 67, 68, 70, 81, 88, 115, 116, 118, 129, 142, 146, 154, 160, 195
Mater et Magistra, 120, 185
Maurras, Charles, 57, 61,
Maximilian, 33
Medina Angarita, Isaías, 131
Meinvielle, Julio, 61, 62
Mendes de Almeida, Cándido, 9, 83, 85–88, 194
Mestizo, 2, 35, 36, 37, 38, 66

Mexico, 12, 30, 32, 33, 147, 164, 172, 173, 175, 183, 184, 186, 187, 190, 192, 195, 198; revolution in, 10, 32, 38, 96, 176, 196, 197
Middle class, 14, 15, 16, 17, 18, 25, 49, 55, 56, 57, 65, 68, 79, 84, 97, 106, 114, 115, 117, 137, 148, 155, 160, 192
Migration, internal, 10, 68, 102, 103
Mikoyan, Anastas I., 156
Mills, C. Wright, 24
MIR. See Movement of the Revolutionary Left
Missile crisis, 158, 176
Mistral, Gabriela, 161
Mitre, Bartolomé, 54, 55
MNR. See National Revolutionary Movement
Mobility, social, 28, 29, 40, 49
Modernization, 2, 10, 11, 17, 19–20, 25, 29, 31, 49, 50, 54, 55, 59, 84, 92, 93, 112, 121, 123, 126, 142, 153, 183, 184, 185, 196–98, 202
Molina Enríquez, Andrés, 37, 38, 41
Monarchy, Brazilian, 77
Montevideo, 122, 123
Morones, Luis, 43
Movement of the Revolutionary Left, 135
Mussolini, Benito, 57, 70

Nacionalismo e desenvolvimento, 9
Nardone, Benito, 128
Nasser, Gamal Abdal, 13, 15, 88
Nasserism, 15, 70, 149
Nation-state system, 203
National Action Party, 46
National Agrarian Institute, 134
National Federation of Chambers of Commerce, 46
Nationalism, continental, 66, 178, 179; definitions of, 3–5; escalation of, 180–82; polycentric organization for, 28, 58–66; relation of ideology to, 26, 27; relation of modernization to, 17, 19, 29, 30, 31, 49, 50, 198; role of key groups in, 15–18; social aspects of, 197–202; varieties of, 6–8, 13–15, 30, 51, 53, 57, 65, 68, 73, 74, 76, 81, 86, 94, 103, 105, 106, 113, 121, 127, 129, 138, 139, 140, 149, 150, 160
Nationalism and Development, 83, 85–88
Nationalist Revolutionary Movement, 25, 139–40, 144, 145–50
National Revolutionary Party, 44
National Peasant Confederation, 45, 46
National Student Union, 89
Nativism, 14, 55, 58, 79, 84
Navarro, Gustavo A., 141
Nazism, 12, 142
Negroes, 2, 86, 166, 176
Netherlands, The, 130
Neutralism, 88, 89. See also Nonalignment; Third Position
New World concept, 163
New York Times, 177, 181
Nitrates, 116, 118
Nobel Prizes, winners of, 2, 161
Nonalignment, 13, 53, 65, 91, 159, 162, 172, 176, 193
Nonintervention, rule of, 12, 47, 193, 194
North Atlantic area, 203
Nueva República, La, 62

OAS. See Organization of American States
Obregón, Alvaro, 41, 42, 43
Odría, Manuel, 25, 110
Oil. See Petroleum
Olaya Herrera, Enrique, 98, 99
Oligarchy, 7, 10, 28, 53, 55, 56, 57, 58, 65, 80, 84, 87, 104, 107, 110, 111, 118, 141, 145, 149, 165, 192, 195
Organization of American States, 12, 74, 90, 91, 168, 179; Charter of, 12, 193
Oribe, Emilio, 169
Oribe, Manuel, 121
ORIT, 174
Orozco, Wistano Luis, 36
Ortega y Gasset, José, 22
ORVE. See Venezuelan Organization
Os Sertões, 79
Ospina Pérez, Mariano, 101, 102
Ostria Gutiérrez, Alberto, 145

Pabón Núñez, Lucio, 102
Palacios, Alfredo, 63
PAN. *See* National Action Party
Pan Americanism, 162
Pan Latin Americanism, 65, 107, 161, 168, 169, 170, 172, 174, 175, 177, 178, 183
Panama, 96
Paraguay, 143
Parties, political, 28, 48, 56, 64, 65, 92, 95, 97, 98, 102, 117, 121, 122, 129, 137, 143, 155, 197
Patch, Richard W., 146
Patiño, Simón, 141, 146
Patria Grande, 161, 164
Patrón, 23, 146
Paz Estenssoro, Víctor, 15, 144, 145, 148, 149, 154
Peasants, 41, 42, 44, 45, 47, 98, 99, 111, 134, 135, 149, 152, 159
Peasants Federation, 134
Pemex, 82, 185
Pensamiento y Acción, 121
Pérez Jiménez, Marcos, 131, 133, 134
Pérez Segrini, Ildegar, 134
Perón, Eva, 69, 195
Perón, Juan Domingo, 10, 15, 24, 53, 60, 65, 66–72, 74, 75, 88, 89, 91, 92, 128, 144, 172, 183, 184
Peronism, 27; after Perón, 72–75, 189. *See also* Perón, Juan Domingo
Peru, 12, 93, 94, 99, 175, 186, 187, 195
Petrobrás, 82, 85, 185
Petroleum, 35, 49, 56, 73, 74, 81, 82, 85, 99, 130, 131, 132, 133, 135, 140, 141, 145, 156, 158, 185
Pinto, Aníbal, 119
PNR. *See* National Revolutionary Party
Polycentrism, 58, 175
Popular Front, 117
Portugal, 86
Positivism, 122
Prado, Javier, 105
Prado, Manuel, 110
Pravda, 89
Prensa, La, 109, 110
Prestes, Luiz Carlos, 92

Primo de Rivera, Miguel, 57
P.T.B. *See* Brazilian Labor Party

Quadragesimo Anno, 120
Quadros, Jânio, 86, 89
Quijada, Ramón, 134

RADEPA. *See* Razón de Patria
Radical party, Argentina, 56–57, 63, 64, 171, 197
Radio broadcasting, 184
Railroads, 39, 77, 81, 125, 151
Ramos, Jorge Abelardo, 71, 72
Ramos, Samuel, 51
Rangel, Domingo Alberto, 135
Raza, 169
Razón de Patria, 143, 144, 145
Rebelión, 148
Reform, agrarian, 44, 45, 48, 97, 99, 104, 110, 111, 116, 126, 132, 133, 147, 151, 154, 157, 159, 196
Reform, Mexican, 34, 35, 36, 37
Reform, structural, 119
Reforma, La. See Reform, Mexican
Regeneración, La, 37
Regional Confederation of Mexican Labor, 42, 43
Republican Democratic Union, 132, 137
Rerum Novarum, 120
Restauración Nacionalista, La, 55
Reston, James, 181
Revolución Social, 36
Rio Defense Treaty, 193
Rivadavia, Bernardino, 54
Rivera, Fructuoso, 121
Rodó, José Enrique, 166, 175
Rodrigues, José Honório, 93
Rojas, Ricardo, 55, 56, 58, 140, 176
Rojas Pinilla, Gustavo, 24, 102
Roosevelt, Franklin D., 47, 150
Roosevelt, Theodore, 7
Rosas, Juan Manuel de, 54, 55, 58, 64, 70, 121
Rose, J. Holland, 4
Rouma, Georges, 140
Royal Dutch Shell, 142
Rubottom, Roy, 157

Rumania, 159
Russia, revolution in, 96

San Martín, José de, 54, 70, 162
Sánchez Bustamante, Daniel, 140
Sánchez Cerro, Luis M., 108, 109, 110
Sánchez Sorondo, Marcelo, 67
Santa Fe, Alberto, 36
Santos, Eduardo, 100, 101
Sanz de Santamaría, Carlos, 175
São Paulo, 93
Sarmiento, Domingo F., 54, 55, 56
Schmidt, Augusto Frederico, 89
Semana Trágica, 61
Sertanismo, 14, 55, 78, 84, 175
Shafer, Boyd, 3
Siles Zuazo, Hernán, 145, 148
Silvert, Kalman H., 4, 14, 17, 180, 201
Sinarquistas, 47
Slavery, 77
Snyder, Louis J., 4, 7
Socialism, 18, 63, 71, 96, 107, 108, 141, 143, 192
Socialist Ideas, 97
Social Studies, 99
Soviet Union, 85, 88, 90, 156, 158, 159, 160, 167, 168, 188, 190, 191, 193
Spain, 12, 57, 63, 64, 75, 97, 104, 166
Stabilization, 73
Standard Oil Company, 85, 141, 142, 194
Statism, 15, 191, 192
Steel mills, 81, 93, 185
Stein, Stanley J., 78
Sturzo, Luigi, 4, 5
Sugar, 151, 152, 157, 160
Switzerland, 126
Syndicalism, 96

Tamayo, Franz, 140
Tannenbaum, Frank, 33, 43
Technology, 10, 50, 92, 163, 192
Texto único, 186
Tin, 140, 141, 146
Third Position, 13, 53, 56, 65, 66, 74, 75, 88, 102, 120, 193

Tierra del Fuego, 187
Tomochic, 36
Toro, David, 143, 144
Traditionalism, 14, 18, 20, 51, 53, 70, 71, 79, 90, 94, 96, 98, 99, 103, 104, 109, 110, 112, 115, 117, 123, 198, 200
Trotskismo. See Trotskyism
Trotsky, Leon, 8
Trotskyism, 8, 15, 71, 148
Turner, Frederick Jackson, 78
Typologies, 201

Ugarte, Manuel, 72, 164
U.N.E. *See* National Student Union
Unión Latino Americana, 164
Unión Liberal, 35
Unión Revolucionaria, 110
United Fruit Company, 98
United Nations, 12, 118, 167, 172, 179; Economic Commission for Latin America, 167
United States, 7, 130, 131, 151, 152, 153, 157, 158, 163, 164, 165, 167, 168, 174, 179, 188; Latin American views of, 10, 35, 56, 65, 66, 85, 88, 96, 156, 160, 175
Universities, 2, 105, 159; students in, 16, 64, 65, 89, 107, 130, 142, 153, 199
University Reform, 65, 164, 165, 177
Urbanization, 2, 10, 19, 23, 24, 55, 81, 93, 102, 115, 123, 167, 168
URD. *See* Republican Democratic Union
Uriburu, José E., 67
Uruguay, 9, 10, 30, 121, 198, 199
Uslar Pietri, Arturo, 137

Value systems, 17, 19, 20, 111, 113, 189, 203
Vargas, Getúlio, 79, 81, 89
Vasconcelos, José, 166, 176
Vendepatria, 10, 14, 18, 56, 64, 118, 182
Venezuela, 30, 129, 170, 185, 187, 195
Venezuelan Organization, 130, 131
Vernon, Raymond, 50
Villalba, Jóvito, 132, 137
Villarán, Manuel Vicente, 105

Villarroel, Gualberto, 145
Volta Redonda, 81, 93

Wars: Mexican-American, 33; Chaco, 140, 142, 146; Spanish American, 166; War of the Pacific, 104, 114, 118, 140; World War I, 78, 96; World War II, 86
Wast, Hugo. *See* Martínez Zuviría, Gustavo
Weber, Alfred, 87
Welfare, social, 127, 128, 189. *See also* Justice, social
Werneck Sodré, Nelson, 79, 80
West, 13, 162, 169, 172, 175, 176

Western Hemisphere idea, 163
Wilson, Henry Lane, 40

Xenophobia, 4, 6, 7, 13, 38, 52, 54, 55, 80, 88, 93, 164, 196

Yacimientos Petrolíferos Fiscales, 56, 82, 185
Yankeephobia, 165. *See also* Anti-Americanism; Xenophobia
YPF. *See Yacimientos Petrolíferos Fiscales*

Zapata, Emiliano, 41
Zea, Leopoldo, 166
Zollverein, 173